FRANK LLOYD WRIGHT
AN ANNOTATED BIBLIOGRAPHY

ART & ARCHITECTURE BIBLIOGRAPHIES 5

Frank Lloyd Wright

An Annotated Bibliography

Robert L. Sweeney

Foreword by Adolf K. Placzek
Avery Library, Columbia University

Los Angeles   HENNESSEY & INGALLS, INC.   1978

Published by

Hennessey & Ingalls, Inc.
8321 Campion Drive
Los Angeles, California 90045
U.S.A.

Library of Congress Cataloging in Publication Data

Sweeney, Robert Lawrence, 1945–
    Frank Lloyd Wright: an annotated bibliography

    (Art & architecture bibliographies; 5)
    1. Wright, Frank Lloyd, 1867–1959—Bibliography.
    I. Series: Art & architecture bibliographies; 5.
Z8986.3.S85 [NA737.W7] 016.72'092'4 78-3727
ISBN 0-912158-57-3

Manufactured in the United States of America
Designed by Laurence McGilvery
Typesetting by Cheryl Ritter

To my mother

CONTENTS

PLATES

FOREWORD

IT is a pleasure to introduce this long-needed and long-awaited bibliography on Frank Lloyd Wright by Robert L. Sweeney, a work of true dedication and love.

Frequently, after a commanding figure departs, interest decreases sharply and others appear to take the center of the stage. The opposite occurred in the case of Frank Lloyd Wright, as if his impact had not been fully realized even when he died at the age of ninety-one. The fascination, the admiration and the controversies which he aroused during his life-time not only continued, but increased. Looking back to him, as though to a mountain top from a growing distance, seemed to reveal new and unnoticed features. Mr. Sweeney's bibliography is indeed such a looking back; and it is indicative of the aliveness of Wright's presence that in the bibliography the number of citations between the year of Wright's death, 1959, and 1977 increased by nearly fifty per cent. Thus, as the literature became more and more voluminous (nationally and internationally) and as mastery of all the sources (old and new) became almost impossible, the need for a bibliographic tool became even greater. It is this that makes Mr. Sweeney's bibliography long-needed. That it was long-awaited must remind us of the amount of time a work of this scope and thoroughness demands. Years of concentrated pursuit—discovering, sleuthing, checking and rechecking and absorbing—have passed until we now have the most complete bibliography on Wright ever done.

It turns out to be a monumental record (everything about Wright turns out to be monumental, although this is not a word he himself would have used). The bibliography contains no fewer than 2,095 entries, spanning almost a century: from the first entry—1886—concerning the nineteen-year-old Wright's part in the construction of a country church to the last entry—1977—dealing with the Historic American Buildings Survey records for the Johnson Wax building in Racine. Between these two entries lies the fabulous story of Wright's early emergence, incredible creativity, tenacity and articulateness, his successes, set-backs, fights, his temporary eclipse and eventual triumph, his death and his continuing enormous posthumous influence. To organize the vastness of the material and to reflect the historic and dramatic sequence of Wright's life, work and impact, Mr. Sweeney has adhered to the chronological order: within this same order are listed pieces *by* Wright (and how eloquent and prolific he was!) as well as pieces *about* him—first books, then periodical articles. Where books have reappeared in new editions, these are entered both with the first edition and in the year of the later edition; book-reviews are listed next to the book. The definitive word (if there is ever such a thing) on the great and seldom correctly described Wasmuth Portfolio of 1910—a decisive publication in Wright's life and in the life of twentieth-century architecture—is told in entry 87.

Except in a few cases where this proved impossible, all entries, many of them out-of-the-way and requiring advanced detective work, have been checked by the author. Errors carried through the years from citation to citation have thus finally been corrected. The bibliography is aiming at as wide a range as possible: only non-Western entries do not make any claim to completeness (a task reserved for another dedicated scholar).

A bibliography can never be the last word. New material will be traced, discovered and annotated (Mr. Sweeney's own annotations are an important feature of his work), and the Frank Lloyd Wright story will continue to be written, as his vision and his work continue to live. But for a long time to come, the following pages will be the basic source-book.

New York, May 1978   ADOLF K. PLACZEK
                              Avery Librarian, Columbia University

ACKNOWLEDGEMENTS

PRIMARY thanks should go to Reginald Hennessey, who suggested that I compile this bibliography and whose prolonged patience made possible its degree of thoroughness. I am grateful to Bernard M. Boyle for advice in the early stages of my task. Bruce Brooks Pfeiffer, archivist of the Frank Lloyd Wright Foundation, was a continuing source of valuable information. Stephen W. Jacobs offered many useful comments on the first draft of the introduction. I have received friendly support from Eugene Streich and from H. Frederick Koeper, whose later criticism of the introduction I especially appreciate. Adolf Placzek has from the beginning been an enthusiastic supporter. That he would consent to write the foreword to this book is a great compliment; another tangible contribution was his insistence on including the building index.

Lloyd Wright graciously recounted incidents in his father's life which clarify and enrich the events of the Wasmuth publications. Several other people close to Wright or his work, including Edgar Kaufmann, Jr., Marjorie F. Leighey, and Elizabeth Coonley Faulkner (who, as a little girl, is familiar in published photographs of the exterior of her parents' house in Riverside), graciously made their collections of Wright material available to me.

Numerous individuals have responded to my written requests for information. Although every letter is appreciated, not all can be acknowledged, but I would especially like to thank Marjorie Winslow Briggs, Howard Dearstyne, Dirk Lohan, Dimitri Tselos, Dr. Auke van der Woud, Ben Weinreb, and Katharine Welch. Also, my conversations with W. R. Hasbrouck, John A. Reed, Elaine Sewell, and Kathryn Smith were valuable in many ways.

Completion of this bibliography would have been impossible without the resources of the Avery Architectural Library at Columbia University and the Burnham Library of Architecture at the Chicago Art Institute. I am grateful to the staffs of both for their help. Much of the final work was completed at Cornell University, and I extend a general thanks to all the librarians there. Judith Holliday of the Architecture and Fine Arts Library also contributed her quick wit, a frequent and welcome relief during the tedium of final checking and rechecking of the work.

I also relied on the collections of the New York Public Library, the Fine Arts Library of the University of Southern California, the libraries of the University of California at Berkeley and Los Angeles, and the Library of Congress. Richard Seidell, of the Newberry Library, Chicago, made me aware of the title page Wright designed for *The Eve of St. Agnes* and also offered detailed clarification on the confusing variant editions of *The Japanese Print* and *Ausgeführte Bauten.* Barbara Ballinger, of the Oak Park Public Library, and Anne E. Williams, of the Kenneth Spencer Research Library, University of Kansas, Lawrence, both assisted with their unique collections.

I am indebted to Laurence McGilvery for his untiring criticism and refinement of the material for publication. Large sections of the manuscript were typed by Gloria Miller, and the typesetting of this book was done by Cheryl Ritter; both of them accomplished demanding tasks with great accuracy and patience. This book is the result of the continued assistance of many people, although I alone am responsible for its content.

INTRODUCTION

FRANK LLOYD WRIGHT had an exceptionally long and active career, which is generally agreed to have fallen into three distinct parts. The pattern of his own activities, the regard in which his work was held, and the character of his times can all be discerned in the extensive record of literature by and about him as set forth in this bibliography.

The first period was one of bold invention and public acclaim. It reached its climax in 1910 with the publication of his architectural drawings in an extraordinary pair of portfolios by the Berlin firm of Ernst Wasmuth (see no. 87 in this bibliography). The excitement generated by that event and by many subsequent publications lasted for more than two decades in Europe, but during this middle period Wright suffered a partial eclipse in the United States.

Wright was the most articulate of modern architects. He was also his own best publicist. Early in his career he began the life-long task of developing and disseminating his own ideas through every available forum. When the public taste in buildings seemed temporarily to have passed him by, he turned vigorously to writing and to teaching through his workshops at Talicsin. Eventually he became known almost as well for his polemic as for his architecture and, in the process, created a public image of himself as vivid and durable as that of any figure in the twentieth century.

By the late 1930s, Wright's star was in the ascendancy again. The first sign was the January, 1938, special issue of *Architectural Forum,* which was devoted completely to his new and unpublished work (no. 457). This was followed in 1942 by the first American monograph on Wright (no. 573). Ironically, this new wave of enthusiasm coincided with the cessation of virtually all architectural activity during World War II, but in January, 1948, with the appearance of a second special issue of *Architectural Forum* (no. 745), the flood of publications on Wright regained its momentum, reaching epic proportions before his death in 1959.

1887–1893: The Early Years, Apprenticeship with Sullivan

"...A boy architect belonging to the family looked after this interior."[1] This passage, published in 1886, is the first recorded reference to Frank Lloyd Wright. It identifies him even at that early date as an architect, and it mentions, though it does not clarify, his contribution to a chapel built for his family in Wisconsin.[2] It establishes his early relationship with the Chicago architect J. L. Silsbee (1845–1913), who designed the building and who later employed Wright as a draftsman. The article from which the passage was taken was written by a family friend, W. C. Gannett, whose essay "The House Beautiful" Wright helped publish in 1896–7. A final connection should be made: Wright's uncle, Jenkin Lloyd Jones (1843–1918), was editor of the religious magazine in which the article was published and was also an influential minister in Chicago.

Early the following year the nineteen-year-old "boy architect" left his home in Madison, Wisconsin, and went to Chicago, determined, as he wrote much later, never to "go near Uncle Jenkin Lloyd Jones nor ask his help nor use his name."[3] The extent to which Wright remained entirely independent of his family connections is debatable, for the fact is that he was unable to find work and finally went to Silsbee's office where he was hired as a tracer. Soon after, a drawing and plan signed "Frank L. Wright, Archt." were reproduced in the *Inland Architect and News Record*, published in Chicago (no. 3). Its editor, Robert Craik McLean, was sympathetic to the work of Sullivan and other local architects. Silsbee's designs were often reproduced, and it may have been his influence that caused McLean to accept Wright's drawings. Six more drawings followed in 1887 and 1888 (nos. 2, 5-9) including Wright's own designs and work done for Silsbee and, subsequently, Adler and Sullivan. These appearances constitute the most important record of his earliest work. Nothing from a brief tenure at

1. William C. Gannett, "Christening a Country Church," *Unity* (Chicago) 17 (28 August 1886): 356-7 (see item no. 1 in this bibliography).

2. Unity Chapel, Helena Valley, Wisconsin. Wright's perspective drawing of this building was published in the 1887 annual of All Souls Church, Chicago (see item no. 4).

3. Frank Lloyd Wright, *An Autobiography* (London, New York, Toronto: Longmans, Green and Company, 1932), p. 63 (see item no. 303).

Beers, Clay and Dutton has come to light.[4]

Wright worked for Adler and Sullivan from 1887 to 1893. He rose rapidly in Sullivan's favor and soon became his chief assistant. A plan published in 1890 (no. 10) of the firm's new offices in the Auditorium tower revealed Wright's space to be next to the master's. That this indication of his status appeared in a national magazine must have been a great source of pride to Wright, for he later reproduced the plan in his autobiography (1932). The few residential commissions accepted by Adler and Sullivan were delegated to Wright. These were given limited attention in the architectural journals, and the designs were not attributed to him. His "bootlegged" houses, done after hours without the consent of his employers and in violation of his contract with them, were not published at the time.

The greatness of Louis Sullivan (1856–1924) lay more in his ability as a theoretician and teacher of architecture than as a designer of buildings, and Wright later paid homage to him. He was the spiritual leader of the group of architects now known as the Prairie School, of which Wright became the dominant figure. Sullivan was also a difficult personality, volatile and alcoholic, and his association with Wright was terminated abruptly and emotionally over the issue of the outside commissions. The two men avoided one another for years, but were reunited around 1913–14.[5]

4. Little information is available on this firm or its members. William Wilson Clay (1849–1926) was born in New York. He graduated from the City College of New York and went to Chicago shortly after the 1871 fire. His first professional association, lasting from 1876 to 1886, was with O. L. Wheelock. A new partnership with Llewellyn B. Dutton (about whom no information has been located) was formed in 1886. In 1888 the third partner, Minard LaFevre Beers (1847–1918) joined the firm. Beers was born and educated in Cleveland and, like Clay, had been attracted to Chicago in 1871. Their work was primarily residential although they did some commercial buildings. They are credited with designing the first steel-frame residence, the W. H. Reid house, built in 1894 in Chicago. The firm existed until 1894. Beers joined the AIA as a Fellow in 1887. Clay became a member of the Western Association of Architects in 1884 and a Fellow of the AIA in 1888. He retired on 1 December 1919. In his autobiography, Wright claimed to have worked for Beers, Clay and Dutton. As the year was 1887, he would have been more precise to have referred only to Clay and Dutton.

5. Kenneth W. Severens, "The Reunion of Louis Sullivan and Frank Lloyd Wright," *Prairie School Review* 12 (no. 3, 1975): 5-21 (see item no. 1991). Tangible evidence of the reunion is the copy of *Ausgeführte Bauten und Entwürfe* which Wright gave Sullivan. The inscription in Wright's hand is reproduced in this article.

1893-1909: Independent Practice, Wright's Star Ascends

Wright began independent practice in 1893. *The Inland Architect and News Record* between 1894 and its demise in 1908 continued to reproduce his work with some regularity, although in only one case are the illustrations accompanied by a descriptive article. The magazine was published by the Western Association of Architects for a professional audience.

Wright's architecture also was featured in the homemaker magazines, which were founded during the late nineteenth and early twentieth centuries. These publications, whose readership included an audience of prospective clients, were strongly influenced by the Arts and Crafts movement, which was then gaining enthusiastic public support in the United States. Their editors strove to improve their readers' taste and stressed naturalness and simplicity in the design of houses and furnishings. The impact was enormous.

One of the most outspoken of these crusaders was Edward W. Bok (1863–1930), editor of the *Ladies' Home Journal.* Beginning in 1895, he published a series of "good" low-cost houses designed by various architects. Working drawings were available, with a guarantee that the houses could be built for the amounts specified. He commissioned three designs from Wright, which were published in 1901 and 1907 (nos. 45, 46, 80). None of these was built as a direct result of their publication.

The other homemaker magazine which opened its pages to Wright was the *House Beautiful.* Wright's own home and studio were described and illustrated in 1897 and 1899 (nos. 26 and 35). Three more articles featuring individual houses were published in 1906 (nos. 62-4). Interestingly, in *The Craftsman,* the editor Gustave Stickley (1858–1942) mentioned Wright only once in passing.

Gallery exhibitions were another important means for an artist to promote his work. The Chicago Architectural Sketch Club, organized in 1885, began a series of annual shows at the Art Institute in 1888. It was reincorporated in 1889 as the Chicago Architectural Club and soon became dominated by the Prairie School architects, who used the club to exchange ideas and to propagandize their work as a revolutionary and cohesive new style. Illustrated catalogues accompanied each show. Wright, although never a member, participated in eight exhibitions between 1894 and

1907 and was represented in several catalogues, notably those of 1900 and 1902 (nos. 37 and 49). His work so dominated the 1902 show and catalogue that the ethical appropriateness of "such a pronounced personal exhibit" was questioned by the *American Architect and Building News* (no. 51).

Early in his career, Wright took to the lecture circuit to further explain his work and theories. "The Architect," depicting the sad state of the profession, was read to the Architectural League of America in 1900. The text was printed in the *Brickbuilder* and was favorably reviewed in other professional journals (no. 42). The following year, Wright's famous lecture "The Art and Craft of the Machine" was given in the Hull House. This was published in the exhibition catalogue of the Chicago Architectural Club (no. 43) and, in slightly revised form, by the Daughters of the Revolution in *The New Industrialism* (no. 50).

By 1900 Wright was the star ascendant among Chicago architects. That year Robert C. Spencer, Jr. (1865–1953), in a well-illustrated article in the *Architectural Review* (Boston), commented favorably on Wright's accomplishments during his first seven years of independent practice (no. 41). Spencer knew his subject well, for the two men had had Chicago offices in the Schiller Building and, later, in Steinway Hall. This was the first critical analysis of Wright's work.

The *Architectural Record* offered its January 1904 issue to Wright, giving him the choice of an author for the article. He first considered Russell Sturgis (1838–1909), but after receiving him in his studio, Wright concluded that Sturgis did not understand his work and decided to seek some younger man.[6] The article did not appear until 1905 and was unsigned (no. 58). A full issue of the *Record* was devoted to Wright in 1908 (no. 85). It includes his philosophical essay "In the Cause of Architecture," followed by fifty-six pages of illustrations.

The number of Wright's commissions continued to increase dramatically in the years up to 1909. This was, of course, his "first golden age,"[7] when he completed some of his greatest works. His buildings were no longer limited geographically to the

6. Nancy K. Morris Smith, "Letters, 1903–1906, by Charles E. White, Jr. from the Studio of Frank Lloyd Wright," *Journal of Architectural Education* 25 (Fall, 1971): 104-5 (see item no. 1860).

7. To use Grant Manson's apt phrase.

Midwest; there were houses as far afield as Santa Barbara, Buffalo, and, possibly, Palm Beach. Sometime in this period Kuno Francke (1855–1930), professor of the history of German culture at Harvard, came to the Oak Park Studio. He had arrived at Harvard in 1884 and founded the Busch-Reisinger Museum of Germanic Culture there in 1902.[8] He was interested in promoting "an artistic interchange between America and Germany," and he conceived of reciprocal art exhibits as one means of accomplishing this.[9] He also traveled to many university campuses across the country to lecture on art.[10] Wright described their meeting:

> He had seen the new type house standing about on the prairies, had asked the name of the architect, time and again, getting the same name for an answer.
>
> A German friend, finally, at the German professor's request, brought Francke and his charming wife to Oak Park for a short visit. Kuno Francke stayed all day, came back the next day.
>
> He, too, as had Mr. Waller and Uncle Dan, wanted me to go to Europe, wanted me to go to Germany to stay and go to work.
>
> "I see that you are doing 'organically,'" he said, "what my people are feeling for only superficially. They would reward you. It will be long before your own people will be ready for what you are trying to give them."[11]

Soon after this visit, Wright was invited by Ernst Wasmuth to send material for a complete monograph of his work. "This proposal of the German publisher, was, I think, one net result of Kuno Francke's visit to the Oak Park workshop—though I never really knew."[12]

Francke was a prolific author, although he apparently did not discuss Wright in any of his published writings. Also, his role in the publication of the portfolio remains unclear. His daughter, Marie Francke Dunlap Smith, who was a freshman at Radcliffe

8. *Dictionary of American Biography*, s.v. "Francke, Kuno."

9. Kuno Francke, "An Artistic Interchange Between America and Germany," *Nation* 86 (30 April 1908): 396.

10. Katharine Welch to author, 13 March 1975. Mrs. Welch is Francke's granddaughter.

11. Wright, p. 164.

12. Ibid., p. 165.

that year, does not remember, though she has indicated that the extensive newspaper coverage at the time concerning her father's relationship with Wright is largely inaccurate.[13] The Wasmuth firm itself is unable to provide substantial information, as its archives were destroyed in November, 1943.[14]

Wright was experiencing some irregularities in his personal life when the German proposal was made. His marriage had deteriorated, and he was openly associating with Mamah Cheney, the wife of a client. He also seems to have reached a point of stagnation in his work:

> This absorbing, consuming phase of my experience as an architect ended about 1909. I had almost reached my fortieth year: weary, I was losing grip on my work and even interest in it. I could see no way out. Because I did not know what I wanted, I wanted to go away. Why not go to Germany and prepare the material for the Wasmuth monograph?...I looked longingly in that direction.[15]

Wright sailed for Europe in September, 1909, accompanied by Mrs. Cheney. They went first to Berlin. Then Wright continued on to Fiesole, Italy, to prepare the publication, with Mrs. Cheney remaining in Berlin. Before leaving Oak Park, Wright asked his son Lloyd (1890–1978) to join him in Florence to help prepare the drawings for the portfolio. Lloyd arrived in November. Fifty-seven years later, he reminisced about his experience:

> I found Father already established in the little Villino "Fortuna" just below the plaza Michelangelo and the David statue—in Florence. Across the street was a walled nunnery with its tinkling bells and olive trees reaching over the walls. The villano [sic] was divided into two parts opening from a tiny inner court. A charming Russian couple who played music with their friends had one apartment and we enjoyed their cultured company. We had the street apartment overlooking the nunnery. There were no rugs on the stone floor and it was cold. The three of us [including Taylor Wooley, a draftsman from the Oak Park studio] set up our tables in

13. Welch.

14. Günther Wasmuth to Linn Cowles, 23 December 1965, Avery Library Columbia University, New York. Also, Dr. Sibylle V. Bockelberg to author, 24 May 1974.

15. Wright, p. 165.

the living room and brought in braziers to warm the room and our freezing hands for it was the end of the winter season and we had to thaw out to do the essential and delicate work.[16]

The work was completed by May, 1910. Wright discussed the publication the following July in correspondence with C. R. Ashbee:

I am to own this work outright—& have bought it because I believe it will be profitable and there is no cleaner way for an architect to find his money than in the sale of his own works in this way. I have a contract with this house for 1,000 copies. Their work is very good—lithography—I must acknowledge but their slow movements drive me to desperation. The German mind is a ponderous affair I find. I thought of giving them up and asking you to help me find someone else but they are doing a little better and I will wait with what patience I can command. 'I must be patient' is a phraze [sic] the Italians use continually—and I will adopt it...There will be some plates printed in grey on cream colored paper, some in sepia on cream—others in grey or sepia on grey paper with white tinted walls—or sky. It is rather large—they employ their largest stones—but I am sick of over-reduction and yearn for a full face in each project.[17]

Ausgeführte Bauten und Entwürfe (*Executed Buildings and Projects*) (no. 87), often called simply the Wasmuth portfolio, made an enormous impact when it appeared in Europe. It must be remembered, however, that its prime audience there was a group of eager and receptive young architects who were already deeply involved in their own progressive movement and were ready for further guidance. Ludwig Mies van der Rohe (1886–1969), who first saw the portfolio in the office of Peter Behrens (1868–1940) where he was working, acknowledged the debt of his generation of architects in an appreciation written for the unpublished catalogue of the Frank Lloyd Wright exhibition held at the Museum of Modern Art in 1940:

16. Lloyd Wright to Mrs. David Cowles, 3 February 1966, Avery Library, Columbia University, New York (quoted with permission of Lloyd Wright). He related virtually the same story to the author in a 1976 conversation.

17. Wright to Ashbee, 24 July 1910. Reprinted in Alan Crawford, "Ten Letters from Frank Lloyd Wright to Charles Robert Ashbee," *Architectural History* 13 (1970): 68 (see item no. 1818).

At this moment, so critical for us, the exhibition of the
work of Frank Lloyd Wright came to Berlin. This comprehensive display and the exhaustive publication of his works
enabled us to become really acquainted with the achievements of this architect. The encounter was destined to prove
of great significance to the European development.[18]

Wright was not the first American architect to receive notice
in Europe. The works of Richardson and Sullivan were already
well known. Also, it is probably erroneous to assume that the
Europeans had had no word of Wright prior to the publication of
the portfolio. The English Arts and Crafts leader C. R. Ashbee
first met Wright in Chicago in November or December, 1900,
while he was on a lecture tour on behalf of the English National
Trust. Then, a German architect, Bruno Möhring, visited the Oak
Park studio in 1904.[19] Wasmuth had published a monograph on
Möhring in 1902 and it is extremely tempting to speculate that
he made the publishers aware of Wright after his visit.[20]

Before Wright undertook the portfolio, the Wasmuth firm con-
tacted him in America requesting material for a *Sonderheft*—a
special issue—to appear in a regular series then in publication. The
material was to consist of photographs of actual buildings and
plans, accompanied by an article written by a German in Cologne.
The portfolio was to present the "office ideal—the architects [sic]
rendering of his vision," the *Sonderheft*, the results.[21] A delay in
obtaining the photographs postponed the work until 1911. For a
time, Wright considered publishing it himself, as he wanted it to
appear simultaneously with the portfolio, and he asked Ashbee if
there were an English house that could do it on short notice.

The monograph was finally published by Wasmuth but, for an
undiscovered reason, it appeared in two different though similar
versions. One was entitled *Ausgeführte Bauten* (no. 96), the other,
Frank Lloyd Wright, Chicago (no. 101). Although some variation
occurred in the illustrative material, the German texts were

18. *In* Philip C. Johnson, *Mies van der Rohe* (New York: The Museum of
Modern Art, 1947), p. 196 (see item no. 686).

19. Smith, p. 105. The architect's name was misspelled Moehing by White.

20. *Bruno Möhring* (Berlin: E. Wasmuth, 1902). (Berliner Kunst. 2 Sonderheft der Berliner Architecturwelt.) This book is one of the series that later
included a work on Wright.

21. Wright to Ashbee.

identical. The introduction, "Frank Lloyd Wright: Eine Studie zu Seiner Würdigung," was by C. R. Ashbee. Wright stayed with the Ashbees in Campden in September, 1910, and during this visit requested the introduction. He later wrote:

> ...I don't mind telling you that my desire to have you say the foreword for me was a pure bit of sentiment on my part—because I liked you and I turned to you at the critical moment...

He continued:

> My conscience troubles me—do not say that I deny my love for Japanese art has influenced me—I admit that it has but claim to have digested it—Do not accuse me of trying to 'adapt Japanese forms' however, *that is a false accusation and against my very religion.* Say it more *truthfully* even if it does mean saying it a little more gently.[22]

The Wasmuth *Sonderheft* of 1911 was advertised in European architectural magazines for several years (plate 4). There is also a third version of this book, similar to the other two, which was published as a catalogue to accompany the exhibition of Wright's work in Berlin in 1910.[23]

1910–1938: European Acclaim, Disillusionment at Home

In addition to his Oak Park studio, Wright maintained a Chicago business office in several different locations over the years. His move to the Fine Arts Building in 1908 placed him in the midst of artists, publishers, and art and book dealers. The sculptor Hermon Atkins MacNeil (1866–1947), creator of the "Dancing Hopi" statuette Wright chose for the entry of the Winslow house, had

22. Wright to Ashbee, 26 September 1910.

23. The existence of this catalogue was mentioned to the author during a conversation with W. R. Hasbrouck, 31 August 1977. Mr. Hasbrouck also referred to his discussion with Mies about the show. But the nature of this exhibition—what was shown, where, and the dates—remains a mystery. Mies mentioned it in the article quoted above. Gropius saw it also (Rosemarie Haag Bletter to author, based on information provided by Edgar Kaufmann, Jr., 7 March 1977). Mies' grandson, Dirk Lohan, stated that he did not recall discussing the show with his grandfather (Lohan to author, 2 December 1976). Howard Dearstyne, a former pupil of Mies, said that he had never heard of it. He added that Mies owned a set of the portfolios but had left it behind in Germany (Dearstyne to author, 2 March 1977).

his studio there. Other tenants were Charles Francis Browne (1859–1920), an artist and editor of a local art magazine, *Brush and Pencil,* in which excerpts of Wright's "The Art and Craft of the Machine" were published in 1901 (no. 47), and his brother, Francis Fisher Browne (1843–1913), publisher of the literary magazine *The Dial,* for whom Wright designed a bookstore in the building.[24]

Upon his return to Chicago in October, 1910, Wright found himself in the center of the city's creative life again. He brought back from Europe several works of the Swedish feminist Ellen Key (1849–1926), which were then enjoying a great vogue and which he and Mrs. Cheney had translated into English. He obtained American publication rights and arranged to have them published by another tenant in the building, Ralph Fletcher Seymour (1876–1966). Three of these works appeared in 1911 and 1912 (nos. 95, 106, 107).[25] The translations were mainly the efforts of Mrs. Cheney (who resumed her maiden name, Borthwick, after her 1911 divorce), but they reflected Wright's own sentiments as well.[26]

Seymour published several other items for Wright, all of them ephemeral and now exceedingly rare. One, mentioned only in

24. It may be useful to note here an advertisement announcing that Browne's Bookstore is open, which appears in *The Dial* issue of 16 November 1907. This contradicts the 1908 date which is always assigned to the design.

25. Another of these translations was published by G. P. Putnam's Sons in 1912 (see item no. 108).

26. According to the records of the University of Michigan, Ann Arbor, Mamah Bouton Borthwick was born in Boone, Iowa on 19 June 1869. She attended the University, receiving a Bachelor of Arts in 1892 and a Master of Arts in 1893. All other biographical information on her seems to derive from articles published in the *Chicago Tribune* during her affair with Wright. After graduation she worked as a librarian in Port Huron, Michigan, leaving in 1899 to marry Edwin H. Cheney. After she came to Chicago she attended lectures at the University of Chicago where for a time she was a student under Robert Herrick. She and Catherine Wright were members of the Nineteenth Century Women's Club. While in Germany she spent part of her time studying in Leipzig. She had other literary interests, including fiction and drama, in addition to feminism and was knowledgable about Goethe. Although she was anxious to become a writer, she produced no original work. A month before her death in 1914, Wright proposed buying the *Weekly Home News,* published in Spring Green, and making her the editor. Lauralee A. Ensign to author, 8 February 1978. *Chicago Tribune,* especially 8 November 1909 and 16 August 1914.

Seymour's autobiography,[27] is a pamphlet published probably in 1911 describing the Wasmuth portfolio and offering it for sale in this country (no. 100; plate 3). A set could be had for $32, payable in installments of four dollars down and four succeeding monthly payments of seven dollars each. Fletcher also published the English version of Wright's introduction to the portfolio to be included in the sets distributed here. In the copies handled by Wasmuth, the introduction appeared only in German translation. The copies intended for this country, brought here with the financial assistance of three clients, Charles E. Roberts, Francis W. Little, and Darwin D. Martin, were largely destroyed in the 1914 fire at Taliesin, where they were stored while awaiting distribution. The work consequently was known better in Europe than in this country.

Another of Wright's works published by Seymour was an important little book entitled *The Japanese Print: An Interpretation* (no. 109; plate 5). It includes a discussion of the elimination of the insignificant, the underlying geometry in nature, and the relation of natural and man-made objects, as demonstrated by the Japanese print artists. In a larger sense, it is a statement of his architectural theories.

The final item Seymour published for Wright was a pamphlet entitled *Experimenting with Human Lives* (no. 149). It was a manifestation of a protest the architect was launching against skyscrapers and other kinds of unsafe buildings in California. The publication was issued in 1923 under the aegis of the Fine Art Society, Olive Hill, Hollywood, California. According to contemporary newspaper accounts, Wright was the president of this group and was ambitious to establish a related school of the fine arts on Olive Hill where he had his architectural studio. The Society was amply financed, but its backers were not made known. This group was to set up a printing plant and send artistic literature to people interested in art in all parts of the world. No other publications of the Society have been located.

Margaret Anderson (1891?–1973), founder and editor of *The Little Review*, also had space in the Fine Arts Building. This liberated woman had worked on the staff of *The Dial*. She then

27. Ralph Fletcher Seymour, *Some Went This Way* (Chicago: Ralph Fletcher Seymour, 1945), p. 125.

established her own magazine, to which Wright contributed $100.[28]
The Little Review was a magazine of the arts, "making no com-
promise with the public taste."[29] When in 1916 Miss Anderson
could find nothing on the arts she considered worthy of publication, she left pages 2-13 of the September issue blank. Wright's
comments on her gesture were included in this issue (no. 135).
She also printed a translation from Goethe with a parenthetical
note that

> (This fragment, a "Hymn to Nature," unknown to us in the
> published works of Goethe, was found in a little bookshop
> in Berlin, and translated into English by a strong man and a
> strong woman whose lives and whose creations have served
> the ideals of all humanity in a way that will gain deeper and
> deeper appreciation.)[30]

Henry Blackman Sell (1889–1974), a young man from Wisconsin, was another participant in the cultural milieu of Chicago in
the years before 1920. As a writer on architecture for the *International Studio,* he was assigned to interview Wright. The two
became friends, and the resulting article appeared in 1915 (no.
127). That same year, Sell's review of *The Japanese Print* was
published in *The Little Review* (no. 111). It has not been noted
in previous studies of Wright. Sell also was interested in the theater and a year earlier had written a pamphlet on the subject.[31]
Finally, it was he who introduced another devotee of the theater,
Aline Barnsdall, to Wright in Chicago. Sell later became editor of
Harper's Bazaar and *Town and Country.*

In the years between 1911 and the mid-1930s, Wright had
increasingly fewer commissions and received comparatively little
recognition in this country. He was dismissed by historians and

28. Margaret Anderson, *My Thirty Years' War: An Autobiography* (New
York: Covici, Friede Publishers, 1930), p. 69.

29. Margaret Anderson, *The Fiery Fountain* (New York: Hermitage House,
1951), p. 6.

30. *The Little Review* 1 (February, 1915): 30 (see item no. 125). It seems
probable that the strong man and strong woman were Wright and Mrs.
Borthwick, although there is no proof. Wright included a portion of this
translation in a eulogy of Mrs. Borthwick published in the *Weekly Home
News. See* Robert C. Twombly, *Frank Lloyd Wright* (New York: Harper &
Row, 1973), p. 137 (see item no. 1920).

31. Henry Blackman Sell, *What Is It All About? A Sketch of the New
Movement in the Theatre* (Chicago: The Laurentian Publishers, 1914).

critics as one who had made a contribution but whose career was now finished. Yet the excitement generated by the publication of his work in Germany continued to be reflected in the European press through the 1920s. Articles appeared regularly in German, Dutch, French, and Czechoslovakian periodicals, and four monographs were published by 1932. Also, the 1910 Wasmuth portfolio was reprinted in smaller format in 1924.

Some of the European architects who made pilgrimages to see Wright's work published their observations upon returning home. After a visit to the United States in 1911, prompted by a special invitation from William Gray Purcell, Hendrik P. Berlage (1856–1934), a reformer of Dutch architecture comparable to the American H. H. Richardson (1838–1886), delivered three speeches in Zurich. These treated Wright's work as something extraordinary, and their subsequent publication did much to introduce his innovations to Europe.[32] Other architects followed. Richard Neutra (1892–1970) came in 1923, and Erich Mendelsohn (1887–1953), recognized from the early 1920s as one of the four or five most important modern architects in Germany, came in 1924. Both men stayed with Wright at Taliesin. Their subsequent books, published in Europe, include numerous examples of Wright's work seen firsthand.[33]

J. J. P. Oud (1890–1960), city architect of Rotterdam from 1918 to 1933 and a member of the de Stijl group, did not visit America, but an analysis he wrote of Wright's influence upon European architecture was included in his important book *Holländische Architektur,* published by the Bauhaus (no. 175). The less well-known Dutch architects Robt. Van't Hoff, who traveled to America and met Wright, and Jan Wils also acknowledged his influence in articles for European magazines (nos. 140, 142, 144).

The most remarkable tribute was a series of seven issues of the magazine *Wendingen* published in 1925 in Amsterdam by Architectura et Amicitia, the counterpart of the Rotterdam de Stijl

32. These articles were responsible for Le Corbusier's introduction to Wright. *See* Sigfried Giedion, *Space, Time and Architecture* (Cambridge, Massachusetts: Harvard University Press, 1967), p. 426.

33. Neutra's books are: *Wie baut Amerika?* (Stuttgart: J. Hoffman, [1927]), and *Amerika* (Wien: A. Schroll, 1930). Those by Mendelsohn are: *Amerika* (Berlin: R. Mosse, 1926), and *Russland, Europa, Amerika* (Berlin: R. Mosse, 1929).

group (no. 168). These issues were later combined into a book and included appreciations by the Amsterdam architect and editor of *Wendingen* H. Th. Wijdeveld (1885–), Lewis Mumford, Berlage, Louis Sullivan, and Rob. Mallet-Stevens, who was a Belgian architect working in Paris. This was the first book on Wright published in English, and he considered it the most beautiful presentation of his work (no. 165).[34] *Wendingen* was in the habit of devoting whole issues to individuals, and architectural subjects were Wijdeveld's main interest. Michel De Klerk was given seven issues and W. M. Dudok five. In an interesting display of syncretism, Wijdeveld placed a cover designed by El Lissitzky on an earlier issue devoted to Wright (no. 143). Wijdeveld himself designed a printed invitation (plate 8) and a poster for the Amsterdam appearance of a major exhibition that toured the U.S. and Europe in 1930 and 1931.

The other books of the period are less important. A German volume, edited by H. de Fries and published in 1926 (no. 172), actually appeared before the compilation of the *Wendingen* issues was complete. Irritated and disappointed in Wright, Wijdeveld wrote (spellings as given):

> ...I heared that you gave a set of the latest designs to a commercial publication in Germany.
>
> I can't help being disappointed about the publication which De Vries made in Germany. Now nothing can be done anymore. My book is ready and we are bussy with wrapping the edition in linnen, bind it in parchment and leather and execute the cover you want. I hope the whole appearance will be up to your standing.
>
> As nothing can be done at present anymore, I would like to make a proposal to you. Can you agree that we publish within one or two years a second volume of the same printing, size and appearance of this book, with a new article from your hand and introduction etc: etc: If os, we will in that way publish the Life-work of a famous architect.... And

---

34. It has been mentioned that the Queen of Holland subsidized this volume, but I have not verified this information. *See* Jim Drought and Wortley Munroe, "Not Without Honor," *Wisconsin Literary Magazine* 28 (February, 1929): 14 (see item no. 218). Mrs. John Lloyd Wright also suggested that this was true in a 1976 conversation with the author.

if so...Please, dont publish your work in other periodicals, but keep it together as a treasure for the second volume.[35]

The de Fries book includes color reproductions of drawings for several of Wright's current projects in California and additional statements from European architects. A book published in France in 1928 was simply a compilation of photographs which had appeared in the periodical *Cahiers d'Art* (no. 201). It includes a "brief and perhaps rather blind foreword"[36] by Henry-Russell Hitchcock in which Wright was assigned a position in the past generation. Lewis Mumford pointed out at the time that it was significant that an American was asked to do the introduction: "—a fact which possibly testifies to the unfamiliarity of the French with Mr. Wright's work, since his influence in France has been negligible..."[37] Another collection of illustrations, this time from *L'Architecture Vivante*, was published in 1932 but added nothing to the existing literature (no. 301).

Although Wright was not completely ignored in the United States after 1910, it is significant that no full-length critical study was completed until 1942. The period before 1914 had been one of architectural vitality in the Midwest and on the West Coast, but by the outset of World War I the Arts and Crafts and related movements had ceased to exist. Since 1893, the eclecticism of the Columbian Exposition had set the prevailing popular taste, and the influence of the Ecole des Beaux-Arts continued to be felt in America through the 1930s. The magazines which had been supportive of the new spirit changed their editorial policies and began publishing traditional designs. Disappointingly, many of the Prairie School architects themselves abandoned their earlier styles, although the progressive movement had been in opposition from its very beginnings to the forces of Beaux-Arts classicism. Among the critics, there were few who were sympathetic to

35. Wijdeveld to Wright, 25 April 1926, Wijdeveld Archives, Architectural Museum, Amsterdam. The second volume proposed by Wijdeveld was not published.

36. Henry-Russell Hitchcock, *In the Nature of Materials* (New York: Duell, Sloan and Pearce, 1942), p. xxxi (see item no. 573).

37. Lewis Mumford, "Frank Lloyd Wright and the New Pioneers," *Architectural Record* 65 (April, 1929): 414 (see item no. 202). Courtesy of *Architectural Record*.

modern architecture (Hitchcock's pioneering study did not
appear until 1929).[38]

By 1928 things had changed. Lewis Mumford observed:

> The energies that worked below the ground so long are now
> erupting in a hundred unsuspected places; and once more
> the American architect has begun to attack the problems of
> design with the audacity and exuberance of a Root, a Sulli-
> van, a Wright. In a sense, we have at long last caught up with
> 1890.[39]

The later 1920s were years of extreme personal hardship for
Frank Lloyd Wright. He had little work and turned to writing,
partially for self-expression and partially to relieve his ever-
mounting financial obligations. In 1927, at the urging of his wife,
he began his autobiography. Portions were completed while he
was in seclusion with his family in Minnesota. Three sections
written for the book were published separately in *Liberty* and
Country Life in 1927 and 1929 (nos. 199, 224, 226). During
roughly the same period, as he later wrote, he was aided by his
friend Michael A. Mikkelsen (1866–1941), editor of the *Architectural Record* from 1914 to 1937, who, upon finding Wright

> ...walking the streets of the big city in nearly every kind of
> distress except a guilty conscience—kindly suggested that I
> write them [a series of articles] offering a sum in payment
> so far beyond the stipends usually paid for contributions
> concerning architecture that it would seem like bragging
> were I to mention it here. Since I have mentioned it at all it
> is bragging—anyway.
>
> I started to write and, wishing also to study, found noth-
> ing on the subject ["matter"] existed in any language as
> interpretation. So all I had to do or could do was to sit down
> and write out of the back of my own head as my own exper-
> ience this series of interpretations.[40]

These thirteen articles appeared in two series in the *Architectural Record* in 1927 and 1928 (nos. 195-8, 206-14). Wright was

38. Henry-Russell Hitchcock, *Modern Architecture: Romanticism and
Reintegration* (New York: Payson & Clarke Ltd., 1929).

39. Lewis Mumford, "American Architecture To-Day," *Architecture* 57
(April, 1928): 181.

40. Frank Lloyd Wright, [introduction], *Taliesin* 1 (no. 1, 1934): 8 (see
item no. 2037).

A real toy—the press—for boys as well as for grown-up rich men. And what *is* the fascination to the average man or boy of seeing his name in type, even on a business or visiting card? It is phenomenal! A secret is there of intense human interest.[43]

Two of Wright's River Forest clients shared with him an enthusiasm for printing. In 1896 William Herman Winslow and Chauncey L. Williams produced an edition of John Keats' *The Eve of St. Agnes* for which Wright designed the title page (no. 22; plate 1).[44] The book was printed on a hand press which was located first in Williams' attic and was then moved into Winslow's stable.

A more ambitious publication of the Auvergne Press, as the enterprise was known, was *The House Beautiful*, an essay by Wright's friend, the Unitarian minister W. C. Gannett. Gannett's theme was a proposal for the betterment of the home, advocating such ideals as simplicity, naturalness, and warmth, all qualities Wright sought in his work. Wright and Winslow worked for nearly three years on this book,[45] the importance of which lies in the page decorations which Wright designed for it (no. 18). Although the designs exhibit several Arts and Crafts characteristics—a double spread title page, red and black printing, and an emphasis on hand craftsmanship—the decorations diverge from the usual Arts and Crafts style. They are rather more innovative and provide an expectedly architectural setting for the text.[46]

43. Wright, p. 34.

44. This title page design is stylistically similar to coeval drawings for the Heller house frieze. Edgar Kaufmann, Jr., has linked the ladies used in the frieze to figure four of Viollet-le-Duc's essay on Roman architecture, with which Wright is known to have been familiar. *See* Kaufmann's "The Fine Arts and Frank Lloyd Wright." In *Four Great Makers of Modern Architecture* (New York: Trustees of Columbia University, 1963), p. 31. A drawing of this frieze was reproduced in *Drawings for a Living Architecture* (New York: Horizon Press for the Bear Run Foundation Inc., and the Edgar J. Kaufmann Charitable Foundation, 1959), p. 246. It was mistakenly identified as being for the Husser house.

45. Wright to Gannett, 27 December 1898, Gannett Collection, University of Rochester Library.

46. Susan Otis Thompson, "The Arts and Crafts Book." *In* Robert Judson Clark, *The Arts and Crafts Movement in America, 1876–1916* (Princeton: Princeton University Press, 1972), pp. 94, 101 (see item no. 1875).

This was a period of literary revival in Chicago. There were several organizations of authors and book collectors, and Wright kept in close contact with them. Chauncey Williams and W. Irving Way were partners in the firm of Way and Williams which published carefully designed books. They, with yet another of Wright's clients, George M. Millard, were charter members of one literary group, the Caxton Club.[47] Wright joined later. Millard and his wife Alice, of whom Wright spoke sympathetically in his autobiography, amassed a notable collection, now in the Huntington Library, San Marino, California, "illustrating the evolution of the book."[48]

Wright designed many publications. Each is a complete package: architecture, graphic design, and text. For an announcement of his practice, printed ca. 1898, Wright integrated a red square, his insignia in numerous incarnations throughout his career, with the printed words to form a unified composition (no. 27, plate 2). Lloyd Wright explained that the square acts as a pivot around which swings the arm of the text.[49] The graphic designs evolved from the early Arts and Crafts influence to bold linear abstractions made with T square and triangle in the 1930s. Among the most striking examples of these later works are the internal title pages for *An Autobiography* (no. 303; plate 9), the dust jacket for *The Disappearing City* (no. 328), and the cover and internal title page (no. 457; plate 11) for the *Architectural Forum* of January, 1938. After this, he relied heavily upon the talent of Eugene Masselink (1911?–1962), whose designs owed much to Wright's influence. One example of Masselink's work is the cover for the January, 1948, issue of the *Architectural Forum* (no. 745).

The year 1932 marked the publication of *The International*

47. *Brush and Pencil* 1 (January, 1898): 107. For Wright's participation *see* Robert C. Twombly, "Frank Lloyd Wright in Spring Green, 1911-1932," *Wisconsin Magazine of History* 51 (Spring 1968): 208 (see item no. 1756). Information on Way and Williams is in Joseph Blumenthal, *The Printed Book in America* (Boston: David R. Godine, in association with the Dartmouth College Library, 1977), pp. 48-50.

48. *The George and Alice Millard Collection Illustrating the Evolution of the Book* (San Marino, California: The Huntington Library, 1939) (see item no. 462).

49. Conversations with author, 1976. Further examples of this composition may be seen on the promotional pamphlet for the Wasmuth portfolios (plate 3), and on *Experimenting with Human Lives* (no. 149).

Style: Architecture Since 1922, by Henry-Russell Hitchcock and Philip Johnson, which was prepared concurrently with the "Modern Architecture" exhibition at the Museum of Modern Art in New York. Wright's work was included with that of the leading modernists. His reaction, entitled "Of Thee I Sing," was published in *Shelter* magazine in April (no. 355). Two months earlier, the same periodical, then known as *T-Square,* had published an attack by Wright on the International Style, which he regarded as no more than another form of eclecticism. The editor, George Howe, saw the article before its appearance and included his own rebuttal in the same issue. Howe's biographer identified this as the single most important clash in the early days of modernism (nos. 341, 353).[50]

The 1930s are peppered with fascinating and seemingly uncharacteristic samples of Wright's literary output. Many were published in obscure periodicals and are all but forgotten. There are, for example, three scenarios whose titles bear repeating: "The Man Who Grew Whiskers" (no. 294), "The Man St. Peter Liked: Those Favored of God Are Those Who Plant and Nurture the Trees He Made" (no. 428), and "The Man Who Paid Cash: A Scenario Wherein a Rich Man Meets an Artist and, For a While, Each Has His Say" (no. 500). There also are several book reviews by Wright, including that of Morrison's biography of Sullivan (no. 394), although their publication was viewed by him as an indication of his own reduced circumstances. He had a literary agent during this period, George Bye (1887–1957) of New York. Little of their association is known, but its existence may partially explain this variety of material.

An activity which has gone unnoticed was Wright's membership on the Board of Consulting Editors of *Arts and Decoration* between January, 1936, and February, 1940, although his presence can hardly be detected in the pages of the magazine. Also unnoted are his responses published in 1934 to a questionnaire on industrial design, a subject of contemporary interest to him.[51] The year 1931 saw the appearance of a reminiscence of the English short story writer Katherine Mansfield (1888–1923) by

50. Robert A. M. Stern, *George Howe* (New Haven and London: Yale University Press, 1975), p. 141.

51. Geoffrey Holme, *Industrial Design and the Future* (London: The Studio Limited and New York: The Studio Publications Inc., 1934), pp. 33-77.

Olgivanna, the architect's wife (no. 299). The two women met at
the Gurdjieff Institute at Fontainebleau-Avon, where Miss Mansfield died. This article, the first published work by Mrs. Wright,
has been cited in subsequent attempts to determine the influence
of Gurdjieff on Wright.

Interest in Wright revived during the 1930s. A major exhibition
of his work toured several European and American cities and received considerable attention from the press. Pauline Schindler
(1893–1977), wife of the California architect R. M. Schindler, who
assisted Wright with the Barnsdall commission, paid tribute to the
master in her article "Modern Architecture Acknowledges the
Light Which Kindled It" (no. 390). Chapters on Wright were included in books by Alexander Woollcott (no. 242), John Dos
Passos (no. 399), and the art critic Thomas Craven (no. 371). The
greatest accolade of all was the special issue of the *Architectural
Forum* published in 1938 and devoted entirely to Wright's recent
work (no. 457). The issue, written and designed by the architect,
was proof of his continuing vitality and creativity. That same
year, Wright's portrait appeared on the cover of *Time* (no. 454),
published by his friend Henry Luce (1898–1967).

1939–1959: The Second Golden Age

If one wishes to identify a single building which marked Wright's
comeback, let it be the Kaufmann house, "Fallingwater," in
Pennsylvania. This was followed soon after by a second tour de
force, the Johnson Wax building in Wisconsin. Both works were
widely published, and photographs of the Kaufmann house were
given a special showing at the Museum of Modern Art (no. 430).
In 1939 Wright was asked to lecture to the Royal Institute of
British Architects. The speeches were published (no. 463) and
were given ample attention in the British press. Numerous other
invitations to speak followed, and he was lavished with honors
throughout the remainder of his life.

A major retrospective of Wright's career was held at the Museum
of Modern Art in 1940. He planned and supervised the installation
of the show with the assistance of a group of students from Taliesin. The museum's Department of Architecture had intended to
issue a catalogue which would have included a great deal of factual
and critical material, including essays by several architects and

architectural historians. Wright, insisting upon "no prejudgments in advance of the show," refused to permit its publication, although it had been intended as a tribute to him.[52]

Henry-Russell Hitchcock's major study of 1942, *In the Nature of Materials,* emerged as a sort of *"ex post facto* catalogue" for the exhibition (no. 573).[53] This detailed and profusely illustrated work is the first American monograph on the architect. Hitchcock, expanding his narrow statement of 1928, describes Wright as the prophet of modern architecture who in 1941 "seems to stand poised for new triumphs at the opening of a great new phase of his career."[54] He wrote that Wright had "physically outlived the generation of the traditionalists,"...and "he seems to be outliving the generation of the great European innovators of the twenties."

The book is the standard work on the architect. The original edition remained in print for nearly a quarter of a century. Its principal shortcoming is that Wright's later work is not within its scope, and a new edition published in 1973 does not treat the period adequately.

In the Nature of Materials was the second of a group of three volumes on Wright published by the fledgling firm of Duell, Sloan and Pearce between 1941 and 1943. The first, *Frank Lloyd Wright on Architecture* (no. 532), was an anthology of his writings, edited from the original manuscripts by Frederick Gutheim. The third was a new, expanded edition of *An Autobiography* (no. 595).[55] A fourth work, Wright's homage to Louis Sullivan, *Genius and the Mobocracy* (no. 750), was published by the firm in 1949.

In spite of the immense amount of material available, the decades of the 1940s and 1950s are, with some exceptions, less

52. Alfred Barr, [letter], *Parnassus* 13 (January, 1941): 3. Mies van der Rohe and Harwell Hamilton Harris were two architects who prepared essays for the catalogue. The catalogue exists as a "ghost" in at least one source. *See* John McAndrew, ed., *Guide to Modern Architecture: Northeast States* (New York: The Museum of Modern Art, [1940]), p. 126. The museum's librarian recently confirmed, however, that it was not published (Inga Forslund to author, 11 September 1975).

53. Hitchcock, *Nature,* p. xxix.

54. Ibid., p. 103.

55. An extremely useful index to this edition was recently compiled. *See* Linn Ann Cowles, *An Index and Guide to "An Autobiography," the 1943 Edition, by Frank Lloyd Wright* (Hopkins, Minnesota: Greenwich Design Publications, 1976).

interesting from a bibliographic viewpoint. Although the architect's own writings never lose their sense of vitality, those published are frequently reworked versions of earlier pieces. His book *When Democracy Builds,* published in 1945 (no. 609), is a new edition of *The Disappearing City* (no. 328). Wright's son John published an irreverent biography of his father in 1946 (no. 648) which is amusing but probably should not be taken too seriously. Both father and son were careless historians.

An exhibition, prepared in response to the Italian admiration of Wright's work which developed after World War II, opened in Florence in 1951 after an American premier in Philadelphia. The show, "Sixty Years of Living Architecture," subsequently was shown in several cities in Europe, the United States, and Mexico. Catalogues including a greeting from Wright were prepared for the individual countries (nos. 833, 861-3, 912, 926, 991). The Philadelphia architect Oscar Stonorov (1905–1970) was responsible for overseeing the exhibition and its attendant publications.[56]

Magazine editors were once again paying attention to Wright's architecture, and much of his current work was published as soon as it was completed. The *Architectural Forum,* having given him a second issue in 1948, followed with still a third in 1951 (no. 854). The number of articles appearing in a single year reached an all-time peak in 1953, a quantity surpassed only in 1959 after his death. Many document the vicissitudes of the Guggenheim Museum, his most controversial and his most frequently published building. Two periodicals in particular should be singled out for their attention to Wright's work. *House and Home* published a number of articles in color featuring his later buildings, which, as Robert Twombly has suggested, would together make an excellent volume; and Elizabeth Gordon, editor of *House Beautiful* between 1942 and 1964, was generous in her presentation of the architect's designs and theories. She published two remarkable and useful special issues on him in 1955 and 1959, each accompanied by a separate, comprehensive bibliography (nos. 1046 and 1264). She also featured the work of his disciples and was an avid propagandist against the "threat" of the International Style.

In 1952 Wright entered into a still-active publishing agreement

56. The often-contentious correspondence between Wright and Stonorov during the time of the exhibitions is in the Archive of Contemporary History, University of Wyoming, Laramie.

with Ben Raeburn of Horizon Press, New York. Raeburn had long been infatuated with *An Autobiography,* and it became his dream to publish Wright's works. He wrote the architect in 1952 and was invited to meet him at the Plaza Hotel.[57] A relationship was established, and since then twenty-three books by Mr. and Mrs. Wright have appeared under Horizon's imprint.

The first Horizon book was *The Future of Architecture* (no. 913), published in 1953. Subsequent works, including new material, anthologies of previous texts, the writings of Mrs. Wright, and a lavish presentation of the architect's drawings, appeared annually through 1960. Books continue to be published, though less regularly.

A detailed study of Wright's work up to 1910, completed with his cooperation and published the year before his death, was looked on with disfavor by him. He extensively and critically annotated his own copy, which is now held by the Wright Foundation in Arizona. This book (no. 1206) by Grant Manson was projected as the first of three volumes covering the architect's career, but the next two did not appear.

1960 to the Present

Several admirable critical studies have been completed since Wright's death. Vincent Scully, in his brief but incisive text of 1960 (no. 1394), analyzed the principles of Wright's designs. Another notable book is that by Norris Kelly Smith, which compares Wright's literary work with his architecture (no. 1636). Leonard K. Eaton's analysis of Wright's clients and those of the traditional architect Howard Van Doren Shaw was published in 1969 (no. 1762). H. Allen Brooks' fine study of the Prairie School was published in 1972 (no. 1869). The assessment of the Usonian houses by John Sergeant (no. 2001) is the first comprehensive study of these buildings.

The biographies of Wright vary widely in quality, a frequently-cited reason being the closely-held archives of the Wright Foundation. The best biographical interpretation is by Robert C. Twombly (no. 1920), although it is marred by its unnecessary condemnation of Wright's successors. The architect's widow, Olgivanna,

57. "Story Behind the Book: 'An Autobiography'," *Publishers Weekly* 212 (25 July 1977): 55 (see item no. 2032).

has written four books which are anecdotal but pleasant to read and offer personal insights into Wright's life. Several of Wright's close associates have seen fit to write about him. None has been as eloquent or perceptive as Edgar Kaufmann, Jr. (1910–   ), a former apprentice of the Taliesin Fellowship and son of the client for "Fallingwater." His first published statement on the architect appeared in 1947; since then he has edited several books on Wright and has contributed numerous articles to periodicals.

The Wright Foundation holds slightly more than nineteen thousand drawings by the architect or his associates. Some three hundred of these were shown at the Museum of Modern Art in 1962 and illustrated in an accompanying catalogue (no. 1489). More recent and unfortunately somewhat repetitious publications include drawings reproduced in color (nos. 2000 and 2023). The value of these works lies in their ability to communicate something of the superb quality of the original drawings.

Horizon Press has issued a high-quality series of works no longer readily available. The Prairie School Press has published a number of reprints, the most handsome being *The House Beautiful* (no. 1530); it also issues the *Prairie School Review.* This quarterly journal, which now appears only sporadically, has brought to light much information about Wright's early work. A new bimonthly, *Frank Lloyd Wright Newsletter,* made its first appearance in February, 1978, as an offshoot of the efforts to restore and adapt Wright's home and studio in Oak Park.

This bibliography spans a ninety-one year time period. Approximately one-third of the references listed have been published in the scant seventeen years following Frank Lloyd Wright's death. Enthusiasm is world wide. There are books in Russian and Arabic and translations of American works in various other languages. Japanese interest is especially strong and dates back to at least 1916, when an edition of the 1910 Wasmuth portfolio was published in Osaka (no. 131). This flood of material, which shows no sign of subsiding, is in itself sufficient testimony to the continuing fascination with Frank Lloyd Wright.

Pacific Palisades, California   ROBERT L. SWEENEY
June, 1978

Explanatory Note

This bibliography is a chronological listing of books and articles by and about Frank Lloyd Wright. Books are listed first, then periodicals, alphabetically by year. Reviews are located under the books to which they apply rather than in the year they appeared. Exhibition catalogues, pamphlets, and ephemera are treated as books, and articles in yearbooks are listed with periodicals.

There has been no attempt to catalogue all the numerous general books on architecture containing separate sections or chapters on Wright, although entries for some especially important ones will be found. Studies of architecture that mention Wright only in passing are ignored. Articles in encyclopedias and other reference books, unpublished doctoral dissertations, and most newspaper articles are similarly omitted.

Publications of the Taliesin Press appeared on a sporadic basis and are unique in nature. They are described in a separate list which comprises Appendix A. Appendix B is an inventory of pertinent material available from the Historic American Buildings Survey in Washington, D. C.

Dimensions are given in centimeters with height preceding width, and all printed pages have been counted in arriving at the total number in each book.

ABBREVIATIONS & LIST OF PERIODICALS

ca., circa
cm., centimeters
del., delixit (drawn by)
dwgs., drawings
ed., editor, edited
ext., exterior
front., frontispiece
i.e., id est (that is)
ill., ills., illustration, illustrations
int., interior
no., nos., number, numbers
no pub., no publisher
n.p., no place
orig., original
p., pp., page, pages
pl., pls., plate, plates
pseud., pseudonym
sup., supplement
vol., vols., volume, volumes

Ja   January
Fe   February
Mr   March
Ap   April
My   May
Je   June
Jy   July
Ag   August
Se   September
O   October
N   November
D   December

Sp   Spring
Su   Summer
Fa   Fall
W   Winter
Au   Autumn

PERIODICALS

AIA J	American Institute of Architects. Journal
Am Arch	American Architect
Am Arch & Build N	American Architect and Building News
Am Inst Plan J	American Institute of Planners. Journal
Am M Art	American Magazine of Art
Am Q	American Quarterly
Arch & Build N	Architect and Building News
Arch & Eng	Architect and Engineer
Arch Assn J	Architectural Association Journal
Arch d'Aujourd'hui	Architecture d'Aujourd'hui
Arch Design	Architectural Design
Arch For	Architectural Forum
Arch R	Architectural Review (London)
Arch R (Boston)	Architectural Review (Boston)
Arch Rec	Architectural Record
Arch Yrbk	Architects' Year Book

Architects' J	Architects' Journal
Art B	Art Bulletin
Art D	Art Digest
Art J	Art Journal
Art N	Art News
Art Q	Art Quarterly
Art in Am	Art in America
Arts & Arch	Arts and Architecture
C Arts & Arch	California Arts and Architecture
Coll Art J	College Art Journal
Creat Art	Creative Art
Engin N R	Engineering News Record
H & H	House and Home
Harper	Harper's Magazine
Hist Pres	Historic Preservation
House B	House Beautiful
Inland Arch	Inland Architect
Inland Arch & N Rec	Inland Architect and News Record
Int	Interiors
JA	Japan Architect
JSAH	Society of Architectural Historians. Journal
Ladies' Home J	Ladies' Home Journal
Landscape Arch	Landscape Architecture
Liturg Art	Liturgical Arts
Mag Art	Magazine of Art
Nat Arch	National Architect (Philadelphia or Detroit, as indicated)
New Repub	New Republic
Northw Arch	Northwest Architect
NYTBR	New York Times Book Review
NYTM	New York Times Magazine
Pac Arch & Build	Pacific Architect and Builder
Pencil P	Pencil Points
Prairie Sch R	Prairie School Review
Progress Arch	Progressive Architecture
RIBA J	Royal Institute of British Architects. Journal
Roy Arch Inst Can J	Royal Architectural Institute of Canada. Journal
Sat R	Saturday Review (of Literature)
W Arch	Western Architect
Wasmuths Monatsh	Wasmuths Monatshefte für Baukunst
Wis Mag Hist	Wisconsin Magazine of History

FRANK LLOYD WRIGHT
AN ANNOTATED BIBLIOGRAPHY

1886

Periodicals

1. Gannett, William C. "Christening a Country Church." *Unity* (Chicago) XVII (28 Ag 1886), pp. 356-7.
   Includes information on Wright's role in the construction of Unity Chapel, Helena Valley, Wisconsin, designed by J. L. Silsbee.

1887

Periodicals

2. "Country Residence for Hillside Estate, Helena Valley, Wis." *Inland Arch & N Rec* X (Ag 1887), hors-texte pl.
   Perspective drawing and plan, signed F. L. Wright, Archt. No text.

3. "Unitarian Chapel for Sioux City, Iowa." *Inland Arch & N Rec* IX (Je 1887), hors-texte pl.
   Perspective drawing and plan, signed Frank L. Wright, Archt. Chicago, Ill. No text.

4. "Unity Chapel, Helena, Wis." In [*Chicago.*] *All Souls Church. Fourth Annual.* Chicago, 1887. P. 33.
   Perspective drawing, signed by Wright.

1888

Periodicals

5. "Houses for Victor Falkenau, Chicago. Adler & Sullivan, Architects, Chicago." *Inland Arch & N Rec* XI (Je 1888), hors-texte pl.

Perspective drawing and plan, signed Frank L. Wright. No text.

6.   "Houses for William Waller, Chicago. J. L. Silsbee, Architect." *Inland Arch & N Rec* XI (My 1888), hors-texte pl. Perspective drawing by Wright. No text.

7.   "Residence at Helena Valley, Wis." *Inland Arch & N Rec* XI (Fe 1888), hors-texte pl.
Hillside Home School building no. 1. Perspective drawings by Wright. No text.

8.   "Residence for J. L. Cochran, Edgewater, Ill. J. L. Silsbee, Architect." *Inland Arch & N Rec* XI (Jy 1888), hors-texte pl. Perspective drawing, signed F. Ll. Wright: del. No text.

9.   "Residence for J. L. Cochrane Esq. J. L. Silsbee, Architect." *Inland Arch & N Rec* XI (Mr 1888), hors-texte pl.
Perspective drawing and plan, signed Frank Ll Wright: Del. No text. This client is the same as the one in item 8, but the name is misspelled here. The houses are different.

1890

Periodicals

10.   "New Offices of Adler & Sullivan, Architects, Chicago." *Engineering and Building Record* XXII (7 Je 1890), p. 5.
Includes floor plans showing location of Wright's office.

1891

Periodicals

11.   "Residence for Mr. James Charnley, Chicago. Adler and Sullivan, Architects." *Inland Arch & N Rec* XVIII (Ag 1891), hors-texte pl.
Perspective drawing of a house now acknowledged to have been designed by Wright. Same as no. 13. No text.

1892

Periodicals

12. "House of James Charnley, Esq., Astor Street, Chicago, Ill."
Am Arch & Build N (International and Imperial editions only)
XXXVIII (31 D 1892), hors-texte pl.
Photograph. No text.

13. "Residence of James Charnley, Esq., Chicago. Adler and
Sullivan, Architects." *Arch Rec* I (Ja-Mr 1892), p. 348.
Perspective drawing of a house now acknowledged to have
been designed by Wright. No text.

1894

Periodicals

14. "Association Notes." *Inland Arch & N Rec* XXIV (D 1894),
p. 48.
A letter, signed by Wright and others, announcing the win-
ners of the Robert Clark Testimonial (see no. 15).

15. "Competition, Robert Clark Testimonial." *Inland Arch &
N Rec* XXIV (Se 1894), p. 17.
Notice of a competition for the best drawing for an art club.
Wright was a member of the judging committee. The same no-
tice also appeared in *Brickbuilder* III (Se 1894), pp. 181-2.

16. "Residence of W. I. Clark, La Grange, Illinois." *Inland Arch
& N Rec* XXIV (Ag 1894), hors-texte pl.
Photograph. No text.

1895

Periodicals

17. "Residence by Architect Frank L. Wright, for Himself, Oak
Park, Illinois." *Inland Arch & N Rec* XXIV (Ja 1895), hors-texte
pl.
Photograph. No text.

1896

Books

18.   Gannett, William C. *The House Beautiful.* In a Setting Designed by Frank Lloyd Wright and Printed by Hand at the Auvergne Press in River Forest by William Herman Winslow and Frank Lloyd Wright during the Winter Months of the Year Eighteen Hundred Ninety Six and Seven. River Forest, [Illinois]: Auvergne Press, 1896-97.
   34.4 x 29 cm., 55 pp.
   This essay by a Unitarian minister and friend of Wright's uncle Jenkin Lloyd Jones had been published prior to its appearance here. The importance of this version lies in its original page decorations in black and red by Wright. The edition of ninety numbered copies signed by Winslow and Wright was printed in the stable Wright designed for Winslow, who was his first independent client. A booklet of fourteen pages sewn to the front endpaper contains illustrations reproducing Wright's photographs of dried weeds. The book was bound in half leather and green cloth. Gannett's name is misspelled Gannet on the title page. The text was reprinted in *My Father Who Is on Earth,* by John Lloyd Wright (no. 648).
   □ A facsimile edition was published by W. R. Hasbrouck, Park Forest, Illinois, 1963 (no. 1530).

REVIEWS of the 1963 edition
19.   Brooks, H. Allen. *JSAH* XXIV (My 1965), pp. 178-80.
20.   Hobson, L. H. *Prairie Sch R* I (no. 1, 1964), p. 17.
21.   Manson, Grant. "An Evocative Experience." *Progress Arch* XLIV (D 1963), pp. 172, 174.

22.   Keats, John. *The Eve of St. Agnes.* With an Appreciation by Leigh Hunt. [River Forest, Illinois]: Auvergne Press, 1896.
   The title page of this edition was designed by Wright and was printed in red and black. A reproduction of it appears on Plate 1 of this volume. The book was published by Winslow and another of Wright's clients, Chauncey L. Williams, in an edition of sixty-five numbered copies.

1897

Periodicals

23. "A Chicago Residence. Frank L. Wright, Architect." *Inland Arch & N Rec* XXIX (Jy 1897), hors-texte pl.
Harlan house. No text.

24. "Designs." U. S. Patent Office. *Official Gazette* LXXXI (7 D 1897), pp. 1773-9.
Patented designs by Wright for the Luxfer Prism Company, Chicago. No text.

25. "Rose-Garden and Residence of Louis H. Sullivan, Architect, Ocean Springs, Miss." *Am Arch & Build N* LV (23 Ja 1897), hors-texte pl.
Photograph of a house now acknowledged to have been designed by Wright. No text.

26. "Successful Houses, III." *House B* I (15 Fe 1897), pp. 64-9.
Wright house, Oak Park.

1898

Books

27. *Frank Lloyd Wright, Architect.* The Rookery, Chicago. Room 1119. Hours Twelve to Two. Telephone Main 2668. Draughting Rooms and Studio at the Corner of Forest and Chicago Avenues. Oak Park, Illinois. Hours Eight to Eleven a.m. Seven to Nine p.m. Telephone Oak Park.
12.3 x 14.3 cm., 4 pp., 1 ill.
A promotional pamphlet printed in red and black on gray paper for Wright's architecture practice. It includes floor plans of the Rookery business office and of the Oak Park studio. An earlier version with annotations in Wright's hand exists in the Avery Library, Columbia University. The announcement is undated. John Lloyd Wright stated that it was published in 1893 (see no. 648, p. 22), a date used again by Twombly (no. 1920, p. 319). It is, however, improbable for two reasons that it appeared before 1898. Wright did not move to the Rookery until

that year, and the draughting rooms and studio mentioned in
the title and illustrated in a plan were constructed between
February and July, 1898. A reproduction of this announcement will be found on Plate 2 of this volume.

Periodicals

28. "Brick and Terra-Cotta Work in American Cities, and Manufacturers' Department." *Brickbuilder* VII (My 1898), pp. 106-8.
      A notice that Wright, George R. Dean, and R. C. Spencer,
Jr. had been chosen by the Central Art Association on behalf
of the Trans-Mississippi Exposition to design a home typical
of American architecture.

29. "Brick and Terra-Cotta Work in American Cities, and Manufacturers' Department." *Brickbuilder* VII (N 1898), pp. 239-41.
      A notice of a collaboration between Wright and Dwight Per-
kins on the design for a new church (Abraham Lincoln Center,
Chicago).

30. "An Interesting Competition." *Inland Arch & N Rec* XXX
(Ja 1898), pp. 63-4.
      Luxfer Prism office building, Chicago (project). The same
information appears in *Am Arch & Build N* LIX (12 Fe 1898),
sup. 189, pp. 1-3.

31. "Interior by Frank Lloyd Wright." *Forms & Fantasies* I
(N 1898), pl. 87.
      Winslow house, River Forest. No text.

32. "Residence at Oak Park, Illinois. Frank L. Wright, Architect." *Inland Arch & N Rec* (photogravure edition only) XXXI
(Je 1898), hors-texte pl.
      Moore house. No text.

1899

Periodicals

33. "Apartment Building, Chicago, F. L. Wright, Architect."

Inland Arch & N Rec (photogravure edition only) XXXII (Ja 1899), hors-texte pl.
Francis Apartments. No text.

34. "Brick and Terra-Cotta Work in American and Foreign Cities, and Manufacturers' Department." *Brickbuilder* VIII (Ja 1899), pp. 16-19.
Includes comment on All Souls Building, Chicago (project), Wright and Dwight H. Perkins, associated architects.

35. Granger, Alfred H. "An Architect's Studio." *House B* VII (D 1899), pp. 36-45.
Wright studio, Oak Park. Also in Dow, Joy Wheeler. *The Book of a Hundred Houses.* Chicago: Herbert S. Stone, 1902 (not seen).

36. "Residence for Mr. Furbeck, Oak Park, Illinois." *Inland Arch & N Rec* (photogravure edition only) XXXIII (Fe 1899), hors-texte pl.
Rollin Furbeck house. Photograph. No text.

1900

Books

37. [Chicago Architectural Club.] *Annual of the Chicago Architectural Club, Being the Book of the Thirteenth Annual Exhibition 1900.* Chicago: Architectural Club, 1900. Pp. 75-84, 156, 159.
An exhibition catalogue containing several illustrations of Wright's work: the Wright studio and the Moore house, Oak Park; the McAfee house, Kenilworth (project); the Eckart and Waller houses, River Forest (projects); the Devin house and the All Souls Building, Chicago (projects).

Periodicals

38. Dean, George R. "Progress before Precedent." *Brickbuilder* IX (My 1900), pp. 91-7.
A discussion concerning the Architectural League of America, with a comment by Wright.

39. "Exhibition of the Chicago Architectural Club and Its Catalogue." *Am Arch & Build N* LXVIII (14 Ap 1900), pp. 12-14.
Includes comment on Wright's work in the exhibition.

40. "Selections from Chicago Architectural Club Exhibition of 1900." *Inland Arch & N Rec* XXXV (Ap 1900), hors-texte pl.
Includes illustrations of Wright's work shown in the exhibition (see no. 37). Comment on this article in *Arch R* (Boston) VII (Je 1900), p. 75.

41. Spencer, Robert C., Jr. "The Work of Frank Lloyd Wright." *Arch R* (Boston) VII (Je 1900), pp. 61-72.
The first critical review of Wright's work written during his seven years of independent practice. Reprinted, see no. 1571.

42. Wright, Frank Lloyd. "The Architect." *Brickbuilder* IX (Je 1900), pp. 124-8.
The text of a speech on the status of the architectural profession, read before the second annual convention of the Architectural League of America, Chicago, 7-9 June 1900. Also in *Construction News* X (16, 23 Je 1900), pp. 518-19, 538-40. Comment in *Am Arch & Build N* LXVIII (16 Je 1900), p. 87, and in *Inland Arch & N Rec* XXXV (Je 1900), p. 43.

1901

Books

43. Wright, Frank Lloyd. "The Art and Craft of the Machine." *In* [Chicago Architectural Club.] *Catalogue of the Fourteenth Annual Exhibition of the Chicago Architectural Club.* In the Galleries of the Art Institute, Michigan Ave. and Adams Street, from Thursday, March Twenty-Eighth, to Monday, April Fifteenth, A.D. MDCCCCI. [Chicago: Architectural Club, 1901.] Unpaged.
The text of a speech read to the Chicago Arts and Crafts Society at Hull House, 6 March, and to the Western Society of Engineers, 20 March 1901. It was read again in 1902 (see no. 50) and was reprinted (see no. 47). The catalogue also includes an announcement that Wright served as a critic for an

Annual Traveling Scholarship awarded by the Architectural Club.

Periodicals

44. "Selected Miscellany." *Brickbuilder* X (Ja 1901), pp. 17-21. Includes notice of a newly formed partnership of Wright and Webster Tomlinson. Also in *Inland Arch & N Rec* XXXVII (Mr 1901), p. 16. A printed announcement of their association exists in the collection of the Avery Library, Columbia University.

45. Wright, Frank Lloyd. "A Home in a Prairie Town." *Ladies' Home J* XVIII (Fe 1901), p. 17.
Reprinted, see no. 1682.

46. Wright, Frank Lloyd. "A Small House with 'Lots of Room in It'." *Ladies' Home J* XVIII (Jy 1901), p. 15.
Reprinted, see no. 1682.

47. Wright, Frank Lloyd. "The Art and Craft of the Machine." *Brush and Pencil* VIII (My 1901), pp. 77-90.
Excerpts from a 1901 speech (see no. 43).

48. Wright, Frank Lloyd. "The 'Village Bank' Series, V." *Brickbuilder* X (Ag 1901), pp. 160-1.
Village Bank in cast concrete. Reprinted, see no. 1682.

1902

Books

49. "The Work of Frank Lloyd Wright." *In* [Chicago Architectural Club.] *The Chicago Architectural Annual Published by the Chicago Architectural Club: A Selection of Works Exhibited at the Art Institute in March of the Year One Thousand Nine Hundred & Two.* [Chicago: Architectural Club, 1902.] Unpaged.
No text. Includes: illustrations of Sullivan house, Ocean Springs; "A Small House with 'Lots of Room in It' " and "A Home in a Prairie Town" (projects for *Ladies' Home J*);

Metzger house, Desbarats, Ontario, Canada (project); Thomas (Rogers) house, and Wright playroom and studio, Oak Park; Hillside Home School building no. 2, Spring Green; Winslow house and stable, and River Forest Golf Club, River Forest; Village Bank in cast concrete (project); Bradley and Hickox houses, Kankakee; Abraham Lincoln Center, and Lexington Terrace (project), Chicago; and Henderson house, Elmhurst.

50. Wright, Frank Lloyd. "The Art and Craft of the Machine." *In* [Daughters of the Revolution. Illinois.] *The New Industrialism.* Chicago: National League of Industrial Art, 1902. Part III, pp. 79-111.

The text of a speech read to the Daughters of the Revolution. It was published previously (see nos. 43 and 47) and was here slightly revised.

Periodicals

51. "Chicago." *Am Arch & Build N* LXXVI (26 Ap 1902), p. 29.

Includes comment on Wright's work in the 1902 exhibit of the Chicago Architectural Club.

52. "Residence, Oak Park, Illinois." *Inland Arch & N Rec* (photogravure edition only) XXXIX (Jy 1902), hors-texte pl.

Thomas house. No text.

1903

Books

53. Harper, William Hudson. *In the Valley of the Clan: The Story of a School.*

An undated pamphlet in the collection of the State Historical Society of Wisconsin, Madison. It includes a description and photographs of the Hillside Home School building no. 2, Spring Green.

Periodicals

54. Spencer, Robert C., Jr. "Brick Architecture in and about Chicago." *Brickbuilder* XII (Se 1903), pp. 178-87.
   Includes: Winslow stable, River Forest; Francisco Terrace, Francis Apartments, and Heller, Husser, and Charnley houses, all in Chicago.

1904

Periodicals

55. Colson, Ethel M. "A Yellow Dining Room." *House B* XV (Mr 1904), pp. 208-10.
   McArthur house, Chicago.

1905

Periodicals

56. "Residence of W. G. Fricke, Oak Park, Ill." *Inland Arch & N Rec* XLVI (Ag 1905), hors-texte pl.
   Photograph. No text.

57. Smith, Lyndon P. "The Home of an Artist-Architect: Louis H. Sullivan's Place at Ocean Springs, Miss." *Arch Rec* XVII (Je 1905), pp. 471-90.

58. "Work of Frank Lloyd Wright, Its Influence." *Arch Rec* XVIII (Jy 1905), pp. 60-5.
   Critical analysis.

1906

Books

59. Johonnot, Rodney F. *The New Edifice of Unity Church, Oak Park, Illinois. Frank Lloyd Wright, Architect.* Descriptive and Historical Matter by Dr. Rodney F. Johonnot, Pastor. [Oak Park]: The New Unity Church Club, 1906.

20 x 23.7 cm., 20 pp., 7 ills.
A descriptive pamphlet designed by Wright with accompanying envelope. Includes text, elevations, and floor plans.
□ Reissued by The Unitarian Universalist Church, Oak Park, 1961. The paper wrapper was modified, the pamphlet was not in an envelope and was slightly smaller, and one illustration was omitted.

60.   [Wright, Frank Lloyd.] *Hiroshige: An Exhibition of Colour Prints from the Collection of Frank Lloyd Wright.* The Art Institute of Chicago, March the Twenty-ninth, Nineteen Hundred Six. 24.8 x 13.5 cm., 12 pp.
An exhibition catalogue with an introduction by Wright and a list of prints in the exhibition. The introduction was reprinted (see no. 532, pp. 21-23).

Periodicals

61.   Heath, William R. "The Office Building and What It Will Bring to the Office Force." *Larkin Idea* VI (N 1906), pp. 10-14.
The text of a speech on the Larkin Company administration building, Buffalo, read to employees of the company.

62.   Percival, C. E. "A House on a Bluff." *House B* XX (Je 1906), pp. 11-13.
Hardy house, Racine.

63.   Percival, C. E. "A House without a Servant." *House B* XX (Ag 1906), pp. 13-14.
Glasner house, Glencoe.

64.   Percival, C. E. "Solving a Difficult Problem: A House at South Bend, Indiana; Frank Lloyd Wright, Architect." *House B* XX (Jy 1906), pp. 20-1.
DeRhodes house.

65.   "Residence, D. D. Martin, Buffalo, N. Y." *Inland Arch & N Rec* XLVII (Jy 1906), hors-texte pl.
Photographs. No text.

66. "Residence of Wm. R. Heath, Buffalo, N. Y." *Inland Arch & N Rec* XLVIII (O 1906), hors-texte pl.
Photographs. No text.

67. Wright, Frank Lloyd. "The New Larkin Administration Building." *Larkin Idea* VI (N 1906), pp. 2-9 and cover.
Reprinted, see no. 1845.

1907

Books

68. Pittsburgh. Architectural Club. *Fourth Exhibition to Be Held in the Carnegie Institute Galleries November, 1907.* Pittsburgh: Architectural Club, 1907. P. 70, ills. follow.
A catalogue which includes a list of Wright's work in the exhibition and illustrations as follow: the Hardy house, Racine; Little house, Peoria; Ullman house (project) and Unity Temple, Oak Park; and Adams house, Highland Park.

Periodicals

69. "House and Studio of Mrs. Mary Lawrence, Springfield, Illinois." *Am Arch & Build N* XCII (24 Ag 1907), hors-texte pls.
Dana house. No text.

70. "House on Lake Avenue, Chicago, Ill." *Am Arch & Build N* (International edition only) XCI (25 My 1907), hors-texte pl.
Albert Sullivan house, now acknowledged to have been designed by Wright. No text.

71. Illsley, Charles E. "The Larkin Administration Building, Buffalo." *Inland Arch & N Rec* L (Jy 1907), p. 4, ills. follow p. 12.
Comment in *Arch R* (Boston) XIV (Jy 1907), p. 184.

72. "The Inscriptions on the Court of the Administration Building." *Larkin Idea* VII (My 1907), pp. 1-2.
Larkin Company administration building, Buffalo.

73. "Our Jamestown Exhibit." *Larkin Idea* VII (Ag 1907), pp. 16-17.

Larkin Company exhibition pavilion, Jamestown, Virginia.

74. "The Pittsburgh Architectural Club's Exhibition." *Am Arch & Build N* XCII (30 N 1907), pp. 175-81.
Includes illustrations of Wright's work in the exhibition (see no. 68).

75. "Remodeled Entrance, The Rookery Building, Chicago." *Inland Arch & N Rec* L (Se 1907), hors-texte pl.
Photograph. No text.

76. "Residence of Arthur Heurtley, Oak Park, Ills. [i.e., Illinois]." *Inland Arch & N Rec* L (N 1907), hors-texte pl.
Photograph. No text.

77. "Residence of Mr. Moore, Oak Park, Ills. [i.e., Illinois]." *Inland Arch & N Rec* L (D 1907), hors-texte pl.
Photograph of Hills house. No text.

78. "Residence of P. A. Beachy, Oak Park, Ills. [i.e., Illinois]." *Inland Arch & N Rec* L (N 1907), hors-texte pl.
Photograph. No text.

79. Twitmyer, Geo. E. "A Model Administration Building." *Business Man's Magazine* XIX (Ap 1907), pp. 43-9.
Larkin Company administration building, Buffalo. Reprinted in abridged form in *Larkin Idea* VII (Ag 1907), pp. 1-8.

80. Wright, Frank Lloyd. "A Fireproof House for $5000." *Ladies' Home J* XXIV (Ap 1907), p. 24.
Reprinted, see no. 1682.

1908

Periodicals

81. "Living Room, House for H. J. Ullman, Oak Park, Ills. [i.e., Illinois], F. L. Wright, Architect." *Inland Arch & N Rec* LI (Ja 1908), hors-texte pl.
Perspective drawing. No text.

82. Sturgis, Russell. "The Larkin Building in Buffalo." *Arch Rec* XXIII (Ap 1908), pp. 310-21.

83. Tallmadge, Thomas E. "The 'Chicago School'." *Arch R* (Boston), XV (Ap 1908), pp. 69-74.
   Mentions Wright as one of the more prominent of a number of architects working in a similar and original manner. Reprinted, see no. 1682.

84. "Unity Temple and Unity House, Oak Park, Ill." *Inland Arch & N Rec* LII (D 1908), hors-texte pls.
   Photographs (description, p. 77).

85. Wright, Frank Lloyd. "In the Cause of Architecture." *Arch Rec* XXIII (Mr 1908), pp. 155-221. (Also issued as offprint.)
   Architectural philosophy, followed by fifty-six pages of illustrations. Comment in *Arch R* (Boston) XV (Ap 1908), pp. 78-80. Reprinted, see no. 1971.

1909

Periodicals

86. "Minneapolis Architectural Club Exhibition." *W Arch* XII (My 1909), pp. 51-5.
   Includes notice of Wright's participation.

1910

Books

87. Wright, Frank Lloyd. *Ausgeführte Bauten und Entwürfe von Frank Lloyd Wright.* [Berlin: Ernst Wasmuth, 1910.]
   64 x 40.5 cm.; 72 plates, 28 with tissue overlays; in two portfolios.
   A total of one hundred plates prepared from drawings made at Wright's Oak Park studio illustrate seventy buildings and projects between 1893 and 1909. Seventy-two of the plates are numbered I through LXIV and include eight plates with a or b numbers. The remaining twenty-eight are tissue overlays

printed with drawings related to the plates to which they are
attached. The plates include perspective views, plans, sections,
and interior and exterior details. The illustrations are printed
variously in brown, gray, gold, and white inks on gray and
white papers and tissue. Each plate and tissue is embossed with
the stamp of Frank Lloyd Wright. Some of the drawings are by
Wright; others are the work of his assistants. According to conversations with Lloyd Wright, the architect's son, the drawings
were taken to Fiesole, Italy, where they were traced in their
original size and scale during the years 1909-1910 by a team of
draftsmen including Lloyd Wright and Taylor Wooley working
under Frank Lloyd Wright's supervision. The tracings were then
photographically reduced or enlarged to a uniform size and the
images transferred to lithographic stones for printing.

Although the buildings and projects are not listed individually in this description, entries for all of them will be found in
the building index.

Wright's introduction appears in German translation (he
neither wrote nor spoke the language) and is dated Florenz,
Italien, 15. Mai 1910. This and the annotated list of plates are
printed on unbound sheets, folded once into loose, consecutive
folio gatherings (40.9 x 32 cm., 31 pp.) and are included in the
portfolios. An English version of the introduction entitled
"Studies and Executed Buildings" was printed in Chicago by
Ralph Fletcher Seymour for inclusion in those sets destined
for distribution in the USA. This version is dated Florence,
Italy, June, 1910 (40.9 x 31.4 cm., 27 pp.). Most of the American sets were damaged or destroyed in a fire at Taliesin, with
the result that the work was far better known and more influential in Europe than in the United States.

The portfolios themselves are gray paper over boards with
cloth at the hinges and the title stamped on the cloth. Some
portfolios have pockets to hold the text. Another edition of
the same year is bound in half leather, with the plates and text
printed on slightly larger, better quality paper.
□ A Japanese edition was published by Seikizen-Kan-Honten,
Osaka, 1916, and edited by Goichi Takeda, a professor at the
Kyoto School of Arts and Crafts whom Wright met on his
first trip to Japan in 1905. This has not been seen by the compiler, and information about it was provided by Bruce Brooks

Pfeiffer of the Frank Lloyd Wright Foundation. A copy in storage at the Foundation has thirty-two plates in one portfolio, but no text or index to indicate the original total number.

□ A second, undated German edition was published in smaller size by Wasmuth, Berlin, [1924]. The plates are kept in their original sequence, but they are reduced to 48.2 x 32.5 cm. They are printed in brown ink on glossy white paper. Wright's embossed stamp is omitted. The text and list of plates are printed on unbound sheets, folded once (36.2 x 26.5 cm., 31 pp.). There is only a single portfolio instead of two, as in the original edition. The portfolio is gray paper over boards, with cloth at the hinges and the title is printed in red ink on the front.

□ An American edition was published by Horizon Press, New York, [1963] under the title *Buildings, Plans and Designs.* The plates are very nearly the size of the 1910 publication, but are printed on tan and gray paper in gold, brown, and gray inks. They are numbered 1 through 100, and arranged in a different sequence. All captions are translated into English. Wright's embossed stamp is omitted. A statement by Wright dated 1957 and a new foreword by William Wesley Peters appear with the original English introduction and list of plates (43.2 x 27.1 cm., 32 pp.). Plate number 72 was omitted in error from the list of plates, but it was published and should be present in the portfolio. The single portfolio is gray paper over boards, with black cloth at the hinges and the title printed on the paper. Twenty-six hundred copies were published, of which twenty-five hundred were for sale. These were divided into five groups numbered one through five hundred, with each group assigned a letter a through e. The copies not for sale were numbered one through one hundred with no accompanying letter.

□ Another American edition was published under the title *Studies and Executed Buildings by Frank Lloyd Wright. Ausgeführte Bauten und Entwürfe von Frank Lloyd Wright.* Palos Park, Illinois: Prairie School Press, 1975. This is a small reproduction of the 1910 edition bound in book form. The pages measure 22.1 x 36.1 cm. They are white, printed in black ink, with the drawings printed only on the recto of each page. The captions are in German, and the numbering and sequence of

the pages follow those of the Wasmuth editions. The German
and English texts and lists of plates are all included with a
comment from the editor on the various editions of this work.

REVIEWS of the 1910, 1963, and 1975 editions
88. Brooks, H. Allen. *JSAH* XXIV (My 1965), pp. 178-80.
.[1963]
89. Hobson, L. Henri. *Prairie Sch R* I (no. 2, 1964), p. 24.
[1963]
90. Schmertz, Mildred F. "Wasmuth's Great Portfolio on
Wright Reprinted." *Arch Rec* CXXXV (Ja 1964), pp. 84,
90. [1963]
91. Schuyler, Montgomery. "An Architectural Pioneer: Review of the Portfolios Containing the Works of Frank Lloyd
Wright." *Arch Rec* XXXI (Ap 1912), pp. 427-36. [1910]
Reprinted in Schuyler, Montgomery. *American Architecture and Other Writings.* Cambridge, Massachusetts: The
Belknap Press of Harvard University Press, 1961. Pp. 634-40.
92. Tafel, Edgar. "Precious Monograph." *Progress Arch* XLVI
(Fe 1965), pp. 240, 244. [1963]
93. Vinci, John. "More on the Work of Frank Lloyd Wright."
Chicago History V (Fall, 1976), pp. 171-2. [1975]

Periodicals

94. "Art Gallery Designed by Frank Lloyd Wright, Architect."
International Studio XXXIX (Fe 1910), pp. xcv-xcvi.
Thurber Art Gallery, Chicago.

1911

Books

95. Key, Ellen. *The Morality of Woman and Other Essays.*
Authorized Translation from the Swedish by Mamah Bouton
Borthwick. Chicago: The Ralph Fletcher Seymour Co., Fine
Arts Building, [1911].
Includes "The Morality of Woman," "The Woman of the
Future," and "The Conventional Woman." During her stay in
Europe with Wright, Mamah Borthwick Cheney translated

several essays by the Swedish feminist Ellen Key. Wright
worked with Mrs. Cheney on one, *Love and Ethics* (see no.
106), and arranged after their return to Chicago to have some
of the translations published by Ralph Fletcher Seymour.

96. Wright, Frank Lloyd. *Frank Lloyd Wright: Ausgeführte
Bauten.* Berlin: Verlegt bei Ernst Wasmuth A. G., 1911.
    30 x 21.3 cm., 141 pp., color front., 193 ills., printed gray
paper wrappers.

    A book of interior and exterior photographs and plans of
Wright's buildings executed before his 1909 departure from
Chicago. It includes in German translation a foreword by C. R.
Ashbee, "Frank Lloyd Wright: Eine Studie zu seiner Würdigung." Wright visited the Arts and Crafts leader in England in
September, 1910, and asked him then to write the introduction. The text ends on page 10. (See also no. 101.) Although
the many buildings illustrated in this book are not listed individually in this description, entries for all of them will be
found in the building index.
    □ A new edition entitled *Frank Lloyd Wright: The Early Work*
was published by Horizon Press, New York, 1968. It includes
an introduction by Edgar Kaufmann, Jr., and a glossary of
terms. Errors in dates and captions have been corrected.
"Frank Lloyd Wright, A Study and an Appreciation" was
printed in C. R. Ashbee's original English text. According to a
publisher's note, the text in the original German edition con-
tained some added material that was not by Ashbee. That material has been reproduced in the original German for this edition, but it has not been translated. Boxed. An undated, less
expensive edition was reissued by Bramhall House, New York.

REVIEWS of the 1968 edition
97. Brooks, H. Allen. *Prairie Sch R* VI (no. 1, 1969), pp. 24-5.
98. Hasbrouck, W. R. *Arch For* CXXX (Je 1969), pp. 84-5.
99. Tafel, Edgar. "Europe's First Knowledge of Wright." *Arch
     Rec* CXLV (Mr 1969), p. 148.

100. Wright, Frank Lloyd. *Ausgeführte Bauten und Entwürfe von
Frank Lloyd Wright.* [Chicago: Ralph Fletcher Seymour.]
    15.2 x 11.4 cm., 7 pp., 3 ills., paper.

An undated announcement which describes the 1910 portfolio (see no. 87), and offers it for sale in the United States.
See Plate 3 in this volume for an illustration of the cover.

101. Wright, Frank Lloyd. *Frank Lloyd Wright, Chicago.* Berlin:
Verlegt bei Ernst Wasmuth A.-G., 1911.
    Cover title. 28.9 x 21 cm., 113 pp., 6 pp. advertising, color
front., 148 ills., printed tan paper wrappers. (8. Sonderheft
der Architektur des XX. Jahrhunderts)
    Variant edition of *Frank Lloyd Wright: Ausgeführte Bauten*
(see no. 96). The photographs differ both in content and quantity. Although the text by Ashbee is the same, it has been reset
in double columns and ends on page nine. Preliminary and final
leaves are advertising material. Colophon: Julius Sittenfeld,
Hofbuchdrucker., Berlin W. The many buildings illustrated in
this book are not listed in this description, but entries for all
of them appear in the building index. No conclusive information has been found which would explain the publication by
the Wasmuth firm of two such similar books in the same year,
but a notice on the cover states that this edition is for sale only
in Europe. An advertisement for the book appears on Plate 4.

Periodicals

102. "City National Bank of Mason City, Iowa, Frank Lloyd
Wright, Architect." *W Arch* XVII (D 1911), p. 105 (ills. follow).
    Comment in *Am Arch* C (27 D 1911), p. 274; and in *Arch R*
    (Boston) XVIII (Ja 1912), p. 11. Reprinted in Brooks, H. Allen.
    *Prairie School Architecture: Studies from 'The Western Archi-
    tect.'* Toronto: University of Toronto Press, 1975. Pp. 3-7.

103. "A Comparison of Master and Pupil Seen in Two Houses."
W Arch XVII (N 1911), p. 95.
    Discussion of the following article.

104. "A Departure from Classic Tradition: Two Unusual Houses
by Louis Sullivan and Frank Lloyd Wright." *Arch Rec* XXX
(O 1911), pp. 326-38.
    Babson (Sullivan) and Coonley houses, Riverside.

1912

Books

105. *For Sale at Oak Park a Forest Avenue Property & a Chicago Avenue Property: Semi-Detached Dwellings for Sale Separately or Together, Partly Finished.*
18.2 x 11.3 cm., 8 pp., 2 ills., paper.
Cover title. A pamphlet which includes descriptions and plans of the Wright house and studio in Oak Park and offers them for sale. The plans reflect the alterations made to the buildings after Wright's return from Europe in 1910 and further changes in the 1920's. The pamphlet is not dated and although it was originally thought to have been published in approximately 1912, information which became available during the typesetting of this text establishes a date of 1925.

106. Key, Ellen. *Love and Ethics.* Authorized Translation from the Original of Ellen Key by Mamah Bouton Borthwick and Frank Lloyd Wright. Chicago: The Ralph Fletcher Seymour Company, [1912].
See annotation for no. 95.

107. Key, Ellen. *The Torpedo under the Ark; "Ibsen and Women,"* by Ellen Key. Authorized Translation from the Swedish by Mamah Bouton Borthwick. Chicago: The Ralph Fletcher Seymour Co., [1912].
Not seen. See annotation for no. 95.

108. Key, Ellen. *The Woman Movement,* by Ellen Key. Translated by Mamah Bouton Borthwick, A. M.; with an Introduction by Havelock Ellis. New York and London: G. P. Putnam's Sons, 1912.
See annotation for no. 95. The book was reprinted by the Hyperion Press, Inc., Westport, Connecticut, 1976 (Pioneers of the Woman's Movement).

109. Wright, Frank Lloyd. *The Japanese Print: An Interpretation.* Chicago: The Ralph Fletcher Seymour Co., Fine Arts Building, 1912.
This book was printed three times by Seymour in 1912. Wright was displeased with the first edition, and all but a few

copies were destroyed. Only two of these three printings have been seen by the compiler, and priority has not been established. Their title pages and bindings differ, but the type settings appear to be the same.

□ One edition (20.8 x 13 cm., 35 pp.) is printed on Japanese paper and bound in tan boards. A crane design appears on the cover and title page. The cover title is printed in dark blue, the design in green. The title page is illustrated on Plate 5 in this volume. On the verso of the title page is the statement: Copyrighted 1912 Ralph Fletcher Seymour Company.

□ Another edition (18.5 cm., 35 pp.) is printed on different paper and bound in tan printed wrappers. The co   'tle is printed in brown. The crane design is omitted fron.   ·h the cover and title page. This edition also lacks the copyri   · statement on the verso of the title page.

□ A new edition was published by Horizon Press, New Yorκ, [1967]. In addition to *The Japanese Print: An Interpretation,* this edition includes the introduction to *Antique Colour Prints from the Collection of Frank Lloyd Wright* (no. 137), the introduction to *The Frank Lloyd Wright Collection of Japanese Antique Prints* (no. 187), and passages from *An Autobiography* (no. 303). According to a publisher's note, the texts reflect Wright's later revisions, and the prints reproduced came from his personal collection. Boxed.

REVIEWS of the 1912 and 1967 editions
110. Kostka, Robert. *Prairie Sch R* IV (no. 4, 1967), pp. 27-9. [1967]
111. Sell, Henry Blackman. "The Artist as Master." *Little Review* I (Ja 1915), pp. 17-19. [1912]

Periodicals

112. Ames, Robert Leonard. "A Western Suburban Home." *American Homes and Gardens* IX (Mr 1912), pp. 86-9.
    Baker house, Wilmette.

113. Berlage, H. P. "Neuere amerikanische Architektur." *Schweizerische Bauzeitung* LX (14, 21, 28 Se 1912), pp. 148-50, 165-7, 178. (Also issued as offprint.)

The texts of three lectures on American architecture delivered by Berlage in Zurich, after a trip to America in 1911. Although he did not meet Wright, he visited several of his buildings. His enthusiasm for Wright's work, particularly the Larkin Company administration building and the Martin house in Buffalo, was apparent in his second speech. Partially reprinted; see no. 172, pp. 74-5. A translation in English was published in Gifford, Don, ed. *The Literature of Architecture: The Evolution of Architectural Theory and Practice in Nineteenth-Century America.* New York: Dutton, 1966. Pp. 606-16.

114. "Daniel Hudson Burnham: An Appreciation." *Arch Rec* XXIII (Ag 1912), pp. 175-85.
Includes a eulogy by Wright, p. 184.

1913

Books

115. [Chicago Architectural Club.] *Book of the Twenty Sixth Annual Exhibition of the Chicago Architectural Club in the Galleries of the Art Institute, Chicago.* May 6 to June 11, 1913. Chicago, Architectural Club, 1913.
Includes illustrations of Lake Geneva Inn, Lake Geneva; and Madison Hotel, Madison (project).

Periodicals

116. Ashbee, C. R. "Taliesin, the Home of Frank Lloyd Wright, and a Study of the Owner." *W Arch* XIX (Fe 1913), pp. 16-19.

117. Lippincott, Roy A. "The Chicago Architectural Club, Notes on the 26th Annual Exhibition." *Arch Rec* XXXIII (Je 1913), pp. 567-73.
Includes comment on Wright's participation, and illustrations from the catalogue (see no. 115).

118. "Residence for D. M. Amberg, Grand Rapids, Mich. H. V. vonHolst, Architect." *W Arch* XX (O 1913), pp. 88, xvii.

Wright made preliminary sketches for this house prior to his departure for Europe.

119. "Residence for E. P. Irving, Decatur, Illinois." *W Arch* XIX (Ap 1913), pp. 38-9, plates follow.
Comment in *Arch R* (Boston) XIX (My 1913), p. 194.

120. "The Studio-Home of Frank Lloyd Wright." *Arch Rec* XXXIII (Ja 1913), pp. 45-54.
"Taliesin," Spring Green. No text.

1914

Books

121. [Chicago. Art Institute.] *The Work of Frank Lloyd Wright.* Work Done Since the Spring of 1911, Only, Is Included in this Exhibit. [Chicago: Art Institute, 1914.]
26.1 x 17.1 cm., 4 pp., paper.
A list of Wright's work in the Twenty-Seventh Annual Exhibition of the Chicago Architectural Club. It includes models, drawings, dwellings, photographs, details of furniture and glass, educational toys, wooden print stands, an essay on the Japanese color print, the essay "In the Cause of Architecture," and foreign publications.

122. *Midway Gardens.* [Chicago: The Midway Gardens Co.], n.d.
Cover title. 15.3 x 22.8 cm., 16 pp., 15 ills., paper.
An undated promotional pamphlet including a description and several photographs of the building not known to have been published elsewhere. A reference to the Gardens' opening in June establishes a publication date of approximately 1914. A copy is located in an uncatalogued collection of Wright ephemera at the Burnham Library of Architecture, Art Institute of Chicago.

Periodicals

123. "Architectural Philosophy of Frank Lloyd Wright." *W Arch* XX (Je 1914), p. 58.

Comment on the following article.

124. Wright, Frank Lloyd. "In the Cause of Architecture, Second Paper." *Arch Rec* XXXV (My 1914), pp. 405-13. (Also issued as offprint.)

1915

Periodicals

125. Goethe, Johann Wolfgang von. "A Hymn to Nature." *Little Review* I (Fe 1915), pp. 30-2.
Translated from German by Wright and Mrs. Cheney during their stay in Europe.

126. Key, Ellen. "Romain Rolland." *Little Review* II (O 1915), pp. 22-30.
Authorized translation from the Swedish by Mamah Bouton Borthwick (Cheney).

127. Sell, Henry Blackman. "Interpretation, Not Imitation: Work of F. L. Wright." *International Studio* LV (My 1915), pp. lxxix-lxxxiii.
Analysis and discussion. Includes photographs of Midway Gardens, Chicago.

128. Wight, Peter B. "Country House Architecture in the Middle West." *Arch Rec* XXXVIII (O 1915), pp. 385-421.
Includes photographs of Wright house, "Taliesin," Spring Green.

129. Wright, Frank Lloyd. "In Response to a Request from the Editor for an Article on Midway Gardens." *Nat Arch* (Philadelphia) V (Mr 1915), pp. 118, 155; pls. 41-3.

1916

Books

130. Milwaukee. The Richards Company. *American System*

Built Houses, Designed by Frank Lloyd Wright. [1916?]
Cover title. 21.5 x 28 cm., 4 pp., paper.
A description of a prefabricated housing project for the
Richards Company. It accompanied drawings of the houses
by Antonin Raymond, which were printed by a Japanese
woodcut process. The pamphlet and the drawings were distributed in an envelope as promotional literature.

131. Wright, Frank Lloyd. *Ausgeführte Bauten und Entwürfe
von Frank Lloyd Wright.* Osaka, Japan: Seikizen-Kan-Honten,
1916.
    See no. 87.

132. Wright, Frank Lloyd. "Non-Competitive Plan." *In* Yeomans,
Alfred B., ed. *City Residential Land Development: Studies in
Planning; Competitive Plans for Subdividing a Typical Quarter
Section of Land in the Outskirts of Chicago.* Chicago: The University of Chicago Press, [1916]. Pp. 95-102. (Publications of
the City Club of Chicago)
    Quadruple Block Plan for *Ladies' Home Journal.* Includes
color drawings of the project.

REVIEW
133. McLean, Robert Craik. "City Residential Land Development." *W Arch* XXV (Ja 1917), pp. 6-8, ills. follow p. 2.

Periodicals

134. "Mueller House, Decatur, Ill." *Arch R* (Boston) XXI
(N 1916), p. 198.
    Photograph. Attributed to H. V. vonHolst; Marion M.
Griffin, associate.

135. Wright, Frank Lloyd. "A Word from Real Art." *Little
Review* III (Se 1916), p. 26.
    Comment by Wright on the wish of the editor, Margaret
Anderson, for the *Little Review* to become a magazine of art.
As she found nothing she considered worthy of publication,
pages 2-13 of this issue were left blank. Reprinted in Anderson,
Margaret. *The Little Review Anthology.* New York: Hermitage
House, 1953. P. 64.

136. Wright, Frank Lloyd. "The American System of House Building." *W Arch* XXIV (Se 1916), pp. 121-3.
 The text of a speech on a prefabricated housing project for the Richards Company, Milwaukee.

1917

Books

137. Chicago. Arts Club. *Antique Colour Prints from the Collection of Frank Lloyd Wright.* The Arts Club of Chicago Exhibition, Fine Arts Building, Beginning November Twelve, Ending December Fifteen.
 Cover title. 21.5 x 15.5 cm., 14 pp.
 A pamphlet which includes an introduction by Wright dated 12 October 1917 and an annotated list of prints in the exhibition. It is bound in tan printed wrappers. The crane design first used for *The Japanese Print* (see no. 109), appears on the cover. The introduction has been reprinted; see no. 109 (1967 edition), no. 532, and no. 1495.

Periodicals

138. *W Arch* XXV (Ja 1917), p. 4.
 Includes notice of Wright's departure for Tokyo in December, 1916, to begin the Imperial Hotel.

1918

Periodicals

139. Oud, J. J. P. "Architectonische beschouwing bij bijlage VIII." *de Stijl* I (no. 4, 1918), pp. 38-41.
 Robie house, Chicago.

1919

Periodicals

140. Hoff, Robt. Van't. "Architectuur en haar ontwikkeling (bij

bijlage VIII)." *de Stijl* II (no. 4, 1919), pp. 40-3.
Unity Temple, Oak Park.

141. Kimball, Fiske. "The American Country House, 1. Practical
Conditions: Natural, Economic, Social." *Arch Rec* XLVI
(O 1919), pp. 299-328.
Includes photographs and plans of Wright house, "Taliesin,"
Spring Green.

142. Wils, Jan. "De nieuwe tijd: eenige gedachten bij het werk
van Frank Lloyd Wright." *Wendingen* II (no. 6, 1919), pp. 14-15.

1921

Periodicals

143. Berlage, H. P. "Frank Lloyd Wright." *Wendingen* IV (no. 11,
1921), pp. 2-18.

144. Wils, Jan. "Frank Lloyd Wright." *Elsevier's Geïllustreerd
Maandschrift* LXI (1921), pp. 217-27.

1922

Periodicals

145. Berlage, H. P. "Frank Lloyd Wright." *Styl* (Prague) IV (no. 1,
1922), pp. 10, 12-15.
Translated by R. Vonka.

146. Mullgardt, Louis Christian. "A Building That Is Wrong."
Arch & Eng LXXI (N 1922), pp. 81-9.
Imperial Hotel, Tokyo. See also no. 152.

147. "Zprávy a Poznàmky." *Styl* (Prague) IV (no. 2-3, 1922),
pp. 57-8, ills. on pp. 28-31.
Imperial Hotel, Tokyo.

1923

Books

148. [Monograph in Japanese on the Imperial Hotel.] Tokyo: 1923.
    Not seen. First mentioned by Henry-Russell Hitchcock, Jr. (see no. 302, p. 39).

149. [Wright, Frank Lloyd.] *Experimenting with Human Lives.* [Chicago: Ralph Fletcher Seymour, 1923.]
    Cover title. 17.7 x 16.5 cm., 12 pp.
    An undated pamphlet written after the 1923 earthquake in Japan. It discusses the inappropriateness of skyscraper construction in seismic zones and then goes on to describe the congestion created by tall buildings in any area, becoming an early argument for decentralization. Partially reprinted; see no. 532. The pages are folded Japanese-style with stapled binding and printed in orange and black. The pamphlet is glued into a printed folder. Printed on this folder is "The Fine Art Society, Olive Hill, Hollywood, California" (the location is that of the Barnsdall house).

Periodicals

150. "The Effect of the Earthquake in Japan upon Construction." *W Arch* XXXII (O 1923), pp. 117-18.
    Includes information on the structure of the Imperial Hotel, Tokyo.

151. "Imperial Hotel, Tokyo, Japan." *Architect* CIX (8 Je 1923), pp. 395-7.

152. "More anent the New Imperial Hotel at Tokio, Japan." *Arch & Eng* LXXII (Fe 1923), pp. 83-4.
    Comment on an article by Louis Christian Mullgardt (see no. 146).

153. Stady, Stanley E. "How Buildings Acted in the Japan Quake." *American Contractor* XLIV (29 D 1923), pp. 16-18.
    Includes Imperial Hotel, Tokyo.

154. Sullivan, Louis H. "Concerning the Imperial Hotel, Tokyo, Japan." *Arch Rec* LIII (Ap 1923), pp. 332-52.

155. Wright, Frank Lloyd. "In the Wake of the Quake; concerning the Imperial Hotel, Tokio, I." *W Arch* XXXII (N 1923), pp. 129-32.
> See also no. 162.

156. Wright, Frank Lloyd. "The New Imperial Hotel, Tokio, Frank Lloyd Wright, Architect." *W Arch* XXXII (Ap 1923), pp. 39-46, pls. 1-14.

1924

Books

157. Wright, Frank Lloyd. *Ausgeführte Bauten und Entwürfe von Frank Lloyd Wright.* [Berlin: Ernst Wasmuth, 1924.]
> See no. 87.

Periodicals

158. Badovici, Jean. "Entretiens sur l'architecture vivante: l'art de Frank Lloyd Wright." *L'Architecture Vivante* II (W 1924), pp. 26-7, pls. 34-5.

159. Floto, Julius. "Imperial Hotel, Tokyo, Japan." *Arch Rec* LV (Fe 1924), pp. 119-23.
> Explanation by the engineer of the Imperial Hotel of the building's structure and its survival of the earthquake.

160. Stone, Jabez K. "The Monument: The Most Talked about Hotel in the World; Tokyo's Unique Survival of Disaster." *Japan* XIII (Ja 1924), pp. 13-17, 37, 40-1, 43, 45.
> Imperial Hotel.

161. Sullivan, Louis H. "Reflections on the Tokyo Disaster." *Arch Rec* LV (Fe 1924), pp. 113-18.

162. Wright, Frank Lloyd. "In the Cause of Architecture: In the

Wake of the Quake; concerning the Imperial Hotel, Tokio" (concluded). *W Arch* XXXIII (Fe 1924), pp. 17-20.

163. Wright, Frank Lloyd. "Louis Henry Sullivan, Beloved Master." *W Arch* XXXIII (Je 1924), pp. 64-6.
    Eulogy. Reprinted in Brooks, H. Allen. *Prairie School Architecture: Studies from 'The Western Architect.'* Toronto: University of Toronto Press, 1975. Pp. 301-3.

164. Wright, Frank Lloyd. "Louis H. Sullivan, His Work." *Arch Rec* LVI (Jy 1924), pp. 28-32.

1925

Books

165. [Wijdeveld, H. Th., ed.] *The Life-Work of the American Architect Frank Lloyd Wright,* with Contributions by Frank Lloyd Wright, an Introduction by Architect H. Th. Wijdeveld and Many Articles by Famous European Architects and American Writers. Santpoort, Holland: C. A. Mees, 1925.
    33 x 32.2 cm., i, 165 pp., front., 197 ills.
    The seven consecutive special issues of *Wendingen* described in no. 168 were bound together as a book. The text includes: "Some Flowers for Architect Frank Lloyd Wright," by H. Th. Wijdeveld; "In the Cause of Architecture" (first paper, March, 1908; second paper, May, 1914; and "The Third Dimension," 1925), by Frank Lloyd Wright; "The Social Back Ground of Frank Lloyd Wright," by Lewis Mumford; "Frank Lloyd Wright," by Dr. H. P. Berlage; "The Influence of Frank Lloyd Wright on the Architecture of Europe," by J. J. P. Oud; "Frank Lloyd Wright et l'architecture nouvelle" (in French), by Rob. Mallet-Stevens; "Frank Lloyd Wright" (in German), by Erich Mendelsohn; "Concerning the Imperial Hotel Tokyo, Japan," and "Reflections on the Tokyo Disaster," by Louis H. Sullivan; and "To My European Co-workers," by Frank Lloyd Wright.
    This book was the first major publication of Wright's work after the 1910-11 German volumes. It includes illustrations of work done between 1902 and 1923. The cloth binding for this volume was designed by Wright. A binding of half leather

was also available.

□ It was reissued in a different binding by A. Kroch & Son, Chicago, [1948].

□ A new edition was published under the title *The Work of Frank Lloyd Wright: The Life-Work of the American Architect Frank Lloyd Wright,* with Contributions by Frank Lloyd Wright, an Introduction by Architect H. Th. Wijdeveld and Many Articles by Famous European Architects and American Writers. 1965 Edition Including an Introduction Written for this Edition by Mrs. Frank Lloyd Wright. [New York]: Horizon Press, 1965. According to a publisher's note, this edition retains the double-fold pages—printed, as in the original, on one side of each sheet—and the specially hinged binding. Some of the original illustrations have been replaced by different views, and the sequence of some plates has been altered. Dates have been added for all buildings. An undated, less expensive edition was reissued by Bramhall House, New York. Another Horizon Press edition was issued with printing on both sides of each page.

REVIEWS of the 1948 and 1965 editions
166. Brooks, H. Allen. *Prairie Sch R* III (no. 1, 1966), p. 24.
[1965]
167. Kienitz, John F. *Wis Mag Hist* XXXII (D 1948), pp. 204-6.
[1948]

Periodicals

168. "Frank Lloyd Wright." *Wendingen* VII (1925, nos. 3, 4, 5, 6, 7, 8, 9), pp. 1-24, 25-52, 53-76, 77-94, 95-118, 119-40, 141-64 and covers.

Wendingen was the organ of the Architectura et Amicitia group in Amsterdam. These seven special issues were devoted to Wright. They were edited by H. Th. Wijdeveld, who also designed the typesetting and the red, black, and white cover which was repeated on each number. A note from the printer and publisher disclaiming responsibility for the cover design was glued inside the first issue. See Plate 6 of this volume for an illustration of the title page of the first issue. The pages were double folded and bound with straw. One page describing the seven issues appeared in each number. The issues were also combined into a bound volume (see no. 165).

169. Hegemann, Werner. "Holland, Wright, Breslau." *Wasmuths Monatsh* IX (no. 4, 1925), pp. 165-7.

170. Moser, W. "Frank Lloyd Wright und amerikanische Architektur." *Werk* V (My 1925), pp. 129-51.

171. Wijdeveld, H. Th. "Uit *Wendingen:* het Wright-boek." *Architectura* XXIX (28 N 1925), pp. 420-3.

Dutch translation of "Some Flowers for Architect Frank Lloyd Wright," the original version of which appeared in *Wendingen* VII (no. 3, 1925).

1926

Books

172. Fries, H. de, ed. *Frank Lloyd Wright: Aus dem Lebenswerke eines Architekten.* Mit Über 100 Abbildungen und 9 Farbentafeln. Berlin: Verlag Ernst Pollak, 1926.

28.8 x 22.4 cm., 80 pp., 98 ills., 9 color pls.

The text contains articles by the editor H. deFries, Wright, Richard Neutra, and excerpts from the speeches of H. P. Berlage delivered after his return from America, all in German. A short bibliography lists European publications. The illustrations consist of work completed prior to Wright's departure for Europe in 1909, and his later buildings and projects in Japan and California. Drawings for the Doheny Ranch Resort and Tahoe Summer Colony projects and the Millard ("La Miniatura") and Freeman houses are reproduced in color. Includes construction photographs of the four California concrete block houses. The book was bound in yellow boards with red cloth spine.

REVIEWS

173. Anonymous. *Der Baumeister* XXV (Ap 1927), pp. B50-1.
174. Anonymous. "Literatura." *Styl* (Prague) VII (no. 2, 1926), p. 40.

175. Oud, J. J. P. "Der Einfluss von Frank Lloyd Wright auf

die Architektur Europas." In *Holländische Architektur.*
München: Albert Langen Verlag, [1926]. Pp. 77-83.
(Bauhausbücher 10)

Periodicals

176. Adler, Leo. "F. L. Wrights neue Baukunst und Mendelsohns
neue Logik." *Wasmuths Monatsh* X (no. 7, 1926), pp. 308-9.

177. Badovici, Jean. "Frank Lloyd Wright." *Cahiers d'Art* I (no. 2,
1926), pp. 30-3.

178. Byrne, Barry. "Frank Lloyd Wright." *Baukunst* (Munich) II
(Fe 1926), pp. 54-5.
Translated by Herman Sörgel.

179. Mendelsohn, Erich. "Besuch bei Wright." *Baukunst* (Munich)
II (Fe 1926), pp. 56-8.

180. Mendelsohn, Erich. "Frank Lloyd Wright." *Wasmuths
Monatsh* X (no. 6, 1926), pp. 244-6.

181. Oud, J. J. P. "De invloed van Frank Lloyd Wright op de
architectuur van Europa." *Architectura* XXX (Fe 1926), pp. 78-
82.
Not seen. From Jaffé, H. L. C. *de Stijl.* Amsterdam: J. M.
Meulenhoff, 1956. See also no. 363.

182. Sörgel, Herman. "Bemerkungen zu Wright." *Baukunst*
(Munich) II (Fe 1926), p. 59.

183. Sörgel, Herman. "Ein internationaler Entwicklungsquer-
schnitt." *Baukunst* (Munich) II (Fe 1926), pp. 43-53.
Includes the work of Wright, Dudok, and Mendelsohn.

184. Wright, Frank Lloyd. "An die europäischen Kollegen."
Werk XIII (1926), pp. 375, 377-80.

185. Wright, Frank Lloyd. "In het belang der architectuur."
Architectura XXX (1926, nos. 12, 13, and 17).

Not seen. Dutch translation of "In the Cause of Architecture" (first paper, March, 1908; second paper, May, 1914; and "The Third Dimension," 1925).

1927

Books

186. New York. Anderson Galleries. *The Anderson Galleries* [Mitchell Kennerley, President]. *489 Park Avenue @ Fifty-ninth Street, New York. Announce the Sale by Auction of the Frank Lloyd Wright Collection of Japanese Antique Prints. "Beauty Abstract in Immaculate Form."* All the Prints in this Collection Are Extraordinarily Fine. Without Exception They Are in Splendid First State, and Most of Them Are Perfect Untrimmed Specimens—Peerless Examples of this Art and Craft. To be Sold by Order of Bank of Wisconsin. Madison, Wisconsin. At Unreserved Public Sale Early in January 1927. A Complete Illustrated Catalogue [Price Two Dollars] Will be Issued and the Exact Dates Announced in Due Course. On Exhibition Prior to the Sale [Week Days 9-6 p.m.—Sundays 2-5 p.m.].
Cover title. 8 pp., 4 ills., paper.
  A pamphlet announcing the sale of Wright's collection of Japanese prints. The copy originally described/seen is undated, but another copy located during the typesetting of this book is dated 1926. Includes excerpts from Wright's introduction to the auction catalogue (see no. 187) and information on Wright and his print collection which does not appear in the catalogue. An untrimmed copy of this pamphlet was not seen, but its dimensions are approximately those of the catalogue.

187. New York. Anderson Galleries. *The Frank Lloyd Wright Collection of Japanese Antique Prints.* Sale Number 2120. Public Exhibition from Wednesday, December Twenty-Ninth. "Beauty abstract in immaculate form." All the Prints in this Collection Are Extraordinarily Fine. Without Exception They are in Splendid First State, and Most of Them Are Perfect Untrimmed Specimens—Peerless Examples of this Art and Craft. To Be Sold by Order of Bank of Wisconsin. Madison, Wisconsin. At Unreserved Public Sale. Thursday, Friday Evenings January Sixth, Seventh,

1927. At Eight-Fifteen. The Anderson Galleries. (Mitchell Kennerley, President.) 489 Park Avenue at Fifty-Ninth Street, New York.
New York: Anderson Galleries, 1927.
    25.2 x 19 cm., xi, 163 pp., front., 91 ills.
    An auction catalogue. It includes an introduction by Wright
which describes the prints, a list of artists, and an annotated
list of the 346 prints to be sold. The introduction was reprinted;
see no. 109 (1967 edition).

Periodicals

188. *L'Architecture Vivante.* (W 1927), pl. 31.
    Millard house, "La Miniatura," Pasadena (photograph).

189. "Auction Reports." *Art N* XXV (15 Ja 1927), p. 12.
    Includes the sale prices and the purchasers of important
items at the auction of Wright's collection of Japanese prints
at Anderson Galleries, New York.

190. Dvořák, Vilém. "The Purpose, Construction and Material in
the Theory of Modern Architecture." *Styl* (Prague) VII (no. 12,
1927), pp. 207-14.
    A discussion of Wright's architecture.

191. "États-Unis." *Cahiers d'Art* II (no. 10, 1927), sup. p. xiii.

192. "Frank Lloyd Wright." *Cahiers d'Art* II (no. 9, 1927), pp.
322-8.
    Photographs of work, later included in Hitchcock's 1928
book (see no. 201). No text.

193. Hilberseimer, Ludwig. "Internationale neue Baukunst."
Moderne Bauformen XXVI (1927), pp. 325-64.
    Includes examples of the work of Wright and European
architects designing in the modern style.

194. Rebori, A. N. "Frank Lloyd Wright's Textile-Block Slab
Construction." *Arch Rec* LXII (D 1927), pp. 448-56.
    Includes a discussion of the 1925 *Wendingen* book (see
no. 165).

195. Wright, Frank Lloyd. "In the Cause of Architecture, I: The Architect and the Machine." *Arch Rec* LXI (My 1927), pp. 394-6. Reprinted, see no. 1971.

196. Wright, Frank Lloyd. "In the Cause of Architecture, II: Standardization, the Soul of the Machine." *Arch Rec* LXI (Je 1927), pp. 478-80. Reprinted, see no. 1971.

197. Wright, Frank Lloyd. "In the Cause of Architecture, III: Steel." *Arch Rec* LXII (Ag 1927), pp. 163-6. Reprinted, see no. 1971.

198. Wright, Frank Lloyd. "In the Cause of Architecture, IV: Fabrication and Imagination." *Arch Rec* LXII (O 1927), pp. 318-24. Reprinted, see no. 1971.

199. Wright, Frank Lloyd. "Why the Japanese Earthquake Did Not Destroy the Hotel Imperial." *Liberty* IV (3 D 1927), pp. 61-6.

1928

Books

200. Frankl, Paul T. *New Dimensions: The Decorative Arts of Today in Words & Pictures.* New York: Payson & Clarke Ltd., [1928].
    The book is dedicated "To a Great American Architect and Creative Artist Frank Lloyd Wright," and includes a foreword by Wright.

201. Hitchcock, Henry Russell. *Frank Lloyd Wright.* Paris: "Cahiers d'Art," [1928].
    28.3 x 23.8 cm., 37 pp., 48 ills. (Collection "Les Maitres de l'architecture contemporaine" no. 1)
    A photo study which includes representations of Wright's work completed between 1902 and 1923. The illustrations appeared previously in *Cahiers d'Art*. The introduction by Hitchcock in French ends on page 6. The book is bound in stiff paper wrappers.

REVIEW
202. Mumford, Lewis. "Frank Lloyd Wright and the New Pioneers." *Arch Rec* LXV (Ap 1929), pp. 414-16.

Periodicals

203. Haskell, Douglas. "Organic Architecture: Frank Lloyd Wright." *Creat Art* III (N 1928), pp. li-lvii.

204. Mumford, Lewis. "American Architecture To-Day, II." *Architecture* LVII (Je 1928), pp. 301-8.
Includes comment on Wright and illustrations of his work.

205. Wright, Frank Lloyd. "Fiske Kimball's New Book: A Review." *Arch Rec* LXIV (Ag 1928), pp. 172-3.
Review of Kimball, Fiske. *American Architecture.* Indianapolis and New York: The Bobbs-Merrill Company, [1928].

206. Wright, Frank Lloyd. "In the Cause of Architecture, I: The Logic of the Plan." *Arch Rec* LXIII (Ja 1928), pp. 49-57.
Reprinted, see no. 1971.

207. Wright, Frank Lloyd. "In the Cause of Architecture, II: What 'Styles' Mean to the Architect." *Arch Rec* LXIII (Fe 1928), pp. 145-51.
Reprinted, see no. 1971.

208. Wright, Frank Lloyd. "In the Cause of Architecture, III: The Meaning of Materials—Stone." *Arch Rec* LXIII (Ap 1928), pp. 350-6.
Reprinted, see no. 1971.

209. Wright, Frank Lloyd. "In the Cause of Architecture, IV: The Meaning of Materials—Wood." *Arch Rec* LXIII (My 1928), pp. 481-8.
Reprinted, see no. 1971.

210. Wright, Frank Lloyd. "In the Cause of Architecture, V: The Meaning of Materials—the Kiln." *Arch Rec* LXIII (Je 1928), pp. 555-61.

Reprinted, see no. 1971.

211. Wright, Frank Lloyd. "In the Cause of Architecture, VI: The Meaning of Materials—Glass." *Arch Rec* LXIV (Jy 1928), pp. 10-16.
Reprinted, see no. 1971.

212. Wright, Frank Lloyd. "In the Cause of Architecture, VII: The Meaning of Materials—Concrete." *Arch Rec* LXIV (Ag 1928), pp. 98-104.
Reprinted, see no. 1971.

213. Wright, Frank Lloyd. "In the Cause of Architecture, VIII: Sheet Metal and a Modern Instance." *Arch Rec* LXIV (O 1928), pp. 334-42.
Reprinted, see no. 1971.

214. Wright, Frank Lloyd. "In the Cause of Architecture, IX: The Terms." *Arch Rec* LXIV (D 1928), pp. 507-14.
Reprinted, see no. 1971.

215. Wright, Frank Lloyd. "Towards a New Architecture." *World Unity* II (Se 1928), pp. 393-5.
Review of Le Corbusier. *Towards a New Architecture.* New York: Brewer and Warren, Inc., [1927].

1929

Periodicals

216. "American Architecture: Correspondence of Walter Pach, Paul Cret, Frank Lloyd Wright and Erich Mendelsohn with Fiske Kimball." *Arch Rec* LXV (My 1929), pp. 431-4.
Concerns Kimball's book, *American Architecture.* Includes a statement from Wright dated Phoenix, Arizona, 30 April 1928, and a reply from Kimball.

217. "The Arizona-Biltmore Hotel, Phoenix, Arizona. Albert Chase McArthur, Architect." *Arch Rec* LXVI (Jy 1929), pp. 19-55.

Although the commission for this building was McArthur's, Wright supervised the design and construction.

218. Drought, Jim, and Wortley Munroe. "Not without Honor." *Wisconsin Literary Magazine* XXVIII (Fe 1929), pp. 14-19.
A biographical essay. The authors' names were pseudonyms for Frederick L. Jochem and Frederick Gutheim, editor, *Wisconsin Literary Magazine.*

219. "Genius, Inc." *Time* XIV (7 O 1929), pp. 45-6.
Profile of Wright, which includes notice of his incorporation.

220. Mendelsohn, Erich. "Frank Lloyd Wright und seine historische Bedeutung." *Das Neue Berlin* IV (Se 1929), pp. 180-1.

221. "Modern Pyramids." *Outlook and Independent* CLIII (30 O 1929), p. 336.
St. Mark's Tower, New York (project).

222. Scharfe, Siegfried. "Theorie und Praxis bei Frank Lloyd Wright." *Wasmuths Monatsh* XIII (Ag 1929), pp. 331-3.

223. "What Architects Are Talking About." *Am Arch* CXXXVI (D 1929), pp. 53-4.
St. Mark's Tower, New York (project).

224. Wright, Frank Lloyd. "A Building Adventure in Modernism." *Country Life* (Garden City, New York) LVI (My 1929), pp. 40-1.
Millard house, "La Miniatura," Pasadena.

225. Wright, Frank Lloyd. "Surface and Mass—Again!" *Arch Rec* LXVI (Jy 1929), pp. 92-4.

226. Wright, Frank Lloyd. "Taliesin: The Chronicle of a House with a Heart." *Liberty* VI (23 Mr 1929), pp. 21-2, 24, 26-9.
Wright house, Spring Green.

227. Wright, Frank Lloyd. "Über das Blech in der Baukunst." *Wasmuths Monatsh* XIII (Ag 1929), pp. 333-41.

228. "Wright's Pyramids." *Time* XIV (28 O 1929), p. 62.
St. Mark's Tower, New York (project).

1930

Periodicals

229. Badovici, Jean. "Frank Lloyd Wright." *L'Architecture Vivante* VIII (Su 1930), pp. 49-76, pls. 26-50.
Included in a book edited by Badovici (see no. 301).

230. Boyd, John Taylor, Jr. "A Prophet of the New Architecture." *Arts and Decoration* XXXIII (My 1930), pp. 56-9, 100, 102, 116.
Interview with Wright.

231. Brock, H. I. "A Pioneer in Architecture That Is Called Modern." *NYTM* (29 Je 1930), pp. 11, 19.

232. "Chicago." *Art N* XXIX (4 O 1930), p. 24.
Comment on exhibition of Wright's work at Chicago Art Institute.

233. "Desert Camp for Frank Lloyd Wright, Arizona. Frank Lloyd Wright, Architect." *Arch Rec* LXVIII (Ag 1930), pp. 188-91.
"Ocatillo," Chandler.

234. "Frank Lloyd Wright and Hugh Ferriss Discuss This Modern Architecture." *Arch For* LIII (N 1930), pp. 535-8.
Radio broadcast at the time of the Contempora exhibition in New York.

235. "Frank Lloyd Wright to the Fore!" *W Arch* XXXIX (Se 1930), p. 152.
From *Time* (see no. 248).

236. Fries, H. de. "Neue Pläne von Frank Lloyd Wright." *Die Form* V (Jy 1930), pp. 342-3.
Also: "Modern Concepts Concerning an Organic Architecture from the Work of Frank Wright," pp. 343-9.

237. Haskell, Douglas. "Frank L. Wright and the Chicago Fair." *Nation* CXXXI (3 D 1930), p. 605.

238. Scharfe, Siegfried. "Wright's Naturalismus." *Wasmuths Monatsh* XIV (Ja 1930), pp. 35-6.

239. "St. Mark's Tower; St. Mark's in the Bouwerie, New York City." *Arch Rec* LXVII (Ja 1930), pp. 1-4.
Includes color reproductions of drawings for this project.

240. "Two Lectures." *Bulletin of the Art Institute of Chicago* XXIV (O 1930), p. 91.
Notice of Wright's lectures delivered in conjunction with an exhibit at the Art Institute, 1 and 2 October 1930. An announcement of the exhibit, held from 25 September to 12 October appeared in the issue of 30 May, p. 80.

241. Voynow, Romola. "Chicagoans, Truth Against the World?" *Chicagoan* VIII (15 Mr 1930), pp. 21-2, 24, 26-7.
Biographical information on Wright.

242. Woollcott, Alexander. "The Prodigal Father." *New Yorker* VI (19 Jy 1930), pp. 22-5.
A profile. Also in Woollcott's *While Rome Burns*. New York: Grosset & Dunlap, [1934]. A condensed version appears in *Reader's Digest* XVII (Se 1930), pp. 388-90.

243. Wright, Frank Lloyd. "Architecture as a Profession Is All Wrong." *Am Arch* CXXXVIII (D 1930), pp. 22-3, 84, 86, 88.
Concerns the status of the individual architect and the firm.

244. Wright, Frank Lloyd. "Beton." *Wasmuths Monatsh* XIV (Ja 1930), pp. 36-42.

245. Wright, Frank Lloyd. "Glas." *Wasmuths Monatsh* XIV (Mr 1930), pp. 135-8.

246. Wright, Frank Lloyd. "In Order to Be Modern." *Architectural Progress* III (D 1930), pp. 6-7.

247. Wright, Frank Lloyd. "The Logic of Contemporary Architecture as an Expression of This Age." *Arch For* LII (My 1930), pp. 637-8. (Also issued as offprint.)
On the need for an appropriate architecture.

248. "Wright's Time." *Time* XV (9 Je 1930), p. 30.
Exhibition in New York. Reprinted, see no. 235.

249. "Zwei kleine Wolkenkratzer." *Wasmuths Monatsh* XIV (Je 1930), pp. 281-3.

1931

Books

250. Wright, Frank Lloyd. *Modern Architecture, Being the Kahn Lectures for 1930.* [Princeton, New Jersey]: Princeton University Press for the department of art and archaeology of Princeton University, 1931.
26.9 x 21 cm., xii, 115 pp., front., 6 ills. (Princeton Monographs in Art and Archaeology)
The texts of six lectures delivered at Princeton University in 1930. Their titles are "Machinery, Materials and Men;" "Style in Industry;" "The Passing of the Cornice;" "The Cardboard House;" "The Tyranny of the Skyscraper;" and "The City." The preface is by E. Baldwin Smith. The book is bound in boards printed with an abstraction designed by Wright in 1927. A list of "Modern Concepts Concerning an Organic Architecture from the Work of Frank Lloyd Wright" appears on the front and back end papers. The speeches have been reprinted in full; see no. 913.
□ A British edition was published by Oxford University Press.
□ Also published in an Italian edition, *Architettura e democrazia.* Traduzione di Giuliana Baracco. Milano: Rosa e Ballo, 1945. (Collezione Il pensiero [4])

REVIEWS of the 1931 edition
251. Anonymous. *Arch For* LIV (My 1931), sup. p. 15.
252. Anonymous. *Landscape Arch* XXII (O 1931), pp. 77-8.
253. Anonymous. *Parnassus* III (My 1931), pp. 38-9.

254. Anonymous. "Tyranny of the Skyscraper." *NYTBR* (31 My 1931), pp. 1, 28.
255. Bauer, Catherine K. "The 'Exuberant and Romantic' Genius of Frank Lloyd Wright." *New Repub* LXVII (8 Jy 1931), pp. 214-15.
256. Bright, John Irwin. *Am M Art* XXIII (Ag 1931), pp. 170-2.
257. Hamlin, Talbot Faulkner. "Artist and Prophet." *Sat R* VII (11 Jy 1931), p. 957.
258. Hamlin, Talbot Faulkner. "Living for the Beautiful." *Outlook and Independent* CLVII (29 Ap 1931), pp. 598-9.
259. "Kunstausstellungen." *Kunst und Künstler* XXIX (Ag 1931), p. 439.
260. Morrow, Irving F. "A Modern Prophet." *C Arts & Arch* XL (N 1931), p. 42.

261. Wright, Frank Lloyd. *Two Lectures on Architecture.* [Chicago]: Art Institute, [1931].

26 x 18.5 cm., 63 pp., front., 8 ills., paper.

The texts of two lectures delivered at the Art Institute, Chicago, 1 and 2 October 1930. Their titles are "In the Realm of Ideas" and "To the Young Man in Architecture." The speeches were reprinted; see no. 913.

Periodicals

262. "American Architect." *Outlook & Independent* CLVII (11 Mr 1931), p. 358.

Comment on Wright's exclusion from the Century of Progress Exposition.

263. "Architect Frank Lloyd Wright naar Europa: een tentoonstelling van zijn werk te Amsterdam." *Bouwkundig Weekblad Architectura* LII (4 Ap 1931).

264. "The Architectural Exhibition for Drawings and Models of Frank Lloyd Wright." *Kokusai-Kenchiku* VII (Ag 1931), p. 1.

Not seen. This issue also includes: a list of executed buildings of Frank Lloyd Wright, compiled by T. Okami, and illustrations of Jones house, Tulsa; San Marcos Water Gardens, Chandler (project); Skelly Gasoline filling station (project);

and St. Mark's Tower, New York (project).

265. "Ausstellungen." *Baugilde* XIII (25 Jy 1931), p. 1190.

266. Bauer, C. K. "The Americanization of Europe." *New Repub* LXVII (24 Je 1931), pp. 153-4.
Wright's influence on European architecture.

267. Bull, Harry Adsit. "Notes of the Month." *International Studio* XCIX (Ag 1931), p. 54.
Notice of exhibition of Wright's work at Prussian Academy of Fine Arts, Berlin.

268. Churchill, Henry S. "Wright and the Chicago Fair." *New Repub* LXV (4 Fe 1931), p. 329.

269. "Frank Lloyd Wright: Ausstellung in der Akademie der Künste, Berlin." *Bauwelt* XXII (2 Jy 1931), p. 914.

270. Gruyter, W. Jos. de. "Frank Lloyd Wright in het Stedelijk Museum te Amsterdam." *Elsevier's Geïllustreerd Maandschrift* LXXXII (Ag 1931), pp. 145-7, pl. xxvii.

271. Landau, Dora. "An American Architect Exhibits in Berlin." *Am M Art* XXIII (Ag 1931), p. 165.
Wright's exhibition at the Prussian Academy of Fine Arts, Berlin.

272. Lotz, Wilhelm. "Frank Lloyd Wright und die Kritik." *Die Form* VI (Se 1931), pp. 357-8.

273. "Models by Frank Lloyd Wright in Berlin Exhibition." *Art N* XXIX (15 Ag 1931), p. 16.

274. Moutschen, J. "Souvenirs sur Frank Lloyd Wright." *Cité et Tekhne* X (N 1931), pp. 41-3.

275. Mumford, Lewis. "Two Chicago Fairs." *New Repub* LXV (21 Ja 1931), pp. 271-2.

276. [Portrait.] *Advertising and Selling* XVII (Jy 1931), sup. p. 40.

277. Robertson, Howard. "Frank Lloyd Wright: Lectures at the Art Institute of Chicago." *Arch & Build N* CXXVIII (16 O 1931), pp. 62-3.

278. Scharfe, Siegfried. "Frank Lloyd Wright." *Baugilde* XIII (25 Jy 1931), pp. 1164-71.

279. Scharfe, Siegfried. "Frank Lloyd Wright über die Stadt der Zukunft." *Baugilde* XIII (25 Jy 1931), pp. 1157-8.

280. Schmidt, Paul F. "Gröse und Niedergang eines Bahnbrechers der modernen Architektur." *Baukunst* (Munich) VII (Ag 1931), pp. 278-9.

281. Schmitz, Marcel. "L'Oeuvre de Frank Lloyd Wright." *Cité et Tekhne* X (N 1931), p. 43.
  Exhibit at Palais des Beaux Arts.

282. "Skyscrapers." *Nation* CXXXIII (30 Se 1931), p. 324.
  Comment on Wright's attack on skyscrapers.

283. "Tentoonstelling Frank Lloyd Wright." *Bouwkundig Weekblad Architectura* LII (23 My 1931), p. 196.

284. "De tentoonstelling van het werk van architect Frank Lloyd Wright." *Bouwkundig Weekblad Architectura* LII (9 My 1931), p. 174.
  Includes reproduction of poster designed by Wijdeveld for exhibition of Wright's work at Stedelijk Museum.

285. Watts, Harvey M. "Don Quixote Atilt at His World." *T-Square* I (N 1931), pp. 14, 34-5.
  A review of the Princeton Lectures. See also no. 342.

286. Wright, Frank Lloyd. "Advice to the Young Architect." *Arch Rec* LXX (Ag 1931), p. 121.
  From *Two Lectures on Architecture* (see no. 261).

287. Wright, Frank Lloyd. "All's Fair, As the Architects View the Lake Front." *Chicagoan* XI (23 My 1931), p. 12.
   Comment on Century of Progress fair in Chicago.

288. Wright, Frank Lloyd. "Die Mechanisierung und die Materialien." *Die Form* VI (Se 1931), pp. 341-9.
   Includes: construction photographs of Jones house, Tulsa; and plans, drawings, and models for "Tent Town for Weekenders."

289. Wright, Frank Lloyd. "Eclectism by Way of 'Taste' Is America's Substitute for Culture." *Tower Town Topics* II (My 1931), p. 19.

290. Wright, Frank Lloyd. "Highlights." *Arch For* LV (O 1931), pp. 409-10.
   Excerpts from a speech on the need for an appropriate American architecture and the correct use of materials, delivered to the Michigan Architectural Society.

291. Wright, Frank Lloyd. "O městu budoucnosti." *Styl* (Prague) XVI (no. 6, 1931), pp. 93-5, 98.
   "The City of the Future," translated from *Modern Architecture* (see no. 250).

292. Wright, Frank Lloyd. "Principles of Design." *Annual of American Design* (1931), pp. 101-4.

293. Wright, Frank Lloyd. "The City." *Architectural Progress* V (O 1931), pp. 4-6, 23; (N 1931), pp. 12-15.
   From *Modern Architecture* (see no. 250).

294. Wright, Frank Lloyd. "The Man Who Grew Whiskers." *New Freeman* III (25 Mr 1931), pp. 38-9.

295. Wright, Frank Lloyd. "To the Young Architect in America." *Architects' J* LXXIV (8 Jy 1931), pp. 48-50.
   From *Two Lectures on Architecture* (see no. 261).

296. Wright, Frank Lloyd. "The Tyranny of the Skyscraper."

Creat Art VIII (My 1931), pp. 324-32.
From *Modern Architecture* (see no. 250).

297. "Wright in Berlin." *Art D* V (1 Jy 1931), p. 12.
Exhibition at Prussian Academy.

298. "Wrightites v. Chicago." *Time* XVII (9 Mr 1931), pp. 63-4.
Note on three meetings held in New York to protest
Wright's exclusion from the Century of Progress Exposition.

299. Wright, Olgivanna. "Last Days of Katherine Mansfield."
Bookman LXXIII (Mr 1931), pp. 6-13.
Mrs. Wright's reminiscences of the English short story
writer. They met at the Gurdjieff Institute at Fontainebleau-
Avon, where Miss Mansfield died.

300. "Wright on a Jury." *Art D* VI (1 O 1931), p. 18.
In Rio de Janeiro to select winning design for Columbus
Memorial Lighthouse, Santo Domingo.

1932

Books

301. Badovici, Jean, ed. *Frank Lloyd Wright: architecte américain.* [Paris]: Éditions Albert Morancé, [1932].
26.9 x 24.3 cm., 77 pp., 114 ills., printed boards.
A review of Wright's work, this book is a compilation of
material which appeared previously in the periodical *L'Architecture Vivante.* The text is in French. Date from Karpel (see
no. 1046).

302. Hitchcock, Henry-Russell. "Frank Lloyd Wright." *In* [New
York. Museum of Modern Art.] *Modern Architecture.* [New
York: Museum of Modern Art, 1932.] Pp. 29-55.
A catalogue, also issued as *Modern Architects,* of an exhibi-
tion held at the Museum of Modern Art in 1932. Wright's
work is included with that of the leading architects of the
International Style. The catalogue includes a 9-page biography
of Wright, a discussion of the model for the "House on the

Mesa," Denver (project) shown in the exhibition, a bibliography, a chronology, a list of work, and 8 pages of illustrations.

303. Wright, Frank Lloyd. *An Autobiography.* London, New
York, and Toronto: Longmans, Green and Company, 1932.
22.6 x 18.1 cm., iv, 371 pp., 65 ills., cloth.
   The first edition of the architect's autobiography. The text
is divided into three sections, each with a separate title page
not included in the pagination. These pages are decorated with
Wright's geometric designs, which are known by the title
"From Generation to Generation." The title page of Book I is
reproduced on Plate 9 of this volume. A fourth section contains a group of photographs of Wright, his family, and his
buildings. Wright designed the black cloth binding and the dust
wrapper.
□ The book was issued again in 1933 in a limp cloth cover edition and was reprinted in 1938.
□ A new edition, partially rewritten and with material added,
was published by Duell, Sloan and Pearce, New York, [1943].
This edition is divided into five sections. A sixth section,
"Broadacre City," was written for the book but was not included. It was published privately by the Taliesin Press in 1943
and 1944 (see nos. 2048 and 2049). The 1943 edition contains
only one photograph.
□ The 1943 edition was published by Faber & Faber and the
Hyperion Press Limited, London, [1945]. A section of photographs is included.
□ The book was translated into French as *Mon autobiographie*
par Frank Lloyd Wright. Traduction de Jules Castier. Éditions
d' Histoire et d' Art, Librairie Plon, Paris, 1955. (Collection
Ars et Historia. Publiée Sous la Direction de René Wittmann)
□ A new American edition was published by Horizon Press,
New York, in 1977. This volume includes revisions and addi-
tions which Wright had made to the preceeding 1943 manuscript. It consists of six sections including the previously
omitted "Broadacre City." There are eighty-two illustrations.
The front endpaper is illustrated with a facsimile page from
the 1943 edition with corrections in Wright's handwriting. The
photograph of Wright on the dust jacket first appeared on the
cover of *Time* (see no. 454).

REVIEWS of the 1932, 1943, 1945, and 1977 editions

304. Anonymous. *AIA J* LXVI (Jy 1977), p. 90. [1977]

305. Anonymous. *Am Arch* CXLI (Je 1932), p. 6. [1932]

306. Anonymous. *Arch For* LVI (My 1932), sup. p. 32. [1932]

307. Anonymous. *Arch For* LXXIX (Se 1943), pp. 120, 124, 128, 132. [1943]

308. Anonymous. "Ego by Frank Lloyd Wright." *Architects' J* CIII (2 My 1946), pp. 336-7. [1945]

309. Anonymous. *Studio* CXXXI (My 1946), p. 160. [1945]

310. Anonymous. "The Autobiography of a Fighting Architect." *NYTBR* (3 Ap 1932), p. 4. [1932]

311. Byrne, Barry. *America* LXIX (19 Je 1943), p. 305. [1943]

312. Cheney, Sheldon. "A Prophetic Artist." *Sat R* VIII (23 Ap 1932), pp. 677-8. [1932]

313. Coit, Elisabeth. *Arch Rec* XCIV (Jy 1943), pp. 26, 28. [1943]

314. Downs, Robert B. "Master Builder: Frank Lloyd Wright's *Autobiography,* 1932." In *Famous American Books.* New York: McGraw-Hill Book Company, 1971. Pp. 283-9. [1932]

315. Goldberger, Paul. "He Had an Answer for Everything." *NYTBR* (19 Je 1977), pp. 13, 43. [1977]

316. Gutheim, F. A. "An Autobiography: From Generation to Generation." *Am M Art* XXV (Jy 1932), pp. 72-3. [1932]

317. Hamlin, Talbot. *Wis Mag Hist* XXVII (D 1943), pp. 227-9. [1943]

318. Howe, George. *Shelter* II (Ap 1932), p. 27. [1932]

319. Kellogg, Louise Phelps. *Wis Mag Hist* XVI (Se 1932), p. 117. [1932]

320. Kimball, F. "Builder and Poet—Frank Lloyd Wright." *Arch Rec* LXXI (Je 1932), pp. 379-80. [1932]

321. Pevsner, Nikolaus. *Burlington Magazine for Connoisseurs* LXXXIX (Je 1947), p. 169. [1945]

322. Pinckheard, John. *RIBA J* LIII (Je 1946), p. 355. [1945]

323. Read, Herbert. "Frank Lloyd Wright." *Arch R* C (Jy 1946), p. 29. [1945]

324. Rienaecker, Victor. "The Philosophy of an Architect."

Apollo XLIII (Je 1946), pp. 137-9; XLIV (Jy 1946), pp. 7-9, 22. [1945]

325. Stoney, Samuel Gaillard. "Portrait of an Artist As Prophet." *Virginia Quarterly Review* VIII (Jy 1932), pp. 435-8. [1932]

326. Wheelwright, John. "Truth against the World." *New Repub* LXXI (29 Je 1932), p. 186. [1932]

327. Wilbur, Susan. "The Life of Frank Lloyd Wright." *Chicagoan* XII (Ap 1932), p. 52. [1932]

328. Wright, Frank Lloyd. *The Disappearing City.* New York: William Farquhar Payson, [1932].

20.9 x 20.9 cm., v, 90 pp., front., 5 ills.

This is the first book in which Wright defined his proposal for a decentralized, agrarian society based on the proper use of the machine. The subject was of continuing concern to him, and the text of this book was rewritten and included in *When Democracy Builds* (see no. 609) and *The Living City* (see no. 1218). The cloth binding and dust wrapper were printed with a graphic pattern designed by Wright. A popular edition was also published.

□ A new edition of *The Disappearing City,* entitled *The Industrial Revolution Runs Away,* was published by Horizon Press, New York, [1969]. It includes a facsimile of Wright's copy of the original edition as subsequently revised in his hand and contains the new text complete with his revisions on the facing pages (publisher's note). 1250 hand-numbered copies were published. Boxed.

REVIEWS of the 1932 edition

329. Agard, Walter R. *Am M Art* XXV (D 1932), p. 364.

330. Anonymous. Portland, Oregon. City Planning Commission, *Plan It* VIII (D 1934), p. 3.

331. Bauer, Catherine K. "When Is a House Not a House?" *Nation* CXXXVI (25 Ja 1933), pp. 99-100.

332. Churchill, Henry S. *Arch Rec* LXXIII (Ja 1933), pp. 12, 14.

333. Haskell, Douglas. *Creat Art* XII (Ja 1933), p. 63.

Periodicals

334. "The Architects' Library." *Arch Rec* LXXI (Ap 1932),
sup. p. 30.
   Announcement of publication of *An Autobiography* and
   Two Lectures on Architecture.

335. "Bookless School Started by Frank Lloyd Wright." *Am
Arch* CXLII (O 1932), p. 26.
   Taliesin Fellowship.

336. "Copyright Window Displays; Frank Lloyd Wright Designs
Displays of His Own Book." *Publishers' Weekly* CXXI (2 Ap
1932), p. 1563.

337. "Frank Lloyd Wright Honored Again." *Arch Rec* LXXI
(Ja 1932), sup. p. 40.
   Selected for representation in the Hall of Living Leaders,
   Thomas Jefferson High School, Brooklyn.

338. "Frank Lloyd Wright Tells of the Broadacre City." *City
Club of Chicago. Bulletin* XXV (15 Fe 1932), pp. 27, 29.

339. Giedion, S. "Les Problémes actuels de l'architecture a
l'occasion d'un manifeste de Frank Lloyd Wright aux architectes
et critiques d'Europe." *Cahiers d'Art* VII (no. 1-2, 1932), pp.
69-73.

340. Haskell, Douglas. "Architecture: News from the Field."
Nation CXXXV (14 D 1932), p. 598.
   Taliesin Fellowship.

341. Howe, George. "Moses Turns Pharaoh." *T-Square* II (Fe
1932), p. 9.
   A response to an article by Wright, (see no. 353). Reprinted,
   see no. 1077.

342. Kuo, Yuan-Hsi. "My Opinion of 'Don Quixote A-Tilt at His
World'." *T-Square* II (Ja 1932), pp. 30-1.
   A response to an article by Harvey M. Watts (see no. 285).

343. "People." *Time* XX (14 N 1932), p. 52.
Note on scuffle with C. R. Sechrest, former laborer at Taliesin, who claimed Wright owed him money.

344. Stone, Peter. "Tooling up." *Shelter* II (My 1932), p. 29.
Includes note on Wright's recent activities.

345. "Taliesin." *Art D* VI (1 Se 1932), p. 27.
Note on formation of Taliesin Fellowship.

346. "Wright Apprentices." *Time* XX (5 Se 1932), p. 33.
Taliesin Fellowship.

347. Wright, F. L. "Myšlenky o architektuře." *Styl* (Prague) XI (no. 12, 1932), pp. 205-7.

348. Wright, Frank Lloyd. "America Tomorrow." *Am Arch* CXLI (My 1932), pp. 14-17, 76.

349. Wright, Frank Lloyd. "A Treatise on Ornament." *Sat R* VIII (21 My 1932), p. 744.
Review of Bragdon, Claude. *The Frozen Fountain.* New York: Alfred A. Knopf, 1932.

350. Wright, Frank Lloyd. "Books That Have Meant Most to Me." *Scholastic* XXI (24 Se 1932), p. 11.

351. Wright, Frank Lloyd. "Broadacre City: An Architect's Vision." *NYTM* (20 Mr 1932), pp. 8-9.

352. Wright, Frank Lloyd. "Caravel or Motorship?" *Arch For* LVII (Ag 1932), p. 90.
On the role of the architect in the machine age.

353. Wright, Frank Lloyd. "For All May Raise the Flowers Now for All Have Got the Seed." *T-Square* II (Fe 1932), pp. 6-8.
Concerns the International Style. Reprinted, see no. 1090.

354. Wright, Frank Lloyd. [Letter.] *T-Square* II (Fe 1932), p. 32.
A response to an article by Norman N. Rice published in *T-Square,* (Ja 1932).

355. Wright, Frank Lloyd. "Of Thee I Sing." *Shelter* II (Ap 1932), pp. 10-12. (Also issued as offprint.)
    Response to the International Exhibition at the Museum of Modern Art. Also in *New Humanist* V (My-Je 1932), pp. 1-5.

356. Wright, Frank Lloyd. "Taste and Autobiography." *Chicagoan* XII (Ap 1932), p. 23.

357. Wright, Frank Lloyd. "The House of the Future." *National Real Estate Journal* XXXIII (Jy 1932), pp. 25-6.
    Excerpts from an address before the Cincinnati convention of the National Association of Real Estate Boards. Reprinted, see no. 1200.

358. Wright, Frank Lloyd. "The Taliesin Fellowship." *London Studio* IV (D 1932), pp. 348-9.

359. Wright, Frank Lloyd. "To the Students of the Beaux-Arts Institute of Design, All Departments." *Architecture* LXVI (O 1932), p. 230.
    A response to an article by Ely Jacques Kahn published in *Beaux Arts Institute of Design* (My 1932), which warned students of the inadvisability of designing in the modern style without understanding the antecedents of its forms.

360. Wright, Frank Lloyd. "Why the Great Earthquake Did Not Destroy the Imperial Hotel." *Creat Art* X (Ap 1932), pp. 268-77.

361. "Wright's Prophesy." *Art D* VI (1 Fe 1932), p. 8.
    Wright's comments on skyscrapers in an interview with S. J. Woolf printed in the *New York Times* (17 Ja 1932).

1933

Periodicals

362. Kostanecki, Michal. "Twórczość arch. Frank Lloyd Wright à." *Architektura i Budownictwo* (Warsaw) IX (no. 6, 1933), pp. 179-87.

363. Oud, J. J. P. "Wplyw Franka Wright'a na architekture europejska." *Architektura i Budownictwo* (Warsaw) IX (no. 6, 1933), pp. 188-9.

364. Persico, Edoardo. "L'architettura mondiale." *L'Italia Letteraria* XI (2 Jy 1933), p. 5.
    Includes references to Wright.

365. Watrous, James. "Taliesin Fellowship." *Am M Art* XXVI (D 1933), pp. 552-3.
    Letter from a visitor to Taliesin.

366. Wright, Frank Lloyd. "Another Pseudo." *Arch For* LIX (Jy 1933), p. 25.
    Century of Progress exposition.

367. Wright, Frank Lloyd. "In the Show Window at Macy's." *Arch For* LIX (N 1933), pp. 419-20.
    Comment on the work of eight "modern" architects.

368. Wright, Frank Lloyd. "The Chicago World Fair." *Architects' J* LXXVIII (13 Jy 1933), pp. 45-7, note on p. 36.

369. Wright, Frank Lloyd. "The City of To-morrow." *Pictorial Review* XXXIV (Mr 1933), pp. 4, 61.

370. "Wright's Rival Fair." *Arch For* LVIII (Ap 1933), sup. p. 32.
    Note on Wright's suggestion that he build a tower of steel and glass opposite the main entrance of the Century of Progress exposition.

1934

Books

371. Craven, Thomas. "An American Architect." In *Modern Art: The Men, the Movements, the Meaning.* New York: Simon and Schuster, 1934. Pp. 273-89.
    A one-chapter biography of Wright.

Periodicals

372. Beal, George Malcolm. "The Taliesin Experiment." *University of Kansas. Graduate Magazine* XXXIII (N 1934), pp. 18-19.

373. "Quelques oeuvres de Frank Lloyd Wright." *Le Document* (Brussels) X (no. 10, 1934), pp. 148-54.
   Robie house, Chicago; Allen house, Wichita; Coonley house, Riverside; Ullman house, Oak Park (project); Martin house, Buffalo; Ennis house, Los Angeles.

374. Wright, Frank Lloyd. "Architecture of Individualism." *Trend* II (Mr-Ap 1934), pp. 55-60.

375. Wright, Frank Lloyd. "The Taliesin Fellowship." *Wisconsin Alumni Magazine* XXXV (Mr 1934), pp. 152-3, 176.

376. Wright, Frank Lloyd. "What Is the Modern Idea?" *Liberty* XI (10 Fe 1934), p. 49.
   Concerns decentralization.

1935

Periodicals

377. Alexander, Stephen. "Frank Lloyd Wright's Utopia." *New Masses* XV (18 Je 1935), p. 28.
   Review of Broadacre City exhibit at National Alliance of Arts and Industry Exposition, New York. See also no. 395.

378. "An Architect Visualizes 'Broadacre City'." *American City* L (Ap 1935), pp. 85, 87.

379. "Broadacre City: Frank Lloyd Wright, Architect." *Am Arch* CXLVI (My 1935), pp. 55-62.
   Photographs of models on view at National Alliance of Arts and Industry Exposition, New York.

380. "Frank Lloyd Wright Addresses N. Y. Decorators." *Interior Decorator* XCV (D 1935), pp. 12-13, 42-4.
   Review of speech.

381. Gloag, John. "Design in America." *Architects' J* LXXXI
(3 Ja 1935), p. 16.
   Account of a visit with Frank Lloyd Wright.

382. Gloag, John. "Frank Lloyd Wright and the Significance of
the Taliesin Fellowship." *Arch R* LXXVII (Ja 1935), pp. 1-2.
   Impressions of a visit to Taliesin in October, 1934.

383. Gloag, John. "Frank Lloyd Wright." *Architects' J* LXXXI
(31 Ja 1935), p. 202.
   Excerpts from a lecture on Wright.

384. "1900-10, House at Oak Park, Illinois." *Arch Rec* LXXVII
(Ap 1935), p. 231.
   Ullman house (project). Reproduced from plate XVI of the
   1910 Wasmuth portfolio.

385. "People." *Time* XXVI (15 Jy 1935), p. 44.
   Wright's comment about Pittsburgh.

386. "Portfolio of Houses: House of Prof. Malcolm Willey in
Minneapolis, Frank Lloyd Wright, Architect." *Arch Rec* LXXVIII
(N 1935), pp. 313-15.
   Photographs and plan.

387. [Portrait.] *Arch & Eng* CXXIII (D 1935), p. 1.
   Included in a special issue on modern architecture, edited
   by Pauline G. Schindler.

388. Roos, Frank J., Jr. "Concerning Several American Architectural Leaders." *Design* XXXVII (D 1935), pp. 2-5, 40.

389. Safford, Virginia. "Home of the Month." *Golfer and Sportsman* XVII (Je 1935), pp. 37-9, 58.
   Willey house, Minneapolis.

390. Schindler, Pauline. "Modern Architecture Acknowledges
the Light Which Kindled It." *C Arts & Arch* XLVII (Ja 1935),
p. 17.
   Tribute to Wright.

391. Shand, P. Morton. "Scenario for a Human Drama, VI: La Machine-à-Habiter to the House of Character." *Arch R* LXXVII (Fe 1935), pp. 61-4.
    Evaluation of Wright's influence on modern architecture. Reprinted, see no. 1359.

392. "The Taliesin Fellowship." *Professional Art Quarterly* II (D 1935), pp. 6-8.

393. Wright, Frank Lloyd. "Broadacre City: A New Community Plan." *Arch Rec* LXXVII (Ap 1935), pp. 243-54. (Also issued as offprint.)

394. Wright, Frank Lloyd. "Form and Function." *Sat R* XIII (14 D 1935), p. 6.
    Review of Morrison, Hugh. *Louis Sullivan: Prophet of Modern Architecture.* New York: The Museum of Modern Art and W. W. Norton & Company, Inc., [1935].

395. Wright, Frank Lloyd. "Freedom Based on Form." *New Masses* XVI (23 Jy 1935), pp. 23-4.
    Response to review of Broadacre City exhibit (no. 377).

396. Wright, Frank Lloyd. "Louis Sullivan's Words and Work." *Arch R* LXXVII (Mr 1935), p. 116.
    Review of Sullivan, Louis. *Kindergarten Chats.* [Lawrence, Kansas]: Scarab Fraternity Press, 1934.

397. Wright, Frank Lloyd. "The Creed of a Modern Architect." *Arch R* LXXVII (Ja 1935), p. 41.
    From "In the Cause of Architecture" series in *Architectural Record* and other essays.

1936

Periodicals

398. Bodley, Ronald V. C. "Imperial Hotel, Tokyo, Japan." *Town and Country* XCI (Ap 1936), pp. 64-5, 113-14.

399. Dos Passos, John. "Grand Old Man." *New Repub* LXXXVII (3 Je 1936), pp. 94-5.
Also in his *The Big Money.* New York: Harcourt, Brace and Company, 1936. Pp. 428-33.

400. Wright, Frank Lloyd. "Apprenticeship-Training for the Architect." *Arch Rec* LXXX (Se 1936), pp. 207-10.
The Taliesin Fellowship. Portrait, p. 179.

401. Wright, Frank Lloyd. "Plan: A Modern Home." *Inland Topics* VII (Ag 1936), pp. 16-17.

402. Wright, Frank Lloyd. "Recollections: United States, 1893-1920." *Architects' J* LXXXIV (16 Jy 1936), pp. 76-8; (23 Jy), pp. 111-12; (30 Jy), pp. 141-2; (6 Ag), pp. 173-4.

403. Wright, Frank Lloyd. "Skyscrapers Doomed? Yes!" *Rotarian* XLVIII (Mr 1936), pp. 10-11, 46-7. (Also issued as offprint.)

404. Wright, Frank Lloyd. "Taliesin: Our Cause." *Professional Art Quarterly* II (Mr 1936), pp. 6-7, 24; (Je 1936), pp. 39-41.

1937

Books

405. Brownell, Baker, and Frank Lloyd Wright. *Architecture and Modern Life.* New York and London: Harper & Brothers Publishers, 1937.
21.7 x 16 cm., v, 339 pp., 24 ills., cloth.
A discussion of the relation of architecture to modern social structure. The authors defined present trends and attempted to predict the future. Baker Brownell was head of the Department of Contemporary Thought at Northwestern University. Chapters I and VII are by Brownell and Wright jointly, II and IV are by Wright, and III, V, and VI are by Brownell.

REVIEWS
406. Anonymous. *Arch For* LXVIII (Ja 1938), p. 18.

407. Duffus, R. "Frank Lloyd Wright's Way to a Better World." *NYTBR* (2 Ja 1938), p. 2.

408. Hamlin, Talbot. "Building for the Future." *Sat R* XVII (18 D 1937), p. 10.

409. Harbeson, John. *Pencil P* XIX (Fe 1938), sup. p. 42.

410. McMahon, A. Philip. *Parnassus* X (Fe 1938), p. 30.

411. Schapiro, Meyer. "Architect's Utopia." *Partisan Review* IV (Mr 1938), pp. 42-7.

412. Tallmadge, Thomas E. "The Brownell-Wright Book." *Architect's World* I (Mr 1938), pp. 131-4.
    Reprinted from the *Evanston Review* (27 Ja 1938).

Periodicals

413. "A Frank Lloyd Wright House at Palo Alto, California Designed to Resist Earthquakes." *Arch & Eng* CXXX (Ag 1937), p. 3.
    Hanna house.

414. "Frank Lloyd Wright Tests a Column, Attends a Convention, Visits the Paris Fair." *Arch For* LXVII (Ag 1937), p. 10.
    Tests column for S. C. Johnson and Son administration building, Racine; invited to All-Union Congress of Soviet Architects.

415. "Frank Lloyd Wright." *Town and Country* XCII (Jy 1937), pp. 56, 85 and cover.
    Portrait. The cover was designed by Wright in 1926/27 for *Liberty,* but was not used at the time. It was one of a series of abstractions which represented the months. It is illustrated on Plate 7 of this volume.

416. Hitchcock, Henry-Russell. "The Architectural Future in America." *Arch R* LXXXII (Jy 1937), pp. 1-2.
    Includes comments on Wright's career. A reply from Eugene Masselink was published in September, p. 114. Another reply from John E. Lautner, Jr., and a rejoinder from Hitchcock were published in November, pp. 221-2.

417. Levin, Meyer. "Master-Builder: Concerning Frank Lloyd

Wright, Stormy Petrel of Architecture." *Coronet* III (D 1937), pp. 171-84.

418. "Office Building for S. C. Johnson and Son, Inc., at Racine, Wisconsin. Frank Lloyd Wright, Architect." *Arch Rec* LXXXI (Fe 1937), sup. p. 36.
Perspective drawing.

419. "Office Building in Wisconsin Designed by Frank Lloyd Wright." *Architects' J* LXXXV (18 Fe 1937), p. 289.
S. C. Johnson and Son administration building, Racine.

420. "Office Building without Precedent." *Engin N R* CXIX (9 D 1937), pp. 956-60.
S. C. Johnson and Son administration building, Racine.

421. "People." *Time* XXX (25 O 1937), p. 68.
Wright's comment on Detroit.

422. "66 Tons with Ease." *Arch Rec* LXXXII (Jy 1937), p. 38.
Test of column for S. C. Johnson and Son administration building, Racine.

423. "Unique Office Structure." *Scientific American* CLVI (My 1937), pp. 316-17.
S. C. Johnson and Son administration building, Racine.

424. "Windowless Building Built by 'Organic' Architecture." *Science Newsletter* XXXII (9 O 1937), pp. 227, 239.
S. C. Johnson and Son administration building, Racine.

425. Wright, Frank Lloyd. "Architecture and Life in the U.S.S.R." *Arch Rec* LXXXII (O 1937), pp. 57-63.
Portrait, p. 5. Impressions from a trip to Russia to serve as an American representative to the All-Union Congress of Soviet Architects. Also in *Soviet Russia Today* VI (O 1937), pp. 14-19. Also in *An Autobiography* (1943), pp. 549-56.

426. Wright, Frank Lloyd. "Building against Doomsday." *Reader's Digest* XXXI (Se 1937), pp. 70-4.

Imperial Hotel, Tokyo. Condensed from *An Autobiography* (see no. 303).

427. Wright, Frank Lloyd. "Per la causa dell'architettura." *Casabella* X (Je 1937), pp. 2-3.

428. Wright, Frank Lloyd. "The Man St. Peter Liked." *Coronet* III (D 1937), p. 91.
   "Those favored of God are those who plant and nurture the trees he made."

429. Wright, Frank Lloyd. "What the Cause of Architecture Needs Most." *Arch R* LXXXI (Mr 1937), pp. 99-100.
   Concerns the need for devotion to a great art, with less emphasis on capitalistic ambitions.

1938

Books

430. New York. Museum of Modern Art. *A New House by Frank Lloyd Wright on Bear Run, Pennsylvania.* New York: Museum of Modern Art, 1938.
   25.5 x 19.1 cm., 17 pp., 14 ills., paper.
   A photo study, published in conjunction with an exhibition of photographs of the Kaufmann house, "Fallingwater." It includes a statement by Wright. This statement and some of the photographs and plans also appeared in the *Architectural Forum* (see no. 457).

Periodicals

431. "Architect Turns Engineer: Frank Lloyd Wright Does Some Pioneering in Reinforced Concrete Design for the Johnson Wax Works at Racine." *Technical America* V (Ja 1938), p. 7.

432. "Art." *Time* XXXI (21 Fe 1938), p. 53.
   Comment on exhibition of photographs of the Kaufmann house, "Fallingwater," Bear Run, at the Museum of Modern Art.

433. "The Conic Dwelling; Appropriate in That Territory Commonly Known as USA, but Often Referred to by Certain Prophets as Usonia." *Federal Architect* VIII (Ap 1938), pp. 31-2, 52.
    Reprinted from *Charette.*

434. "Fallingwater, een landhuis van Frank Lloyd Wright." *Bouwkundig Weekblad Architectura* LIX (23 Ap 1938), pp. 137-8.
    Kaufmann house, "Fallingwater," Bear Run.

435. "Fallingwater: Kaufmann House, Pennsylvania, Frank Lloyd Wright." *Kokusai-Kentiku* XIV (Ap 1938), pls. 149-56.
    Reprinted from *Architectural Forum,* January, 1938 (see no. 457).

436. " 'Fallingwater', vivienda en Pensilvania, arq. Frank Lloyd Wright." *Nuestra Arquitectura* (O 1938), pp. 336-45.
    Kaufmann house.

437. Finetti, Giuseppe de. "L'America di Frank Lloyd Wright." *Rassegna di Architettura* X (Fe 1938), pp. 49-61.

438. "Frank Lloyd Wright, Architect: House for $5,000–$6,000 Income." *Arch For* LXIX (N 1938), pp. 331-5.
    The *Life* house (see no. 447).

439. "Frank Lloyd Wright." *Architect's World* I (Fe 1938), p. 6.
    Discussion of the special issue of the *Architectural Forum* devoted to Wright (see no. 457).

440. "Frank Lloyd Wright." *Arkitekten* (Finland) (1938), pp. 120-1.
    From *Architectural Forum,* January, 1938 (see no. 457).

441. "Frank Lloyd Wright at Williamsburg." *Mag Art* XXXI (O 1938), p. 597.
    Exhibit at College of William and Mary.

442. "Frank Lloyd Wright Designs a Honeycomb House." *Arch Rec* LXXXIV (Jy 1938), pp. 59-74.

P. 74: Paul R. and Jean S. Hanna, "Frank Lloyd Wright Builds Us a Home."

443. "Frank Lloyd Wright Exhibition Planned." *Pencil P* XIX (Se 1938), sup. p. 40.
At College of William and Mary.

444. Giolli, Raffaelo. "L'ultimo Wright." *Casabella-Costruzioni* X (Mr 1938), pp. 1, 4-19, 40 and cover.

445. Hamlin, Talbot F. "F. L. W.–An Analysis." *Pencil P* XIX (Mr 1938), pp. 137-44.
Includes discussion of: Kaufmann house, "Fallingwater," Bear Run; Hanna house, Palo Alto; and S. C. Johnson and Son administration building, Racine. A condensed version appeared in *Architect's World* I (Ap 1938), pp. 159-63.

446. "Letters." *Arch For* LXVIII (Fe 1938), pp. 42, 86.
Responses to the special issue of the *Forum* devoted to Wright published in January (see no. 457). The letters are from Hugh S. Morrison, Ernest Born, M. Lincoln Schuster, Ralph Walker, Joseph K. Boltz, J. H. Phillips, Bayard Wilson, W. W. Wurster, Tom Maloney, Gilman Lane, Mishal A. Securda, Jacob Moscowitz, Armistead Fitzhugh, T. W. Brooks, Quentin F. Haig, William H. Scheick, Mendel Glickman, Louis Brustein, and William Heyl Thompson.

447. "*Life* Presents in Collaboration with the *Architectural Forum* Eight Houses for Modern Living Especially Designed by Famous American Architects for Four Representative Families Earning $2,000 to $10,000 a Year." *Life* V (26 Se 1938), pp. 45-65.
Includes design by Wright, pp. 60-1.

448. Meyer, Ernest L. "Frank Lloyd Wright." *Scholastic* XXXII (12 Fe 1938), pp. 21 E, 24 E.
Also published in the *New York Post.*

449. Mumford, Lewis. "The Sky Line—at Home, Indoors and Out." *New Yorker* XIII (12 Fe 1938), p. 31.

Comments on: Kaufmann house, "Fallingwater," Bear Run; Willey house, Minneapolis.

450. Patterson, Augusta Owen. "Three Modern Houses, No. 3: Owner, Edgar J. Kaufmann, Pittsburgh; Architect, Frank Lloyd Wright." *Town and Country* XCIII (Fe 1938), pp. 64-5, 104.

451. "People." *Time* XXXII (7 N 1938), p. 37.
Wright's comment on Williamsburg.

452. Peterson, Jay. "Nature's Architect." *New Masses* XXVI (8 Fe 1938), pp. 29-30.
Review of exhibition of photographs of Kaufmann house, "Fallingwater," at Museum of Modern Art.

453. Seckel, Harry. "Frank Lloyd Wright." *North American Review* CCXLVI (Au 1938), pp. 48-64.
Biographical information.

454. "Usonian Architect." *Time* XXXI (17 Ja 1938), pp. 29-32 and cover.
Biographical information. Cover photograph of Wright by Valentino Sarra. Responses from readers: 31 Ja, pp. 2, 4-5; 21 Fe, pp. 10, 12.

455. "Wright and Center." *Arch For* LXVIII (Je 1938), sup. p. 10.
Florida Southern College, Lakeland.

456. "Wright Dissents Again." *Art D* XIII (1 O 1938), p. 23.

457. Wright, Frank Lloyd. "Frank Lloyd Wright." *Arch For* LXVIII (Ja 1938), sup. pp. 1-102 and cover.
A special issue, written and designed by Wright, devoted to his new and unpublished work. Includes: Wright house, "Taliesin," and the Taliesin Fellowship complex, Spring Green; Willey house, Minneapolis; Barnsdall kindergarten, "Little Dipper," Los Angeles; "Memorial to the Soil" chapel, Wisconsin (project); Kaufmann house, "Fallingwater," Bear Run; Kaufmann office, Pittsburgh; Marcus house, Dallas (project); St. Mark's Tower, New York (project); Johnson house,

"Wingspread," and farm group, Racine; Wright desert dwelling and studio, "Ocatillo," and San Marcos in the Desert, Chandler (project); Hanna house, Palo Alto; "House on the Mesa," Denver (project); Lusk house, Huron (project); Jacobs house I, Madison; Bramson dress shop, Oak Park (project); Parker garage, Janesville (project); Capitol Journal office building, Salem (project); Midway Gardens furniture (project); and S. C. Johnson and Son administration building, Racine. Bibliography. Black and red cover and fold-out title page designed by Wright. The internal title page is illustrated on Plate 11 of this volume. Spiral binding. This issue elicited numerous comments from readers, see no. 446.

458. Wright, Frank Lloyd. "Ideas for the Future." *Sat R* XXXII (17 Se 1938), pp. 14-15.
    Review of Fuller, R. Buckminster. *Nine Chains to the Moon.* Philadelphia: J. B. Lippincott Co., [1938].

459. Wright, Frank Lloyd. "No Real Honor." *Mag Art* XXXI (Je 1938), p. 368.
    Letter concerning Thomas Jefferson memorial.

460. "Wright's Newest." *Art D* XII (1 Fe 1938), p. 13.
    Kaufmann house, "Fallingwater," Bear Run.

1939

Books

461. Chase, Mary Ellen. "The Hillside Home School." In *A Goodly Fellowship.* New York: The MacMillan Company, 1939. Pp. 85-121.
    One chapter describes a school run by Wright's aunts, Jane and Nell Lloyd-Jones at Hillside, Wisconsin.

462. San Marino, California. The Huntington Library. *The George and Alice Millard Collection Illustrating the Evolution of the Book.* Acquired for the Huntington Library by a group of their friends. [1939.]
    A pamphlet prepared for presentation to the doners. It

includes a description of the Millard house, "La Miniatura," while Mrs. Millard lived there and an essay on the Millard Memorial Collection. Seventy-five copies were printed by the Ward Ritchie Press.

463. Wright, Frank Lloyd. *An Organic Architecture: The Architecture of Democracy.* The Sir George Watson Lectures of the Sulgrave Manor Board for 1939. [London]: Lund Humphries & Co., [1939].
    27.8 x 20.1 cm., viii, 56 pp., color front., 25 ills., cloth.
    The texts of four lectures delivered by Wright at the Royal Institute of British Architects in May, 1939. Discussion with the audience followed two of the lectures; this also was printed fully. The book includes a bibliography and lists of buildings and projected work.
□ Reprinted, 1941.
□ A facsimile edition was published by Lund Humphries, London, and MIT, Cambridge, in 1970. According to a publisher's note, only the title page, copyright page, binding, and jacket were altered in appearance.
□ An Italian edition entitled *Architettura organica, l'architettura della democrazia* was published by Muggiani, Milano, 1945.

REVIEWS of the 1939 and 1970 editions
464. Anonymous. *Art and Industry* XXVIII (Je 1940), p. 190. [1939]
465. Anonymous. *Cahiers d'Art* XV (nos. 3-4, 1940), p. 76. [1939]
466. Carter, Ernestine. "The Prophet of Taliesin." *Arch R* LXXXVII (Ap 1940), p. 148. [1939]
467. Pawley, Martin. "FLW, 1939." *Arch Design* XL (Se 1970), pp. 473-4. [1970]
468. Yanul, Thomas. *Prairie Sch R* VIII (no. 1, 1971), p. 19. [1970]

Periodicals

469. Abercrombie, Patrick. "Frank Lloyd Wright." *RIBA J* XLVII (11 D 1939), p. 44.
    Criticism of London lectures.

470. Carter, E. J., and Naum Gabo. "Frank Lloyd Wright." *Focus* I (Su 1939), pp. 49-52.
From a discussion which followed Wright's London lectures.

471. Castagna, John F. "Bertram Goodhue and Frank Lloyd Wright—Their Ideals and Their Influence in 'the Arts'." *New York University School of Architecture Bulletin* II (Se 1939), pp. 35-44.

472. Delafon, S. Gille. "L'Architecte américain Frank Lloyd Wright présente à Paris un film de ses oeuvres." *Beaux Arts* (9 Je 1939), p. 1.

473. "Exhibition at Building Centre." *Builder* CLVI (5 My 1939), p. 858.

474. Farrar, Benedict. "Answers Frank Lloyd Wright." *Arch & Eng* CXXXVI (Fe 1939), pp. 74-5.
Response from the president of the St. Louis chapter of the American Institute of Architects to Wright's criticism of buildings in St. Louis.

475. "Frank Lloyd Wright Again." *Arch & Eng* CXXXVI (Mr 1939), p. 4.
Wright's responses to questions after a lecture in Washington, D. C.

476. "Frank Lloyd Wright." *Architects' J* LXXXIX (11 My 1939), pp. 756-7.
Comments on Wright's London lectures. Reprinted; see no. 480.

477. "Frank Lloyd Wright, Architecture Club Dinner." *Builder* CLVI (5 My 1939), p. 855.
Remarks made at the dinner.

478. "Frank Lloyd Wright." *Builder* CLVI (28 Ap 1939), p. 789.
Wright's itinerary while in London to deliver the Watson lectures.

479. "Frank Lloyd Wright." *RIBA J* XLVI (22 My 1939), p. 700.

Discussion of the London lectures (1939).

480. "Frank Lloyd Wright Takes England." *Arch For* LXXI (Ag 1939), sup. pp. 22-3.
From *Architects' Journal* (no. 476).

481. Fuller, Kathryn Handy. "Home of the Month." *Golfer and Sportsman* XXIV (N 1939), pp. 24-5, 45-6.
Wright house, "Taliesin," Spring Green.

482. "The Future of Cities." *Spectator* CLXII (12 My 1939), pp. 793-4.
Comment on Wright's opinion of cities.

483. Herrick, George. "A 'Functional' Office Building, U. S. A." *Builder* CLVI (5 My 1939), pp. 857-8.
S. C. Johnson and Son administration building, Racine.

484. Kahn, Albert. "The Wizard of Taliesin." *Arch & Eng* CXXXIX (D 1939), p. 75.
S. C. Johnson and Son administration building, Racine.

485. "Lloyd Wright." *Arch & Build N* CLVIII (12 My 1939), p. 141.
Comment on Wright's London lectures.

486. Morley-Horder, P. "American Architecture." *Journal of the Royal Society of Arts* LXXXVII (26 My 1939), p. 732.
Summary of the following article.

487. Morley-Horder, P. "Mr. Frank Lloyd Wright's Visit." *RIBA J* XLVI (22 My 1939), p. 743.
Letter commenting on Wright's London lectures.

488. "Mr. Frank Lloyd Wright." *RIBA J* XLVI (8 My 1939), p. 643.
Comment on Wright's visit to London.

489. "New Frank Lloyd Wright Office Building Shows Shape of Things to Come." *Life* VI (8 My 1939), pp. 15-17.

S. C. Johnson and Son administration building, Racine.

490. Newnham, Peter. "Letter from America." *Arch Assn J* LXVI (O 1939), pp. 59-63.

491. "Notes and News." *Builder* CLVI (26 My 1939), p. 983.
Note on transfer of an exhibit of Wright's work from the Building Centre to the Architectural Association, London.

492. "Office Building Goes Functional." *Business Week* (6 My 1939), pp. 24, 29-30.
S. C. Johnson and Son administration building, Racine.

493. "Offices & Factories." *Architectural Design and Construction* IX (Je 1939), pp. 232-3.
S. C. Johnson and Son administration building, Racine.

494. Pevsner, Nikolaus. "Frank Lloyd Wright's Peaceful Penetration of Europe." *Architects' J* LXXXIX (4 My 1939), pp. 731-4.
Wright's influence on European architects.

495. "Rural Housing Project." *Arch & Eng* CXXXVI (Ja 1939), p. 58.
Usonia I, master plan, Lansing.

496. "Usonia Comes to Ardmore When Frank Lloyd Wright Invents a Four-Family House with Kitchens as Control Rooms, Floors as Radiators." *Arch For* LXXI (Ag 1939), pp. 142-3, sup. p. 30.
Suntop Homes, Ardmore. A reply from Vernon Harrison was published in October, sup. p. 82.

497. Wright, Frank Lloyd. "Mr. Frank Lloyd Wright at the A. A." *Arch Assn J* LIV (My 1939), pp. 268-9.
Wright's address to the school.

498. Wright, Frank Lloyd. "Organic Architecture, Mr. Lloyd Wright's First-Fourth 'Watson' Lectures." *Builder* CLVI (5, 12, 19 My 1939), pp. 856; 907, 909-10; 932, 951-4.

499. Wright, Frank Lloyd. "Speech to the A.F.A.; 600 Federal Architects Assembled in the Ball Room of the Mayflower Hotel at Washington, D. C., October 25, 1938." *Federal Architect* IX (Ja 1939), pp. 20-3.

Text of a speech on America's failure to develop its own culture. It includes comments on Williamsburg, government buildings, and the Jefferson Memorial.

500. Wright, Frank Lloyd. "The Man Who Paid Cash." *Coronet* V (Ja 1939), pp. 175-6.

"A scenario wherein a rich man meets an artist and, for a while, each has his say."

501. Wright, Frank Lloyd. "To the Fifty-Eighth." *RIBA J* XLVI (16 O 1939), pp. 1005-6.

Reply to criticism of London lectures. Also in *Architectural Review* LXXXVI (N 1939), pp. 223-4.

1940

Books

502. Boston. Institute of Modern Art. *Frank Lloyd Wright: A Pictorial Record of Architectural Progress.* Supplement to the Loan Exhibition Held by the Institute of Modern Art at 270 Dartmouth Street, Boston. January 24–March 3, 1940. With Notes Selected from the Published Writings of the Architect and a Foreword by Joseph Hudnut, Dean of the Faculty of Design, Harvard University. [Boston, The Institute of Modern Art, 1940.]

19.1 x 25.4 cm., 62 pp., 50 ills., paper.

A catalogue for an exhibition of plans, photos, blueprints, and drawings.

Periodicals

503. "Ardmore Housing Development—under Protest." *Business Week* (13 Jy 1940), p. 34.

Suntop Homes, Ardmore.

504. Bliven, Bruce, Jr. "Frank Lloyd Wright." *New Repub* CIII (9 D 1940), pp. 790-1.

505. "Bostonians Turn Out for Wright." *Pencil P* XXI (Fe 1940), sup. p. 60.

Comment on Wright's lecture sponsored by the Boston Architectural Club and the Institute of Modern Art, January, 1940.

506. Brown, Milton. "Frank Lloyd Wright's First Fifty Years." *Parnassus* XII (D 1940), pp. 37-8.

A review of "Two Great Americans" exhibit at the Museum of Modern Art. A reply from Alfred Barr was published in volume XIII (Ja 1941), p. 3.

507. "A City for the Future." *Time* XXXVI (25 N 1940), p. 58.

Exhibit at Museum of Modern Art, New York.

508. Decker, Paul. "Prophet Not without Honor." *C Arts & Arch* LVII (Fe 1940), p. 15.

Comment on speech delivered by Wright at dedication of May Omerod Harris Hall of Architecture and Fine Arts, University of Southern California.

509. "Fall Exhibit." *Pencil P* XXI (O 1940), sup. p. 58.

"Two Great Americans," Museum of Modern Art, New York.

510. "Frank Lloyd Wright: The Residence of Mr. and Mrs. George D. Sturges, Brentwood, Calif." *C Arts & Arch* LVII (Ap 1940), pp. 14-15 and cover.

511. Hamlin, Talbot. "Frank Lloyd Wright." *Nation* CLI (30 N 1940), pp. 541-2.

"Two Great Americans" exhibit, Museum of Modern Art, New York.

512. Hamlin, Talbot F. "Recent Developments in School Design." *Pencil P* XXI (D 1940), pp. 768-82.

Includes Wright house, "Taliesin West," Scottsdale.

513. Hitchcock, Henry-Russell, Jr. "Wright's Influence Abroad." *Parnassus* XII (D 1940), pp. 11-15.

Analysis of the influence of Wright's work published in

European books and periodicals.

514. Hunter, Paul. "Mr. Wright Goes to Los Angeles." *Pencil P* XXI (Mr 1940), sup. pp. 34, 36.

Comment on the architect's activities while in Los Angeles for the dedication of a new Hall of Architecture and Fine Arts, University of Southern California.

515. "In the General Office." *Interior Decorator* XCIX (Ja 1940), pp. 28-30.

S. C. Johnson and Son administration building, Racine.

516. "Lead Flashing for an Ultra-Modern Office Building." *Lead* X (Ja 1940), p. 10.

S. C. Johnson and Son administration building, Racine.

517. Mather, Alan. "The Perennial Trail Blazer." *Pencil P* XXI (D 1940), sup. p. 16.

Review of "Two Great Americans" exhibit, Museum of Modern Art, New York.

518. "Mr. Frank Lloyd Wright, the Taliesin Fellowship, and Taliesin West." *Arizona Highways* XVI (My 1940), pp. 4-15.

Includes an introduction by Raymond Carlson, p. 2, and "To Arizona," by Wright (reprinted, see no. 767).

519. "New Design for Worship." *Newsweek* XVI (1 Jy 1940), p. 38.

Community Church, Kansas City.

520. "Notes & Topics." *Architects' J* XCI (11 Ap 1940), p. 379.

A description of the annual trip made by the Taliesin Fellow-ship from Wisconsin to Arizona.

521. Patterson, Augusta Owen. "3 Modern Houses, No. 1: Owner, Herbert F. Johnson, Jr., Racine; Architect, Frank Lloyd Wright." *Town and Country* XCV (Fe 1940), pp. 52-7.

"Wingspread."

522. "People." *Time* XXXV (5 Fe 1940), p. 40.

Wright's comment on Los Angeles.

523. "Rumor." *Arch For* LXXIII (O 1940), sup. p. 2.
Crystal Heights, Washington, D. C. (project).

524. Schelling, H. G. J. "De amerikaansche architect Frank Lloyd Wright." *Bouwkundig Weekblad Architectura* LXI (17 Ag 1940), pp. 255-61.

525. "Something New in Churches." *Time* XXXVI (2 D 1940), pp. 38, 40.
Community Church, Kansas City.

526. Udall, Mary C. "Wright: Great U.S. Architect; First Comprehensive Exhibition at Boston's Modern Institute." *Art N* XXXVIII (24 Fe 1940), pp. 6-7.

527. Wright, Frank Lloyd. "Chicago's Auditorium Is Fifty Years Old." *Arch For* LXXIII (Se 1940), sup. pp. 10, 12.
A slightly longer version of this article, typed on Taliesin stationery and signed by Wright, exists in the Burnham Library, Chicago. Also in *Builder* (no. 529).

528. Wright, Frank Lloyd. [Letter]. *Christian Century* LVII (13 N 1940), pp. 1419-20.
Concerning American defense of England.

529. Wright, Frank Lloyd. "Louis Sullivan and the Chicago Auditorium; Frank Lloyd Wright's Reminiscences." *Builder* CLIX (27 D 1940), p. 617.
Same as no. 527.

530. "Wright Goes to Washington with a $15,000,000 Surprise." *Newsweek* XVI (25 N 1940), p. 48.
Crystal Heights (project).

531. "Wright in Boston." *Art D* XIV (15 Fe 1940), p. 28.
Exhibition at Institute of Modern Art.

1941

Books

532. Wright, Frank Lloyd. *Frank Lloyd Wright on Architecture: Selected Writings, 1894–1940.* Edited with an Introduction by Frederick Gutheim. New York: Duell, Sloan and Pearce, 1941. 21.1 x 21.2 cm., xviii, 275 pp., cloth.

An anthology of Wright's writings, edited from the original manuscripts. The material is arranged chronologically from the dates on the manuscripts. A list of the published writings of Wright from 1900 to 1940 is included.

□ A British edition was published by Meridian Books: Mayflower, London.

□ A paperbound edition was published by Grosset and Dunlap, New York, 1960.

REVIEWS of the 1941 and 1960 editions

533. Anonymous. *Arch For* LXXIV (Je 1941), sup. pp. 34, 88. [1941]

534. Anonymous. *Liturg Art* IX (Ag 1941), p. 83. [1941]

535. Coit, Elisabeth. *Arch Rec* LXXXIX (Je 1941), p. 28. [1941]

536. Duffus, R. L. "Frank Lloyd Wright on Men and Stones." *NYTBR* (3 Ag 1941), pp. 3, 10. [1941]

537. Lautner, John. *C Arts & Arch* LVIII (Je 1941), p. 14. [1941]

538. Mock, Elizabeth. "Frank Lloyd Wright's Writings." *Mag Art* XXXIV (Je-Jy 1941), pp. 330, 332. [1941]

539. Seward, John C. *Pencil P* XXII (N 1941), sup. p. 66. [1941]

540. Weinberg, Robert C. *Am Inst Plan J* XXVII (N 1961), p. 354. [1960]

Periodicals

541. Argan, Giulio Carlo. "L'autobiografia di Wright." *Casabella-Costruzioni* XIV (Je 1941), pp. 2-3.

542. "An Arizona Dwelling by Frank Lloyd Wright." *Arizona Highways* XVII (O 1941), pp. 6-11.

Pauson house, Phoenix.

543. "Britain Honors Wright." *Arch & Eng* CXLIV (Ja 1941), p. 56.
    Recipient of Royal Gold Medal for Architecture.

544. Donner, Peter F. R. "Criticism." *Arch R* XC (Ag 1941), pp. 68-70.
    Discussion of the Watson Lectures (no. 463).

545. Fell, H. Granville. "An American Architect Honoured." *Connoisseur* CVII (Fe 1941), pp. 80-1.
    Wright to be recipient of Royal Gold Medal for Architecture.

546. "Frank Lloyd Wright: A Leader in American Art." *Design* XLII (Ja 1941), pp. 19-20.

547. "Frank Lloyd Wright." *Arch & Build N* CLXV (10 Ja 1941), p. 16.
    Nominated to receive Royal Gold Medal for Architecture, 1941.

548. "Frank Lloyd Wright's Newest Creation: A College Chapel Designed to Express the Significance of a Name—Florida." *Arch & Eng* CXLVI (Jy 1941), pp. 34-6.
    Anne Pfeiffer Chapel, Florida Southern College, Lakeland.

549. Gutheim, F. A. "First Reckon with His Future: Frank Lloyd Wright's Exhibit at the Modern Museum." *Mag Art* XXXIV (Ja 1941), pp. 32-3.
    Review of "Two Great Americans" exhibit, Museum of Modern Art, New York.

550. Gutheim, Frederick. "Frank Lloyd Wright: Prophet of Decentralization." *Free America* V (Ap 1941), pp. 8-10.

551. Hamlin, Talbot F. "A Pot Pourri for Architects." *Pencil P* XXII (Ja 1941), pp. 55-8.
    Includes comment on "Two Great Americans" exhibit, Museum of Modern Art, New York.

552. Hitchcock, Henry-Russell. "Frank Lloyd Wright at the

Museum of Modern Art." *Art B* XXIII (Mr 1941), pp. 73-6. (Also issued as offprint.)

Review of "Two Great Americans" exhibit, Museum of Modern Art, New York.

553. "The Immobile Idea: Home Grown." *Architects' J* XCIV (24 Jy 1941), pp. 56-7.

Wright house, "Taliesin West," Scottsdale.

554. Kantorowich, Roy. "Architectural Utopias: The City Planning Theories of Frank Lloyd Wright and Le Corbusier." *Task* (Cambridge) I (no. 2, 1941), pp. 30-5.

Also in *South African Architectural Record* (no. 590).

555. McArthur, Albert Chase. [Letter.] *Arch Rec* LXXXIX (Je 1941), p. 7.

Concerns published assertions that Wright designed the Arizona Biltmore Hotel, Phoenix, with a statement by Wright.

556. "A Major Prophet of Architecture." *Country Life* (London) LXXXIX (18 Ja 1941), p. 49.

557. "New Home Is Frank Lloyd Wright Product." *Real Estate* XVI (22 Mr 1941), p. 17.

Lewis house, Libertyville.

558. [Portrait.] *Pencil P* XXII (Mr 1941), sup. p. 17.

On Wright's receipt of the Royal Gold Medal for Architecture.

559. "Royal Gold Medal for Architecture." *Studio* CXXI (Fe 1941), p. 60.

Nomination of Wright.

560. "The Royal Gold Medal." *RIBA J* XLVIII (13 Ja 1941), pp. 37-8.

Awarded to Wright; includes a brief review of his career.

561. "The Royal Gold Medal—Nomination of Mr. Frank Lloyd Wright." *Builder* CLX (10 Ja 1941), p. 26.

562. "Royal Medal Comes to America." *Arch For* LXXIV (Fe 1941), sup. p. 10.
    Includes list of previous American recipients.

563. " 'Taliesin West', Arizona, by Frank Lloyd Wright." *Architects' J* XCIII (13 Mr 1941), pp. 177-8.
    Wright house, Scottsdale.

564. Tselos, Dimitris. "Frank Lloyd Wright." *Art in Am* XXIX (Ja 1941), pp. 42-3.
    Criticism of "Two Great Americans" exhibit, Museum of Modern Art, New York.

565. "Tulsa Home of Editor Richard Lloyd Jones." *National Geographic* LXXIX (Mr 1941), p. 305.
    Photograph showing the original color of the house which was intended to blend with Oklahoma's red soil.

566. Wright, Frank Lloyd. "America! Wake Up!" *Progressive* V (21 Je 1941), p. 2.

567. Wright, Frank Lloyd. "Mumford Lectures." *Sat R* XXIV (23 Ag 1941), pp. 15-16.
    Review of Mumford, Lewis. *The South in Architecture: Lectures in Alabama.* New York: Harcourt, Brace & Co., 1941.

568. Wright, Frank Lloyd. "Organic Architecture." *Common Sense* X (Ap 1941), pp. 108-9, 118.

569. Wright, Frank Lloyd. "The American Quality; with a Picture Section of Outstanding Works." *Scribner's Commentator* X (O 1941), pp. 35-46.

570. "Wright over London." *Arch For* LXXV (Ag 1941), sup. p. 68.
    Excerpts from Wright's article for the *News Chronicle* on rebuilding London. Also issued as a *Taliesin Square-Paper* (see no. 2042).

571. "Wright Plans Community Church." *Arch & Eng* CXLIV

(Fe 1941), p. 6.

Community Church, Kansas City. Reprinted from *Illinois Society of Architects. Bulletin.*

1942

Books

572. Derleth, August. "The Shining Brow." In *The Wisconsin: River of a Thousand Isles.* New York, Toronto: Farrar & Rinehart Inc., [1942]. Pp. 301-8.

A chapter which gives biographical information on Wright.

573. Hitchcock, Henry-Russell. *In the Nature of Materials: 1887-1941, the Buildings of Frank Lloyd Wright.* New York: Duell, Sloan and Pearce, 1942.

21.2 x 21.2 cm., xxxv, 143 pp., color front., 413 ills., cloth.

A survey of Wright's architecture from 1887 to 1941, completed with the architect's supervision, and intended as a replacement for the never-published catalogue of the exhibition of his work at the Museum of Modern Art in 1940. It includes an historical analysis, a chronological list of projects and completed buildings with addresses, and numerous photographs and plans especially redrawn by members of the Taliesin Fellowship for this book. Although the list of illustrations calls for 413 illustrations, figure numbers 227, 270, 272, 306, 319, 326, and 354 were omitted. The frontispiece photograph of Taliesin West was reversed and was not corrected in later printings. The projects and buildings discussed in this book are not listed in this description, but entries for all of them will be found in the building index.

□ A British edition was published by Elck, Ltd., London, 1958.
□ A new edition was published by DaCapo, New York, 1973. It includes a new foreword and bibliography by Hitchcock, as well as his "The Later Work of Frank Lloyd Wright, 1942-1959," reprinted from *Architecture: Nineteenth and Twentieth Centuries* (see no. 1532). A bibliography from 1969 to 1972, compiled by William G. Foulks, Avery Library, was added. (Da Capo Press Series in Architecture and Decorative Art, vol. 28)

REVIEWS of the 1942, 1958, and 1973 editions

574. Anonymous. *American Artist* VI (Se 1942), p. 39. [1942]

575. Anonymous. *Arch For* LXXVI (Je 1942), sup. p. 14. [1942]

576. Brett, Lionel. "The Cyma and the Hollyhock." *Arch R* XCIII (Mr 1943), pp. 80-1. [1942]

577. Byrne, Barry. *Liturg Art* XI (Fe 1943), p. 49. [1942]

578. Coit, Elisabeth. *Arch Rec* XCI (Je 1942), p. 80. [1942]

579. de Long, David G. *Architecture Plus* I (My 1973), pp. 13-14. [1973]

580. Hartwell, Frances. *C Arts & Arch* LIX (My 1942), pp. 4-5. [1942]

581. Newcomb, Rexford. *JSAH* III (O 1943), pp. 51-2. [1942]

582. Seward, John C. *Pencil P* XXIII (Je 1942), pp. 128, 130. [1942]

583. Tomkinson, Donald H. *RIBA J* LXVI (O 1959), pp. 438-9. [1958]

584. Townsend, R. L. *RIBA J* LVI (Mr 1949), pp. 236-7. [1942]

585. Tunnard, Christopher. *Landscape Arch* XXXII (Jy 1942), pp. 168-9. [1942]

Periodicals

586. Chambers, Wm. S., Jr. "Innovation in College Chapel Architecture." *Architectural Concrete* VIII (no. 1, 1942), pp. 16-17.
    Anne Pfeiffer Chapel, Florida Southern College, Lakeland.

587. "Flight to the Valley of the Sun." *Harper's Bazaar* LXXVI (Ja 1942), pp. 40-1, 45-7.
    Fashion photography, with the Pauson house, Phoenix, as a background.

588. "Frank Lloyd Wright Builds a Desert House for Miss Rose Pauson in Phoenix, Arizona." *C Arts & Arch* LIX (Ap 1942), pp. 18-19.

589. Goodman, Paul & Percival Goodman. "Frank Lloyd Wright on Architecture." *Kenyon Review* IV (W 1942), pp. 7-28.

590. Kantorowich, Roy. "The Modern Theorists of Planning: Le Corbusier, Frank Lloyd Wright, etc." *South African Architectural Record* XXVII (Ja 1942), pp. 6-15.
Also in *Task* (no. 554).

591. Moser, Werner. "Over het werk van architect F. L. Wright." *De 8 en Opbouw* XIII (N 1942), pp. 137-40.

592. [Portrait.] *Life* XIII (9 N 1942), p. 109.

593. "Usonian Evolution." *Time* XXXIX (4 My 1942), p. 67.
Biographical information; note on 1942 book *In the Nature of Materials* (see no. 573).

1943

Books

594. Harvard University. William Hayes Fogg Art Museum. *Masters of Four Arts: Wright, Maillol, Picasso, Strawinsky.* An Exhibition May 4–May 29 and a Concert May 7. Fogg Museum of Art. Harvard University. [Cambridge], 1943.
24 x 16.3 cm., 21 pp., 3 ills., paper.
An exhibition catalogue.

595. Wright, Frank Lloyd. *An Autobiography.* New York: Duell, Sloan and Pearce, [1943].
See no. 303.

1944

Periodicals

596. "Frank Lloyd Wright Is Designing Building for Guggenheim Collection." *Arch & Eng* CLVII (Je 1944), p. 4.

597. Hitchcock, Henry-Russell. "Frank Lloyd Wright and the 'Academic Tradition' of the Early Eighteen-Nineties." *Journal of the Warburg and Courtauld Institutes* VII (Ja-Je 1944), pp. 46-63. (Also issued as offprint.)

Discussion of Wright's experiments with academic classical design. Includes: the Charnley and Blossom houses, Chicago; Library and Museum, Milwaukee (project); and Amusement Park, Wolf Lake (project).

598. Kienitz, John Fabian. "The Romanticism of Frank Lloyd Wright." *Art in Am* XXXII (Ap 1944), pp. 91-101.

599. Miller, Joseph (photographer). "The Sun Country." *Arizona Highways* XX (N 1944), pp. 2-9.
Arizona Biltmore Hotel, Phoenix (photographs). No text.

600. "New York Discovers an Architect." *Arch For* LXXX (Ap 1944), p. 70.
Guggenheim Museum.

601. Pope, Loren. "Wright's Influence on Housing." *Michigan Society of Architects, Weekly Bulletin* XVIII (5 Se 1944), p. 3.

602. [Portrait.] *Pencil P* XXV (Ap 1944), p. 14.
Photograph by T. H. Robsjohn-Gibbings.

603. "Slum of the Soul." *Arch For* LXXX (Ja 1944), pp. 104, 106.
Wright's comment on Chicago and tomorrow's house.

604. Wright, Frank Lloyd. "American Forum of the Air—What Are the Air Waves Saying?" *AIA J* I (Ap 1944), pp. 176-82.
Excerpts from a discussion on rebuilding cities or encouraging decentralization, broadcast coast-to-coast, 29 February 1944.

605. Wright, Frank Lloyd. "Viewpoints: To the Mole." *Mag Art* XXXVII (D 1944), pp. 310, 312-15.
Reply to an editorial by Robert Moses published in the *New York Times Magazine* (18 June 1944). The *Times* solicited the reply, then declined to publish it.

1945

Books

606. Wright, Frank Lloyd. *An Autobiography*. London: Faber & Faber and the Hyperion Press Limited, [1945].
  See no. 303.

607. Wright, Frank Lloyd. *Architettura e democrazia*. Traduzione di Giuliana Baracco. Milano: Rosa e Ballo, 1945.
  See no. 250.

608. Wright, Frank Lloyd. *Architettura organica, l'architettura della democrazia*. Milano: Muggiani, 1945.
  See no. 463.

609. Wright, Frank Lloyd. *When Democracy Builds*. Chicago: University of Chicago Press, [1945].
  26 x 18.9 cm., x, 131 pp., 11 ills., cloth.
  A revised and expanded edition of *The Disappearing City* (no. 328). It reflects the architect's continuing dissatisfaction with centralization and the economic basis of our society. Illustrations of the model for Broadacre City are included.
  □ A British edition of the first U.S. edition was published by Cambridge University Press, London, 1945.
  □ A revised edition with new material added was published by The University of Chicago Press, Chicago, 1945, and was reprinted in 1947 and 1951.
  □ A German version of the revised edition was published under the title *Usonien: When Democracy Builds*. Berlin: Gebr. Mann, 1950.

REVIEWS of the American and British 1945 editions
610. Anonymous. *Arch For* LXXXIII (Jy 1945), pp. 156, 160, 164.
611. Anonymous. *Arch Rec* XCVII (My 1945), p. 120.
612. Anonymous. *Connoisseur* CXVII (Mr 1946), p. 61.
613. Anonymous. *Design* XLVII (Ja 1946), p. 24.
614. Anonymous. *Studio* CXXX (O 1945), p. 128. [British]
615. Comey, Arthur C. *Landscape Arch* XXXVI (O 1945), pp. 38-9.

616. Creighton, Thomas H. *Pencil P* XXVI (Se 1945), pp. 118, 120.
617. Hamlin, Talbot. *Gazette des Beaux Arts* XXX (Se 1946), p. 187.
618. Harvey, W. Clifford. "Mr. Wright on His Customary Crusade." *Christian Science Monitor Magazine* (28 Jy 1945), p. 14.
619. Kahn, Ely Jacques. "Realistic Dreams for Tomorrow." *Sat R* XXVIII (19 My 1945), p. 26.
620. Mawn, Lawrence E. *Arts & Arch* LXII (Je 1945), pp. 14, 44, 46.
621. Mawn, Lawrence E. *Liturg Art* XIII (Ag 1945), p. 86.
622. McCausland, Elizabeth. *Mag Art* XXXIX (D 1946), pp. 385-6. [Revised ed.]
623. Pinckheard, John. *RIBA J* LIII (Je 1946), p. 355.
624. Zucker, Paul. *Journal of Aesthetics and Art Criticism* IV (Mr 1946), p. 196.

Periodicals

625. "American Small House Exhibition at the Museum of Modern Art." *Architects' J* CII (30 Ag 1945), p. 159.
Glass house, "Opus 497" (project).

626. "Architects on the Ramp-Age." *Harper* CXCI (O 1945), pp. 388, 390.
Guggenheim Museum, New York.

627. Cook, Theodore N. "Museum in a Spiral." *Christian Science Monitor Magazine* (3 N 1945), p. 7.
Guggenheim Museum, New York.

628. "Frank Lloyd Wright's Museum." *Art D* XIX (1 Ag 1945), p. 3.
Guggenheim Museum, New York.

629. "Frank Lloyd Wright's New Museum Plan." *Art N* XLIV (15-31 O 1945), p. 29.
Guggenheim Museum, New York.

630. "Guggenheim Art Museum Plans Spiral Building." *Museum News* XXIII (1 Se 1945), pp. 1-2; (1 O 1945), p. 1.

631. "Houses for the People." *Pencil P* XXVI (Se 1945), pp. 59-66.
Includes Glass house, "Opus 497" (project), published in *Ladies' Home Journal* (see nos. 636 and 644).

632. Kienitz, John F. "Fifty-two Years of Frank Lloyd Wright's Progressivism, 1893-1945." *Wis Mag Hist* XXIX (Se 1945), pp. 61-71 and cover.

633. "Made in Japan, U.S.-Designed." *Time* XLVI (24 Se 1945), p. 46.
Imperial Hotel damaged during war.

634. [Model of S. R. Guggenheim Museum of Non-Objective Painting.] *Art D* XX (15 O 1945), p. 15.

635. "Monolithic Masterpiece." *Arch For* LXXXIII (O 1945), p. 9.
Models of Guggenheim Museum; note that Imperial Hotel survived bombing.

636. Murdock, Henrietta. "Accent on Living." *Ladies' Home J* LXII (Je 1945), p. 141.
Glass house, "Opus 497" (project).

637. "Un Musée en spirale: le musée d'art Guggenheim." *Mouseion* sup. CI (D 1945), pp. 3-4.

638. "Museum à la Wright." *Time* XLVI (23 Jy 1945), p. 72.
Guggenheim Museum, New York.

639. "News." *Arch For* LXXXIII (Ag 1945), p. 8.
Guggenheim Museum, New York.

640. "Optimistic Ziggurat." *Time* XLVI (1 O 1945), p. 74.
Guggenheim Museum, New York.

641. Patterson, Augusta Owen. "A Frank Lloyd Wright House for Connecticut." *Town and Country* C (D 1945), pp. 129-31, 219.
   Loeb house, Redding (project).

642. Ponti, Gio. "Un sogno una realtà." *Stile* no. 54 (1945), pp. 2-5.

643. "Post-war Buildings." *Art N* XLIV (Ag 1945), p. 6-7.
   Guggenheim Museum, New York.

644. Pratt, Richard. "Opus 497." *Ladies' Home J* LXII (Je 1945), pp. 138-9.
   Glass house, "Opus 497" (project).

645. "Speaking of Pictures...New Art Museum Will be New York's Strangest Building." *Life* XIX (8 O 1945), pp. 12-13, 15.
   Guggenheim Museum, New York.

646. "When Democracy Builds." *Milwaukee Art Institute Bulletin* XVIII (N 1945), pp. 1-2.
   Description of exhibit of models, photographs, and drawings.

647. Wright, Frank Lloyd. "On Organic Architecture." *Michigan Society of Architects. Weekly Bulletin* XIX (10 Ap 1945), pp. 8-9.
   The text of a lecture read to the Michigan Society of Architects, 22 March 1945.

1946

Books

648. Wright, John Lloyd. *My Father Who Is on Earth.* New York: G. P. Putnam's Sons, [1946].
   21 x 14.1 cm., 195 pp., 14 ills., cloth.
   A biography by the architect's second son. It includes the text of *The House Beautiful,* the book designed by Frank Lloyd Wright and printed by him and William Herman Winslow in 1896-1897 (see no. 18).

REVIEWS

649. Anonymous. "Fabulous Father." *Arch Rec* XCIX (My 1946), p. 26.

650. Anonymous. "Great Papa." *Time* XLVII (1 Ap 1946), p. 55.

651. Anonymous. *La Jollan* I (23 O 1946), p. 11.

652. Anonymous. "Life with Father Wright." *Newsweek* XXVII (8 Ap 1946), p. 90.

653. Kahn, Ely Jacques. "Life, More or Less, with Father." *Sat R* XXIX (13 Ap 1946), p. 52.

654. Sanders, Mary. *Arch For* LXXXIV (My 1946), pp. 156, 158.

Periodicals

655. "Another Frank Lloyd Wright Building Is Planned by Johnson Wax." *Arch For* LXXXIV (Fe 1946), p. 10.
   S. C. Johnson and Son research tower, Racine.

656. "Antologia di Frank Lloyd Wright." *Stile* I (Ja 1946), pp. 1-5.

657. Carlo, Giancarlo de. "L'insegnamento di Frank Lloyd Wright." *Domus* no. 207 (Mr 1946), pp. 21-4.

658. "Country House in Connecticut, U.S.A., Designed by Frank Lloyd Wright." *Architects' J* CIV (19 Se 1946), pp. 213-14.
   Loeb house, Redding (project).

659. "Éclairage d'un musée: The Modern Gallery, New York. Frank Lloyd Wright, architecte." *Techniques et Architecture* VI (no. 1-2, 1946), pp. 66-7.
   Guggenheim Museum.

660. "Frank Lloyd Wright e l'architettura europea." *Stile* no. 5 (My 1946), pp. 7-13.

661. Gordon, Elizabeth. "One Man's House." *House B* LXXXVIII (D 1946), pp. 186-96, 235.
   Wright house, "Taliesin West," Scottsdale.

662. Harriman, Georges. "Die Bauten Frank L. Wrights." *Bauhelfer* I (Jy 1946), pp. 17-18.

663. "A Haven for Work." *Northwest Architect* X (no. 4, 1946), pp. 16-17.
     S. C. Johnson and Son research tower, Racine.

664. "House at Bloomfield Hills, Michigan." *Progress Arch* XXVII (O 1946), pp. 67-70.
     Affleck house.

665. "House in Connecticut." *Arch For* LXXXIV (Je 1946), pp. 83-8.
     Loeb house, Redding (project). See also "Letters to the Editor," August, p. 34.

666. "Meet Frank Lloyd Wright." *House B* LXXXVIII (Je 1946), pp. 76-7, 163.

667. Middeldorf, Ulrich. "Architecture as an Art: Prologue to a Lecture by Frank Lloyd Wright." *Coll Art J* VI (Au 1946), pp. 37-40.

668. Mies van der Rohe. "A Tribute to Frank Lloyd Wright." *Coll Art J* VI (Au 1946), pp. 41-2.
     Italian version in *Emporium* (see no. 732).

669. "The Modern Gallery; the World's Greatest Architect, at 74, Designs the Boldest Building of his Career." *Arch For* LXXXIV (Ja 1946), pp. 81-8.
     Guggenheim Museum, New York.

670. "The Most Influential Design Source of the Last 50 Years." *House B* LXXXVIII (D 1946), p. 185.

671. "Le Musée en spirale." *Arts* (Paris) (22 Mr 1946), p. 1.
     Guggenheim Museum, New York.

672. Nelson, George. "Wright's Houses." *Fortune* XXXIV (Ag 1946), pp. 116-25.

"Taliesin," Spring Green, and "Taliesin West," Scottsdale.
Text reprinted in *Problems of Design*. New York: Whitney
Publications, 1957. Pp. 110-13.

673. "New York Modern Art Gallery Models." *Arch & Eng*
CLXVI (Ag 1946), p. 8.
Includes note on J. J. Polivka, consulting engineer for the
Guggenheim Museum, New York, and S. C. Johnson and Son
research tower, Racine.

674. "Uma original concepção arquitectonica." *Arquitectura
Portuguesa* XXXIX (Ap 1946), pp. 19-21.
Guggenheim Museum, New York.

675. "Project for a Week-end House by Frank Lloyd Wright."
Architects' J CIV (25 Jy 1946), p. 67.
A model displayed in the "Exhibition of Regional Building
in the United States" at Heal's, London.

676. Sargeant, Winthrop. "Frank Lloyd Wright: The Titan of
Modern Architecture Still Flings His Houses and His Insults at
Backward Colleagues." *Life* XXI (12 Ag 1946), pp. 84-8, 90,
93-4, 96.
Also in *Nuova Città* I (O-N 1946), pp. 22-31. Translated by
Giusta Nicco Fasola.

677. Sargeant, Winthrop. "Titan of Modern Architecture."
Reader's Digest XLIX (N 1946), pp. 31-5.
Condensed from *Life*, see no. 676.

678. V-G. "De S. R. Guggenheim Foundation te New York."
Phoenix (Amsterdam) I (no. 2, 1946), p. 27.

679. "Work and Theories of Frank Lloyd Wright." *Listener*
XXXVI (12 D 1946), pp. 837-40.
Includes: "Organic Architecture," by J. M. Richards; "In-
fluence in This Country," by Lionel Brett; and "The Right to
Be Oneself," by Frank Lloyd Wright.

680. Wright, Frank Lloyd. "Democratie et architecture."

Chantiers I (D 1946), p. 3.

From *When Democracy Builds* (no. 609), translated by Stéphanie Chandler.

681. Wright, Frank Lloyd. "The Modern Gallery for the Solomon R. Guggenheim Foundation: New York City." *Mag Art* XXXIX (Ja 1946), pp. 24-6.

682. Wright, Frank Lloyd. "The Right to Be One's Self." *Husk* (Mount Vernon, Iowa) XXVI (D 1946), pp. 37-40.

Text of a speech delivered at the Fifteenth Annual *New York Herald Tribune* Forum on current thought in New York. Also in *Marg* (see no. 718).

683. Wright, Frank Lloyd. "To a Hero Nation: Ireland." *Architecture in Ireland. Yearbook for 1946.* Pp. 29-30.

684. Wright, John Lloyd and Donald Koehler. [Letters.] *Arch For* LXXXV (N 1946), p. 44.

Concerns the Imperial Hotel, Tokyo.

685. "Wright Makes It Right." *Time* XLVIII (1 Jy 1946), p. 73.

Comment on exhibition of model for Loeb house, Redding (project) at Museum of Modern Art, New York.

1947

Books

686. Mies van der Rohe. "Frank Lloyd Wright." *In* Johnson, Philip C. *Mies van der Rohe.* New York: The Museum of Modern Art, [1947]. Pp. 195-6.

A tribute, written in 1940, intended for the unpublished catalogue of the exhibition of Wright's work at the Museum of Modern Art.

687. Zevi, Bruno. *Frank Lloyd Wright.* Milano: Il Balcone, 1947. 16.7 x 12 cm., 134 pp., 43 ills., paper. (Architetti del movimento moderno. 3)

Includes a list of principal work through 1946 and a bibliography through 1945.

□ A revised and expanded edition was published by Il Balcone, Milano, 1954. It contains a list of principal work through 1953 and a bibliography.

REVIEWS of the 1947 edition

688. Anonymous. *Emporium* CVII (Je 1948), p. 279.
689. Maurogordato, Franca. *Progress Arch* XXIX (O 1948), pp. 138, 140.

Periodicals

690. Argan, Giulio Carlo. "Introduzione a Wright." *Metron* no. 18 (1947), pp. 9-24.

691. "Awards." *Arch For* LXXXVII (Jy 1947), p. 64.
Wright elected to membership in the National Institute of Arts and Letters.

692. Baldwin, Guy H. "Modernism, 1906, Part I." *Empire State Architect* VII (Ja-Fe 1947), pp. 8, 21.
Larkin Company administration building, Buffalo.

693. Baldwin, Guy H. "Modernism, 1906, Part II." *Empire State Architect* VII (Mr-Ap 1947), pp. 8, 19.
Martin house, Buffalo.

694. Danes, Gibson. "Architectural Sculpture Today." *Mag Art* XL (My 1947), pp. 170-5.
Includes examples of Wright's work.

695. "Design for the Solomon R. Guggenheim Foundation: New York." *Arch & Build N* CXC (25 Ap 1947), pp. 70-3.

696. "Florida Southern College, Designed by Frank Lloyd Wright." *Architects' J* CVI (25 D 1947), pp. 559-61.

697. Hadley, Homer M. [Letter.] *Arch For* LXXXVI (Fe 1947), p. 22.
Concerns the Imperial Hotel, Tokyo.

698. Hansen, Preben. "Fra Wren til Wright." *Bonytt* VII (no. 7-8, 1947), pp. 127-31.

699. "Happy Mortuary." *Time* XLIX (27 Ja 1947), p. 63.
Daphne Funeral Chapels, San Francisco (project).

700. Hitchcock, Henry-Russell, Jr. "Notes on Wright Buildings in Buffalo." *Albright Art Gallery, Gallery Notes* XI (Je 1947), pp. 18-21.
Larkin Company administration building, Martin, Barton, Heath, and Davidson houses.

701. Hitchcock, Henry-Russell, Jr. "The Architecture of Bureaucracy & the Architecture of Genius." *Arch R* CI (Ja 1947), pp. 3-6.

702. "Houses U.S.A., the Modern Pioneers." *Arch For* LXXXVI (My 1947), pp. 81-8.
Includes examples by Wright.

703. Huggler, Max & Georg Schmidt. "Das Guggenheim-Museum von Frank Lloyd Wright in New York." *Werk* XXXIV (Je 1947), pp. 188-92.

704. "New Members of Arts Institute." *Nat Arch* (Detroit) III (Fe 1947), p. 4.
Wright's election to the National Institute of Arts and Letters.

705. "News." *Arch For* LXXXVII (Ag 1947), p. 12.
Rogers Lacy Hotel, Dallas (project).

706. "Planners' Platform." *Arch For* LXXXVI (Ap 1947), p. 13.
"Top-rank professionals spend two days talking about what kind of environment they would plan for modern society—if they had a chance."

707. Portela, Francisco V. "La arquitectura di Frank Lloyd Wright." *Norte* VII (Ja 1947), unpaged.

708. [Portrait.] *Arch For* LXXXVI (Fe 1947), p. 12.
Wright elected to membership by National Institute of Arts and Letters.

709. [Portrait.] *Arch Rec* CI (Ap 1947), p. 98.
At conference on Planning Man's Physical Environment, Princeton, 5 and 6 March.

710. "Presentation of Royal Gold Medals for the War Years."
RIBA J LIV (My 1947), pp. 351-7.

711. Salter, L. J. [Letter.] *Arch For* LXXXVI (Ja 1947), p. 34.
Concerns the Imperial Hotel, Tokyo. "A full account of the 1923 earthquake may be found in the *Pasadena Star-News*, September 26, 1923, signed by Lehmann Hisey."

712. Sholta, Jan. [Letter.] *Arch For* LXXXVI (My 1947), pp. 26, 28.
Concerns the liveability of Wright's designs. Replies from Edgar Kaufmann and George [Gregor] S. Affleck, July, p. 22.

713. Stranger, M. A. "Ronde huizen en een rond museum."
Kroniek van Kunst en Kultuur VIII (no. 3, 1947), pp. 85-6, 95.
Guggenheim Museum, New York.

714. Troller, Norbert. [Letter.] *Arch For* LXXXVI (Ap 1947), p. 22.
Concerns the Guggenheim Museum, New York, and Loeb house, Redding (project).

715. Winston, Elizabeth. "Advocates of Modern Design Rally Strongly to the Defense of Frank Lloyd Wright." *Michigan Society of Architects, Weekly Bulletin* XXI (22 Jy 1947), p. 1.

716. Wright, Frank Lloyd. "Building a Democracy." *Albright Art Gallery, Gallery Notes* XI (Je 1947), pp. 14-18.
Reprinted from *A Taliesin Square-Paper* (see no. 2053).

717. Wright, Frank Lloyd. "Notes and Comments." *Architects' J* CVI (28 Ag 1947), p. 183.

A response to a request for comments on the design for the UN headquarters.

718. Wright, Frank Lloyd. "On the Right to Be One's Self." *Marg* I (Ja 1947), pp. 20-4, 47.

Text of a speech delivered at the Fifteenth Annual *New York Herald Tribune* Forum on current thought in New York. Also in *Husk,* see no. 682.

719. Wright, Frank Lloyd. "Planning Man's Physical Environment." *Berkeley, A Journal of Modern Culture* (no. 1, 1947), pp. 5, 7.

720. Wright, Frank Lloyd. "We Must Shape True Inspiration." *NYTM* (20 Ap 1947), p. 59.

Concerning the new building for the United Nations.

1948

Books

721. [Wright, Lloyd.] *Huntington Hartford Presents...* N.p.: no pub., [1948].

28 x 21.5 cm., 16 pp., 3 ills., paper.

Cover title. A pamphlet describing the Huntington Hartford cottage group hotel resort center, Hollywood (project), "...a beautiful new hotel in the Hollywood Hills...recreation in ideal circumstances...a step foreward [sic] in the progress of an entire region." It includes text, an elevation, a site plan, and an aerial photograph of the site. The graphics for the pamphlet were designed by Lloyd Wright and Eugene Masselink.

Periodicals

722. "Ahead of His Time." *Time* LI (9 Fe 1948), pp. 68-9.

Comment on the issue of *Architectural Forum* devoted to Wright, January, 1948 (no. 745).

723. "Architects in the News This Month." *Nat Arch* (Detroit) IV (D 1948), pp. 3-4.

Wright to receive Gold Medal of the American Institute of

Architects; to speak at Michigan Building Industry banquet.

724. Churchill, Henry S. "Notes on Frank Lloyd Wright." *Mag Art* XLI (Fe 1948), pp. 62-6.
Analysis of the relationships between Wright's architecture and philosophy.

725. Churchill, Henry S. "Un notable arquitecto: Frank Lloyd Wright." *Revista Excelsior* (Lima) XIV (Je-Jy 1948), p. 43.

726. "Frank Lloyd Wright: A Reassessment." *Builder* CLXXIV (5 Mr 1948), pp. 274-6.
A reply from P. Taylor and a rejoinder were published 26 March and 9 April, pp. 367-8, 431.

727. "Frank Lloyd Wright et l'O. N. U." *Arch d'Aujourd'hui* XIX (Ja 1948), p. xv.
Comment on design for U. N. headquarters.

728. "Frank Lloyd Wright on Hospital Design." *Modern Hospital* LXXI (Se 1948), pp. 51-4 and cover.

729. Gilmore, William. "Frank Lloyd Wright." *Art et Industrie* (no. 11, 1948), pp. 31-4.

730. Hicks, Clifford B. "Architecture from the Ground Up." *Popular Mechanics* LXXXIX (Ap 1948), pp. 164-8, 256.
Taliesin Fellowship.

731. Kennedy, Sighle. "Frank Lloyd Wright." *Arch For* LXXXIX (Se 1948), p. 200.
Review of film "California Architecture."

732. Mies van der Rohe. "Un tributo a F. L. Wright." *Emporium* CVII (Mr 1948), p. 119.
Reprinted from *College Art Journal* (no. 668).

733. Mock, Elizabeth B. "Taliesin West." *House and Garden* XCIV (Ag 1948), pp. 52-5.
Wright house, Scottsdale.

734. Pope, Loren. "The Love Affair of a Man and His House."
House B XC (Ag 1948), pp. 32-4, 80, 90.
   Pope house, Falls Church.

735. [Portrait.] *Arch For* LXXXVIII (Ja 1948), p. 54.

736. [Portrait by Henri Cartier-Bresson.] *Harper's Bazaar*
LXXXII (Mr 1948), p. 200.

737. Stillman, Seymour. "Comparing Wright and Le Corbusier."
AIA J IX (Ap, My 1948), pp. 171-8, 226-33.

738. Stowell, Kenneth K. "Basis for the Highest Honor." *Arch
Rec* CIV (N 1948), p. 91.
   Wright to receive Gold Medal of the American Institute of
Architects.

739. "Taliesin West, arkitekten Frank Lloyd Wrights vinterbostad
i Arizona." *Byggmästaren* (Stockholm) no. 1 (1948), pp. 8-12.

740. Thomas, M. Hartland. "American Review: Frank Lloyd
Wright." *Arch Design* XVIII (Ap 1948), pp. 83-8.

741. "Usonia Homes: Every Family Has an Acre." *Arch For*
LXXXIX (O 1948), p. 16.
   Usonia II: master plan, executed in part, Pleasantville.

742. Whitcomb, Mildred. "Begin with a Hoe: An Interview with
Frank Lloyd Wright." *Nation's Schools* XLII (N 1948), pp. 20-4.

743. Wright, Frank Lloyd. "A New Success Ideal." *Berkeley*
(Berkeley) no. 3 (Mr 1948), p. 2.
   Broadacre City (project). Excerpted from *Taliesin* (see no.
2040).

744. Wright, Frank Lloyd. "Die moderne Galerie der Guggenheim-
Stiftung in New York." *Kunst* (Munich) I (1948), pp. 111-13.

745. Wright, Frank Lloyd. "Frank Lloyd Wright." *Arch For*
LXXXVIII (Ja 1948), pp. 65-156, editor's note, p. 54.

The second issue of the *Forum* devoted to Wright's work; the first appeared in January, 1938. Includes: the Usonian houses (listed individually in the building index); Taliesin West, Scottsdale; Stevens plantation, Yemassee; Huntington Hartford play resort-sports club, Hollywood (project); Adelman laundry plant, Milwaukee (project); Butterfly Bridge, Spring Green (project); S. C. Johnson and Son research tower, Racine; Daphne Funeral Chapels, San Francisco (project); Sarabhai Calico Mills Store, Ahmadabad (project); Rogers Lacy Hotel, Dallas (project); Florida Southern College, Lakeland; Guggenheim Museum, New York; Cloverleaf Housing Project, Pittsfield (project); Co-operative Homesteads, Detroit (project); desert spa for Elizabeth Arden, Phoenix (project); Parkwyn Village, master plan, executed in part, Kalamazoo; Unitarian Church, Madison; and Usonia I, master plan, Lansing. Cover abstraction designed by Eugene Masselink.

746. "Wright Homes for Westchester." *Arch Rec* CIV (N 1948), pp. 10, 170.
    Usonia II: master plan, executed in part, Pleasantville.

1949

Books

747. Chicago. Art Institute. Burnham Library of Architecture. *Buildings by Frank Lloyd Wright in Six Middle Western States: Illinois, Indiana, Iowa, Michigan, Minnesota, Wisconsin.* Chicago: Art Institute of Chicago, 1949.
    28 x 21.6 cm., ii, 12 pp., paper.
    An annotated list.
    □ A revised edition was published by the Art Institute, Chicago, 1954.
    □ A further revision, entitled *Guide to Chicago & Midwestern Architecture,* was published by the Art Institute, Chicago, 1963. This edition contains "Buildings by Frank Lloyd Wright in Seven Middle Western States, 1887-1959: Illinois, Wisconsin, Indiana, Michigan, Minnesota, Iowa, Ohio," and "A Selective Guide to Chicago Architecture Adapted from Lists Prepared by John Replinger and Allan Frumkin." A loose, folded map of downtown Chicago is laid in.

748. [Hartford, Connecticut. The New Theatre Corporation.]
The New Theatre. [1949.]
   28.5 x 21.8 cm., 8 pp., 6 ills., paper.
   A pamphlet, enclosed in an envelope, which describes the
design of the theatre and the corporation to be formed to
build and operate it. It includes: a statement from Wright;
perspective, elevation, and section drawings; and photographs
of the model. Two loose sheets, not included in the collation,
are laid in. One describes the stock, its distribution, and voting
powers. The other is a contract to be given to an investor.

749. Hartford, Connecticut. Wadsworth Atheneum. *The New
Theatre, Frank Lloyd Wright, Architect.* Hartford: Wadsworth
Atheneum, 1949.
   23.3 x 15 cm., 3 pp., 2 ills., paper.
   An announcement, distributed by mail, of an exhibition of
the model, plans, and renderings of this 1949 project. A statement by Wright is included.

750. Wright, Frank Lloyd. *Genius and the Mobocracy.* New York:
Duell, Sloan and Pearce, [1949].
   25.4 x 20.2 cm., xiii, 113 pp., 38 ills., cloth.
   A biography of Louis Sullivan. It includes reproductions of
drawings by Sullivan which he gave, just before his death in
1924, to Wright.
   □ A Canadian edition was published by Wm. Collins Son & Co.
Canada Ltd., Toronto.
   □ A new edition was published by Horizon Press, New York,
1971. According to a publisher's note this enlarged edition
contains, in addition to the thirty-nine drawings from the original edition: two drawings by Frank Lloyd Wright incorporated in the text; a separate section of twenty drawings, nineteen by Louis Sullivan and one by Frank Lloyd Wright, all
hitherto unpublished; fifty-four photographs; and two essays
by Louis Sullivan on Frank Lloyd Wright's work.
   □ The British version of this new edition was published by
Secker & Warburg, Ltd., London, 1972.

REVIEWS of the 1949, 1971, and 1972 editions
751. Anonymous. "Frank Lloyd Wright on Louis Sullivan."

Arch For XCI (Ag 1949), pp. 94-7 and cover. [1949]

752. Anonymous. *Roy Arch Inst Can J* XXVI (Se 1949), p. 304. [Canadian]

753. Anonymous. "Sullivan Recalled." *Progress Arch* XXX (O 1949), p. 106. [1949]

754. Anonymous. "Wright's Sullivan." *Arch Rec* CVI (Ag 1949), p. 28. [1949]

755. Hamlin, Talbot. "A Great American Architect Pays Tribute to His Teacher." *NYTBR* (10 Jy 1949), p. 3. [1949]

756. Hasbrouck, Wilbert R. *Prairie Sch R* VIII (no. 3, 1971), pp. 14-18. [1971]

757. Morrison, Hugh. *Mag Art* XLIV (Ap 1951), pp. 154-5. [1949]

758. Sharp, Dennis. "In His Master's Steps." *Design* no. 284 (Ag 1972), p. 73. [1972]

759. Spitz, David. "The Mob in Wrong with Wright." *Sat R* XXXII (3 Se 1949), p. 21. [1949]

760. Tafel, Edgar. *AIA J* LVII (Mr 1972), pp. 62-3. [1971]

Periodicals

761. "A. I. A. Meets in Houston." *Arch For* XC (Ap 1949), sup. p. 17.
Receives gold medal of A. I. A.

762. "Architect Wright Given Gold Medal." *Arch & Eng* CLXXVI (Ja 1949), p. 31.

763. Blake, Peter. "Architect from the Prairies." *NYTM* (5 Je 1949), pp. 24-5.
Summary of Wright's career.

764. Bouverie, David Pleydell. "New Theatre, Hartford, Connecticut." *Arch R* CVI (Se 1949), p. 193.

765. Breit, Harvey. "Talk with Frank Lloyd Wright." *NYTBR* (24 Jy 1949), p. 11.

766. "Brick—Known and Loved Best." *Brick and Clay Record*

CXV (N 1949), pp. 33, 68, 70.
Interview with Wright on the use of brick in construction.

767. Carlson, Raymond. "Frank Lloyd Wright and Taliesin West."
Arizona Highways XXV (O 1949), pp. 4-9.
This issue also includes two articles by Wright: "To Arizona,"
pp. 10-11 (excerpted from *Arizona Highways*, May, 1940); and
"Living in the Desert," pp. 12-15.

768. "Citation with the Gold Metal to Frank Lloyd Wright." *AIA
J* XI (Ap 1949), p. 163.

769. "The Eighty-First Convention of the American Institute of
Architects, Houston, Texas, March 15th to 18th, 1949." *Arch
Rec* CV (My 1949), pp. 86-7.
The convention at which Wright was awarded the gold medal.

770. "Frank Lloyd Wright: A. I. A. Will Give Belated Honor to
World's Great Architect." *Arch For* XC (Ja 1949), p. 14.

771. "Frank Lloyd Wright." *Arch d'Aujourd'hui* XX (Je 1949),
p. v.

772. "Frank Lloyd Wright." *Proyectos y Materiales* V (Se-O
1949), pp. 18-20, 60-1.

773. "Homenaje al Maestro Frank Lloyd Wright." *Arquitectura*
(Havana) XVII (Je 1949), pp. 185-7.

774. Johnson, Philip. "The Frontiersman." *Arch R* CVI (Ag
1949), pp. 105-10.

775. Kennedy, Sighle. "Wright's Hartford Theater Shown in a
New York City Museum Exhibit." *Arch For* XC (My 1949), pp.
162-3.
New Theatre, Hartford (project).

776. Laporte, Paul M. "Architecture and Democracy." *Arch
Yrbk* III (1949), pp. 12-19.

777. Lewis, Lloyd. "The New Theater." *Theatre Arts* XXXIII (Jy 1949), pp. 32-4.

778. "Medal for a Titan." *Newsweek* XXXIII (28 Mr 1949), pp. 74-5.
Awarded Gold Medal of American Institute of Architects.

779. Moloobhoy, Sherrif. "Offices and Stores for Calico Mills, Ahmedabad." *Marg* III (no. 2, 1949), pp. 14-16.
Sarabhai Calico Mills store (project).

780. "Museum Shows Large Model of Wright's Theater." *Arch Rec* CV (My 1949), p. 156.
New Theatre, Hartford (project), at Museum of Modern Art.

781. Nelson, George. "Mr. Roark Goes to Hollywood: A Comment on Warner Brothers' Attempt to Interpret Frank Lloyd Wright to the Masses." *Interiors* CVIII (Ap 1949), pp. 106-11.

782. "The New Curiosity Shop." *Architects' J* CX (10 N 1949), pp. 512, 516.
Morris gift shop, San Francisco. A comparison with Richardson's Glessner house, Chicago, was published 8 December, p. 639.

783. Pellegrini, Enrico. "Il gusto del liberty." *Domus* no. 239 (O 1949), pp. 10-11, 17.

784. [Portrait.] *Arch For* XCI (Jy 1949), p. 14.

785. [Portrait.] *Arch d'Aujourd'hui* XX (Mr 1949), p. IX.

786. "The Prophet Honored in His Own Country." *Esquire* XXXI (Ja 1949), pp. 42-3.
Portrait by Yousuf Karsh.

787. Roche, Mary. "Chairs Designed for Sitting." *NYTM* (21 Ag 1949), pp. 34-5.

788. Stoddard, Donna M. "Frank Lloyd Wright Designs a College."

Design L (Je 1949), pp. 12-13, 23.
Florida Southern College, Lakeland.

789. "Théâtre á Hartford, Frank Lloyd Wright." *Arch d'Aujourd'hui* XX (My 1949), p. 26.

790. "To Frank Lloyd Wright, the Gold Medal." *AIA J* XI (Mr 1949), pp. 114-15.

791. Townsend, Robert. "Frank Lloyd Wright: On His Eightieth Birthday." *Arch Assn J* LXV (O 1949), pp. 64-9.

792. Wright, Frank Lloyd. "Acceptance Speech of Frank Lloyd Wright upon Receiving the Gold Medal for 1948." *AIA J* XI (My 1949), pp. 199-207.
Also in *Progressive Architecture* XXX (My 1949), pp. 24, 26.

793. Wright, Frank Lloyd. "A los jóvenes arquitectos." *Arquitectura* (Havana) XVII (N 1949), p. 315.

794. Wright, Frank Lloyd. "I Don't Like Hardware." *Hardware Consultant and Contractor* XIII (My 1949), pp. 22, 24, 26, 28.
The text of a speech read at the Fourth Annual Pacific Coast Regional Conference of the National Contract Hardware Association, Arizona Biltmore Hotel, Phoenix. This issue contains other references to Wright. Also in *Weekly Bulletin, Michigan Society of Architects* XXIII (16 Ag 1949), pp. 1-3.

795. Wright, Frank Lloyd. "Sullivan against the World." *Arch R* CV (Je 1949), pp. 295-8.
A chapter from *Genius and the Mobocracy* (no. 750).

796. Wright, Frank Lloyd. "Tribute to L. Lewis." *Theatre Arts* XXXIII (Jy 1949), p. 32.

797. "Wright's First Theater Design." *Interiors* CVIII (Ja 1949), p. 12.
New Theatre, Hartford (project).

798. "Wright to Receive Gold Medal." *Arch Rec* CV (Fe 1949), p. 158.

1950

Books

799. Wright, Frank Lloyd. *V. C. Morris.* [N.p.: no pub., 1950?] 28.6 x 21.5 cm., 12 pp., 8 ills.
   A pamphlet describing the Morris gift shop, San Francisco. It includes articles by Mr. and Mrs. V. C. Morris, Edgar Kaufmann, Jr. (transcribed from an article in *Art News*), Elizabeth Mock (transcribed from an article in *Architectural Forum*), and Frank Lloyd Wright.

800. Wright, Frank Lloyd. *Usonien: When Democracy Builds.* Berlin: Gebr. Mann, 1950.
   See no. 609.

Periodicals

801. "American Landscape, III." *Harper* CC (Mr 1950), pp. 98-100.

802. "Annual Prize-Giving, Presentations by Mr. Frank Lloyd Wright." *Arch Assn J* LXVI (Ag-Se 1950), pp. 32-42.

803. "China and Gift Shop for V. C. Morris, San Francisco." *Arch For* XCII (Fe 1950), pp. 79-85 and cover.

804. "The Contemporary Domestic Interior: Frank Lloyd Wright." *Interiors* CIX (Jy 1950), pp. 66-9.
   Pauson house, Phoenix.

805. "Cooper Union Honors Wright." *Interiors* CIX (Mr 1950), pp. 166, 168.
   Awarded Peter Cooper Medal.

806. "Down with the East." *Time* LVI (25 Se 1950), p. 77.
   New Theatre, Hartford (project).

807. "Early Wright Structure Goes under Hammer." *Northw Arch* XIV (no. 1, 1950), p. 43.
Larkin Company administration building, Buffalo.

808. "The End of an Era." *Empire State Architect* X (Mr-Ap 1950), p. 27 and cover.
Dismantling of the Larkin Company administration building, Buffalo.

809. "Frank Lloyd Wright in Zürich." *Werk* XXXVII (Se 1950), sup. pp. 128-9.

810. "Glass House for Researchers." *Fortune* XLI (Fe 1950), p. 16.
S. C. Johnson and Son research tower, Racine.

811. Jordan, R. Furneaux. "Lloyd Wright in Britain." *Builder* CLXXIX (24 N 1950), p. 540.

812. Jordan, Robert Furneaux. "A Great Architect's Visit to Britain." *Listener* XLIV (28 Se 1950), pp. 415-16.
To be guest of honor at the prize-giving of the Architectural Association School.

813. Kaufmann, Edgar, Jr. "Wright Setting for Decorative Art." *Art N* XLVIII (Fe 1950), pp. 42-4.
Morris gift shop, San Francisco.

814. "Laboratory Tower for S. C. Johnson & Company." *Arch & Build N* CXCVIII (1 D 1950), pp. 582-3.

815. Lamoreaux, Jeanne. "Taliesin...Rural Workshop for Master Builders." *Harvester World* XLI (Ag 1950), pp. 2-8 and cover.
Also in *Charette* (Pittsburgh), September, 1950, pp. 14-17.

816. Loeb, Gerald. "A Stockbroker Meets F. LL. W." *Arch For* XCIII (Ag 1950), pp. 24, 28.

817. Maza, Aquiles. "Miguel Angel del siglo XX." *Arquitectura* (Havana) XVIII (Ap 1950), pp. 122-35.

818. Moya, Luis. "Frank Lloyd Wright." *Revista Nacional de Arquitectura* X (Mr 1950), pp. 103-8.

819. [Portrait.] *Time* LVI (24 Jy 1950), p. 38.

820. "Research Tower at Wisconsin Designed by Frank Lloyd Wright." *Architects' J* CXI (2 Fe 1950), pp. 150-2.
    S. C. Johnson and Son research tower, Racine.

821. "Solomon R. Guggenheim Memorial Museum Designed by Frank Wright." *Arch & Eng* CLXXX (Fe 1950), p. 6.

822. [Statue at Taliesin.] *Architects' J* CXI (13 Ap 1950), p. 445.
    Chinese figure placed on roof.

823. "Unusual Research Tower under Construction in Racine." *Nat Arch* (Detroit) VI (Ag 1950), p. 7.
    For S. C. Johnson and Son.

824. "Wax Research and Development Tower, Racine, Wisconsin." *Arch & Eng* CLXXXIII (D 1950), pp. 20-4.
    For S. C. Johnson and Son.

825. "Wright Campus Blooms in Fla." *Art D* XXIV (15 Ap 1950), p. 13.
    Florida Southern College, Lakeland.

826. Wright, Frank Lloyd. "An Adventure in the Human Spirit." *Motive* XI (N 1950), pp. 30-1.
    An address given during Founder's Week at Florida Southern College.

827. Wright, Frank Lloyd. "July 14. AA School Annual Prize-giving, Bedford Square, W.C. I." *Architects' J* CXII (27 Jy 1950), pp. 86-7.
    Text of a speech by Wright. Also in *Architectural Design* XX (Ag 1950), pp. 219, 232, and *Builder* CLXXIX (21 Jy 1950), p. 97.

828. Wright, Frank Lloyd. [Speech at Southern Conference on

Hospital Planning, Biloxi, Mississippi, 1949.] *Proceedings, Southern Conference on Hospital Planning* (22 Fe 1950), pp. 103-14.
Also broadcast over radio station WLOX (Mutual Broadcasting System).

829. "Wright's Core-Supported Tower Unveiled in Photographs: Research and Development Tower Added to Group Designed for S. C. Johnson & Son, Inc., Racine, Wis., by Frank Lloyd Wright, Architect." *Arch Rec* CVIII (D 1950), pp. 11a-b.

830. Zevi, Bruno. "Frank Lloyd Wright and the Conquest of Space." *Mag Art* XLIII (My 1950), pp. 186-91.
Translated by Edgar Kaufmann from the introduction to Zevi's *Architetti del movimento moderno, vol. III: Frank Lloyd Wright* (see no. 687).

831. Zevi, Bruno. "Mies van der Rohe e Frank Ll. Wright, poeti dello spazio." *Metron* no. 37 (Jy-Ag 1950), pp. 6-18.

1951

Books

832. [First Unitarian Society. Committee on Publications & Publicity.] *Meeting House of the First Unitarian Society of Madison, Wisconsin.* [Madison: First Unitarian Society, 1951.]
21.6 x 18.3 cm., 12 pp., 6 ills.
A descriptive pamphlet.

833. Firenze, Italy. Palazzo Strozzi. *Mostra di Frank Lloyd Wright; dialogo: "Broadacre City."* Studio italiano di storia dell'arte. May 15, 1951. As previewed at Gimbel Brothers, Philadelphia, Pa., January, 1951.
21.9 x 21.4 cm., 5 pp., paper.
Text of a conversation between Wright and Oskar Stonorov about Broadacre City (project).

834. Troedsson, Carl Birger. *Two Standpoints of Modern Architecture: Wright and Le Corbusier.* Göteborg: Elanders Boktryckeri Aktiebolag, 1951.

20 pp., 14 ills. (Chalmers Tekniska Högskolas Handlingar. Avd. Arkitektur I. Nr. 113, 1951)
Original not seen.

Periodicals

835. "Architect F. L. Wright." *Art D* XXV (15 Fe 1951), p. 16.
"Sixty Years of Living Architecture" exhibit at Gimbel Brothers, Philadelphia.

836. "The Architecture of Frank Lloyd Wright at Florida Southern College; Architecture of Robert Law Weed, A.I.A., at Florida Southern College." *Nat Arch* (Detroit) VII (Ap 1951), pp. 4-6.

837. Argan, G. C. "De tentoonstelling van F. L. Wright te Florence." *Forum* (Amsterdam) XI (N 1951), pp. 298-304.

838. Bottoni, Piero. "Alla direzione della rivista Metron, Roma." *Metron* XLIII (Se-D 1951), p. 6.
Letter.

839. "Business and Culture." *Newsweek* XXXVII (5 Fe 1951), p. 76.
Exhibition at Gimbel Brothers, Philadelphia.

840. "Frank Lloyd Wright." *Arts* (Paris) no. 321 (27 Jy 1951), p. 8.
Exhibition in Florence.

841. "Frank Lloyd Wright in Italia." *Urbanistica* XXI (no. 7, 1951), p. 57.

842. [Frank Lloyd Wright.] *Metron* no. 41-2 (My-Ag 1951), pp. 19-87 and cover.
Includes articles by Wright and Giuseppe Samonà. The article by Samonà appears in English translation in *Architects' Year Book* (see no. 964) and as a preface to *Drawings for a Living Architecture* (see no. 1265).

843. Goulder, Grace. "Home by Frank Lloyd Wright, Architec-

tural Innovator." *Cleveland Plain Dealer Pictorial Magazine* (28 O 1951).

Not seen. From Karpel (see no. 1046). Weltzheimer house, Oberlin.

844. Grafly, Dorothy. "The Artist and the Architect." *American Artist* XV (My 1951), pp. 45, 59-61.

Notes on Wright's career and the exhibit "Sixty Years of Living Architecture."

845. Hamlin, Talbot. "Frank Lloyd Wright in Philadelphia." *Nation* CLXXII (10 Fe 1951), pp. 140-1.

"Sixty Years of Living Architecture" previewed at Gimbel Brothers. Also in *Journal of the American Institute of Architects* XV (Ap 1951), pp. 169-72.

846. Kaufmann, Edgar, Jr. "Frank Lloyd Wright at the Strozzi." *Mag Art* XLIV (My 1951), pp. 190-2.

847. "Laboratoire de recherches á Racine, Wisconsin." *Arch d'Aujourd'hui* XXII (O 1951), pp. vi-vii.

S. C. Johnson and Son research tower, Racine.

848. "Lots Are Circular in This 50-House Group." *House and Garden* XLIX (Fe 1951), pp. 52-5, 100, 111.

Usonia II: master plan, executed in part, Pleasantville.

849. "People." *Arch For* XCV (D 1951), p. 64.

Wright elected to American Academy of Arts and Letters.

850. "La polemica su Wright." *Metron* XLIII (Se-D 1951), pp. 8-10.

851. Ragghianti, Carlo L. "Letture di Wright." *Edilizia Moderna* no. 47 (D 1951), pp. 17-28.

Exhibit at Palazzo Strozzi, Florence.

852. Roth, Alfred. "Geschenkartikel-Laden in San Francisco." *Werk* XXXVIII (D 1951), pp. 379-82.

Morris gift shop, San Francisco.

853. Wright, Frank Lloyd. "Force Is a Heresy." *Wisconsin Athenaean* II (Sp 1951), pp. 10-11.

854. Wright, Frank Lloyd. "A Four-Color Portfolio of the Recent Work of the Dean of Contemporary Architects, with His Own Commentary on Each Building." *Arch For* XCIV (Ja 1951), pp. 73-108 and cover. (Also issued as offprint.)

   Includes: S. C. Johnson and Son research tower, Racine; Walter house, Quasqueton; Adelman house, Fox Point; Jacobs house 2 and Pew house, Madison; Friedman house, Pleasantville; Anne Pfeiffer Chapel and library, Florida Southern College, Lakeland. The offprint was distributed in connection with the exhibition "Sixty Years of Living Architecture."

855. Wright, Frank Lloyd. "The Southwest Christian Seminary." *Seminary News* V (Ag 1951), pp. 1-4.

   Southwest Christian Seminary, Phoenix (project).

856. Wright, Frank Lloyd. "When Free Men Fear." *Nation* CLXXII (2 Je 1951), pp. 527-8.

857. [Wright presented with the Italian Star of Solidarity decoration.] *Arch For* XCV (Ag 1951), p. 68.

1952

Books

858. Moser, Werner M. *Frank Lloyd Wright: Sechzig Jahre lebendige Architektur; Sixty Years of Living Architecture.* Winterthur: Verlag Buchdruckerei Winterthur AG., [1952].

   29.2 x 21.2 cm., 100 pp., front., 157 ills. (part color), cloth.

   The text includes: "Gedanken über die Architektur Frank Ll. Wrights," and "Anmerkungen zur Charakteristik der Bauten F. Ll. Wrights," by Werner M. Moser; "Werklied aus dem Jahre" (1896), "Aus dem Vorwort zum Buch *When Democracy Builds*," "Über die Lehrzeit des Architekten" (1936), "Über Romantik in der Architektur und über die Funktion der Maschine im menschlichen Leben," "Zur Frage, warum die Fachleute das Wesen seiner Architektur," and "Falling

Water" (in English), by Frank Lloyd Wright; "Aus einem
Dialog über "Broadacre City," by Wright and Oskar Stonorov;
"Notizen über die Frank-Lloyd-Wright-Ausstellung," by Sto-
norov; "Wir bauen mit Frank Lloyd Wright," by Herbert
Jacobs; "Frank Lloyd Wright baut uns ein Heim," by Paul R.
and Jean S. Hanna; and "Leben der Studenten in Taliesin-
West," by Peter Steiger. A paperback edition also was pub-
lished.

REVIEWS
859. Anonymous. *Arch For* XCVII (D 1952), pp. 158, 166.
860. Sachs, Lisbeth. *Werk* XXXIX (Ag 1952), sup. pp. 111-12.

861. Munich. Haus der Kunst. *Frank Lloyd Wright: 60 Jahre
Architektur.* Veranstalter, Ausstellungsleitung München E. V.,
Haus der Kunst, [1952].
    24 x 17 cm., 71 pp., front., 36 ills., paper.
    A catalogue for the traveling exhibit "Sixty Years of Living
Architecture." It includes: "To Germany" (in English), by
Wright, dated 1 May 1952; "Aus einem Dialog über "Broad-
acre City," by Wright and Oskar Stonorov; "Bemerkungen zu
den Frank Lloyd Wright-Ausstellungen," by Stonorov; and
"Zum Katalog für die Frank Lloyd Wright-Ausstellung in
München Mai 1952," by Otto Bartning. The final leaves are
advertising material.

862. Paris. Ecole Nationale Supérieure des Beaux-Arts. *Exposition de l'oeuvre de Frank Lloyd Wright.* Paris: Avril, 1952.
    21.5 x 21.5 cm., 14 pp., 1 ill., paper.
    A catalogue for the traveling exhibit "Sixty Years of Living
Architecture."

863. Rotterdam. Academie van Beeldende Kunsten en Technische
Wetenschappen. *Frank Lloyd Wright.* Rotterdam: Ahoy'-gebouw,
1952.
    21.3 x 21.2 cm., 24 pp., front., 15 ills., paper.
    A catalogue for the traveling exhibit "Sixty Years of Living
Architecture." It includes "To Holland" (in English), by
Wright, dated 1 June 1952, and "FLLW," by J. J. P. Oud.

864. Wright, Frank Lloyd. *Taliesin Drawings: Recent Architecture of Frank Lloyd Wright Selected from His Drawings.* Comments by Edgar Kaufmann, Jr. [New York]: Wittenborn, Schultz, Inc., [1952].

22.2 x 27.8 cm., 63 pp., front., 57 ills. (Problems of Contemporary Art No. 6)

A book of drawings of nineteen structures, only eight of which had been published previously according to the introduction. The illustrations were selected with Wright's guidance and were reproduced from negatives of the original drawings. The book is bound in stiff paper wrappers.

REVIEWS

865. Anonymous. *Arch For* XCVIII (Ja 1953), p. 168.

866. Anonymous. *H & H* III (Fe 1953), p. 146.

867. Smith, Herbert L., Jr. "Wright's Renderings." *Arch Rec* CXIII (Mr 1953), p. 48.

868. Soby, James Thrall. "Unaging Frank Lloyd Wright." *Sat R* XXXV (4 O 1952), pp. 58-9.

869. Strutt, James. *Roy Arch Inst Can J* XXX (Ag 1953), p. 243.

Periodicals

870. "Der amerikanische Ausdruck." *Der Spiegel* VI (17 Se 1952), pp. 28-33 and cover.

"Sixty Years of Living Architecture" exhibition.

871. "Arquitectura moderna norteamericana." *Cortijos y rascacielos* II (no. 72, 1952), pp. 37-40.

872. Carlo, Giancarlo de. "Wright e l'Europa." *Sele Arte* I (Se-O 1952), pp. 17-24.

873. Champigneulle, Bernard. "Frank Lloyd Wright à Paris." *Art & Décoration* no. 28 (1952), pp. 21-4.

874. Champigneulle, Bernard. "Le Plus Illustre des architectes américains Frank Lloyd Wright est venu à Paris prêcher la croisade contre le gratte-ciel." *Figaro Littéraire* (12 Ap 1952), p. 9.

875. Dufet, Michel. "L'Architecte le plus étonnant: FL. Wright présente à bientôt ses travaux à Paris." *Arts* (Paris) no. 352 (28 Mr 1952), p. 9.

876. Eckstein, Hans. "Zu den F. L. Wright-Ausstellungen in Europa." *Bauen und Wohnen* no. 3 (Je 1952), p. 159.

877. "Exhibitions: Influences of Mies and Wright." *Interiors* CXII (N 1952), pp. 8, 10.

878. "15-Story Glass Research Tower Built on Concrete Core." *Building Digest* XII (D 1952), pp. 404-5.
    S. C. Johnson and Son research tower, Racine.

879. "Fighting the Box." *New Yorker* XXVIII (5 Jy 1952), p. 16.
    Observations on Wright's speech to a students' symposium at the eighty-fourth annual convention of the American Institute of Architects.

880. "First Unitarian Church, Madison, Wisconsin. Frank Lloyd Wright, Architect." *Arch For* XCVII (D 1952), pp. 85-92.

881. "Florida Southern College Revisited for Glimpses of the Administration Group in Wright's Organic Campus." *Arch For* XCVII (Se 1952), pp. 120-7.
    Includes essays by Wright and Ludd M. Spivey.

882. "FLW in New Kind of Exhibit." *Arch Rec* CXI (Mr 1952), p. 374.
    Photographs of buildings for S. C. Johnson and Son, Racine, exhibited at Museum of Modern Art, New York.

883. "FLW Plans Block House: Any Man Can Build It." *Arch Rec* CXI (Fe 1952), p. 26.

884. "Frank Lloyd Wright." *Architecture Française* XIII nos. 123-4 (1952), pp. 3-72 and cover.
    A special issue published to coincide with the exhibit "Sixty Years of Living Architecture" at the Ecole des Beaux-Arts, Paris. It includes articles by Wright, Jean Morey, and L.-G. Noviant.

885. "Frank Lloyd Wright à Paris." *Arch d'Aujourd'hui* XXII (Ap 1952), p. xxxiii.
    "Sixty Years of Living Architecture" exhibit at Ecole des Beaux-Arts.

886. "Frank Lloyd Wright, architecte américain." *Construction Moderne* LXVIII (Je 1952), pp. 224-5.

887. "Frank Lloyd Wright's Masterwork." *Arch For* XCVI (Ap 1952), pp. 141-4.
    Guggenheim Museum, New York.

888. "Frank Lloyd Wright: Zürich." *Werk* XXXIX (Mr 1952), sup. pp. 26-8.
    "Sixty Years of Living Architecture" exhibit at Kunsthaus.

889. "Guggenheim Museum Files Revised Building Plans." *Museum News* XXX (15 My 1952), p. 1.

890. "That Haunted House." *Northw Arch* XVI (N-D 1952), pp. 3, 16, 18.
    Remodeling of Hills house, Oak Park.

891. Henning, Heinrich. "Frank Lloyd Wright, 60 Jahre lebendige Architektur." *Neue Stadt.* VI (no. 9, 1952), pp. 388-97.

892. Hitchcock, Henry-Russell. "The Evolution of Wright, Mies and Le Corbusier." *Perspecta* no. 1 (Su 1952), pp. 8-17.

893. " 'Honestly Arrogant' F. LL. W. Restates Lifelong Creed." *Arch Rec* CXI (My 1952), p. 14.

894. "A House by Frank Lloyd Wright for Mr. and Mrs. Herman T. Mossberg in South Bend, Ind. William Reinke, General Contractor." *H & H* II (D 1952), pp. 66-73 and cover.

895. "Journey to Taliesin West." *Look* XVI (1 Ja 1952), pp. 28-31.

896. Kaufmann, Edgar, Jr. "Three New Buildings on the Pacific

Coast." *Arch Yrbk* IV (1952), pp. 55-63.
Includes Morris gift shop, San Francisco.

897. Leitl, Alfons. "Baukunst zwischen Mies und Frank Lloyd Wright." *Baukunst und Werkform* no. 2-3 (1952), pp. 36-60.
1. "Diskussion um ein Haus von Mies van der Rohe."
2. "Frank Lloyd Wright in Europa." Discussion: no. 6-7, pp. 82-4.

898. Martinie, A. H. "Frank-Lloyd Wright, inventeur de la maison dans l'espace triomphe à Paris." *Arts* (Paris) no. 355 (17-23 Ap 1952), p. 7.
Exhibition at the Ecole des Beaux-Arts.

899. "Nautilus's Prune." *New Yorker* XXVIII (12 Jy 1952), pp. 20-1.
Conversation with Wright.

900. "New Display Method Reveals FLW's Work in 3 Dimensions." *Arch For* XCVI (Mr 1952), p. 78.
Buildings for S. C. Johnson and Son, Racine, exhibited at Museum of Modern Art, New York.

901. "New Honors for FLW." *Arch Rec* CXI (Ja 1952), p. 22.
Elected to membership in American Academy of Arts & Letters; given Centennial Award for the Northwest Territory.

902. Ottolenghi, Marinella. "Istantànee da un viaggio negli U.S.A." *Metron* VII (no. 47, 1952), pp. 15-17.
Unitarian Church, Madison.

903. [Portrait.] *Harper's Bazaar* LXXXV (Je 1952), pp. 70-1.

904. Reed, Henry H., Jr. "Frank Lloyd Wright Conquers Paris and Vice Versa." *Arch Rec* CXII (Jy 1952), p. 22.
"Henry H. Reed, Jr. analyzes reviews of Beaux Arts exhibit; even Communists bow to 'most famous American architect'."

905. "Residenza F. Ll. Wright a Taliesin East." *Metron* VII (no. 47, 1952), p. 18.

906. Schelling, H. G. J. "Tentoonstelling Frank Lloyd Wright te Rotterdam." *Bouwkundig Weekblad* LXX (22 Jy 1952), pp. 231-2.

907. Torcapel, John. "A propos de Frank Ll. Wright." *Werk* XXXIX (O 1952), pp. 330-2.
 Impressions of "Sixty Years of Living Architecture" exhibit at Kunsthaus in Zurich.

908. Wright, Frank Lloyd. "Book Reviews." *Arch For* XCVI (Ap 1952), pp. 212, 216, 220.
 Wright wrote an article for the *American Peoples Encyclopedia Year Book,* 1951. It is reprinted here in its entirety.

909. Wright, Frank Lloyd. "Organic Architecture Looks at Modern Architecture." *Arch Rec* CXI (My 1952), pp. 148-54, foldout page containing reproductions of several drawings.
 Also in Puma, Fernando, ed. *7 Arts.* Garden City, New York: Permabooks, 1953. Pp. 64-74. A translation was published in *Byggekunst* XXXIV (no. 10, 1952), pp. 192-5.

910. Wright, Frank Lloyd. "The Word on Design." *Interiors* CXII (D 1952), pp. 116, 150, 152, 154, 156, 158, 160, 162, 164, 166.
 Includes comments from *An Organic Architecture: The Architecture of Democracy* (no. 463), compiled by Edgar Kaufmann, Jr.

1953

Books

911. [Wright, Frank Lloyd.] *Frank Lloyd Wright at the National Institute of Arts and Letters by the Recipient of the Gold Medal for Architecture, May 27, 1953.* N.p.: no pub., 1953.
 21.4 x 21.4 cm., 6 pp., paper.
 An exhibition catalogue.

912. Wright, Frank Lloyd. *Sixty Years of Living Architecture.* [New York], The Solomon R. Guggenheim Museum, [1953].
 21.5 x 21.5 cm., 36 pp., front., 50 ills., paper.

A catalogue for the traveling exhibit "Sixty Years of Living Architecture."

913. Wright, Frank Lloyd. *The Future of Architecture.* New York: Horizon Press, 1953.

25.3 x 20.1 cm., 326 pp., front., 35 ills., cloth.

A collection of Wright's statements on architecture between 1930 and 1953. It includes: "A Conversation" with Hugh Downs (broadcast 17 May 1953 by the National Broadcasting Company); "Some Aspects of the Past and Present of Architecture," and "Some Aspects of the Future of Architecture" (from *Architecture and Modern Life,* no. 405); "Modern Architecture" (The Princeton Lectures, no. 250); "Two Lectures on Architecture" (The Chicago Art Institute Lectures, no. 261); "An Organic Architecture" (The London Lectures, no. 463); and "The Language of an Organic Architecture" (1953; reprinted, see no. 2068).

□ An undated, less expensive edition was reissued by Bramhall House, New York.

□ A British edition was published by the Architectural Press, London, 1955.

□ A Russian edition entitled *Budushchee arkhitektury* was published in 1960.

□ A French edition was published as *L'Avenir de l'architecture.* Traduit de l'américain par Marie-Françoise Bonardi. [Paris]: Gonthier, [1966].

□ A German edition was published under the title *Die Zukunft der Architektur.* München-Wien: Albert Langen-Georg Müller, 1966.

REVIEWS of the 1953, 1955, and German editions

914. Andrews, Wayne. "Great Uncompromiser." *Sat R* XXXVI (14 N 1953), pp. 15-16. [1953]

915. Anonymous. *H & H* V (Mr 1954), p. 174. [1953]

916. Colquhoun, Alan. "Organic Prophecy." *Arch R* CXVIII (D 1955), pp. 401-2. [1955]

917. "Frank Lloyd Wright, *Die Zukunft der Architektur.*" *Das Kunstwerk* XX (Fe-Mr 1967), pp. 65-6. [German, 1966]

918. Gaebler, Max David. *USA Tomorrow* I (O 1954), p. 90. [1953]

919. Goble, Emerson. "Wright Lectures on Architecture."
Arch Rec CXIV (D 1953), pp. 46, 48. [1953]

920. Hamlin, Talbot. "To Be Victoriously Himself." *NYTBR*
(1 N 1953), p. 7. [1953]

921. Kauten, Mat. *Progress Arch* XXXV (Fe 1954), pp. 174,
178. [1953]

922. Knapp, William. "The Testament of Frank Lloyd Wright."
Reporter X (19 Ja 1954), pp. 38-40. [1953]

923. Read, Herbert. "Against the Betrayal of Architecture."
New Repub CXXIX (2 N 1953), pp. 20-1. [1953]

924. Stevens, Thomas. *RIBA J* LXIII (Fe 1956), p. 159. [1955]

925. Tintner, Adeline. "Wright Speaks." *Art D* XXVIII (1 Fe
1954), p. 33. [1953]

926. [Wright, Frank Lloyd.] *The Usonian House, Souvenir of the
Exhibition: 60 Years of Living Architecture, the Work of Frank
Lloyd Wright.* [New York], The Solomon R. Guggenheim Museum, [1953].
19 x 25.2 cm., 10 pp., 10 ills.

A pamphlet describing the Usonian house built as part of
the exhibit "Sixty Years of Living Architecture," New York.
It includes "Concerning the Usonian House," by Wright, dated
12 November 1953.

Periodicals

927. Andrews, Wayne. "Looking at the Latest of Frank Lloyd
Wright." *Perspectives USA* no. 4 (Su 1953), pp. 115-25.

928. Andrews, Wayne. "The Recent Work of Frank Lloyd Wright."
Marg VII (D 1953), pp. 5-10.

929. "Another Gold Medal for Wright." *Arch Rec* CXIV (Jy 1953),
p. 16.

Awarded 1953 Gold Medal for Architecture of the National
Institute of Arts & Letters.

930. Brett, Lionel. "Wright in New York." *New Repub* CXXIX
(16 N 1953), pp. 19-20.

"Sixty Years of Living Architecture" exhibit.

931. d'Harnoncourt, Rene. [Letter.] *Arch Rec* CXIV (Se 1953), p. 12.
    A response to Wright's "In the Cause of Modern Architecture" (see no. 975). Also in *Interiors* CXIII (Se 1953), pp. 163-5.

932. "Exhibition at Guggenheim Museum." *Art N* LII (O 1953), p. 44.

933. "Frank Lloyd Wright and 1,000,000 Houses a Year." *H & H* III (Mr 1953), p. 105.
    Comment on Wright's innovations.

934. "Frank Lloyd Wright: At 84, Still Fighting." *Business Week* (17 O 1953), pp. 30-1.

935. "Frank Lloyd Wright Builds in the Middle of Manhattan, Shows How to Make a Small, Simple House Rich and Spacious." *H & H* IV (N 1953), pp. 118-21.
    Usonian house, built as part of the exhibit "Sixty Years of Living Architecture."

936. "The Frank Lloyd Wright Campus." *Bulletin of Florida Southern College, Lakeland* LXIX (Ap 1953), unpaged and cover.
    Includes a reprint from *Architectural Forum.*

937. "Frank Lloyd Wright Exhibits 60 Years' Work." *Arch For* XCIX (O 1953), p. 45.
    "Sixty Years of Living Architecture," New York.

938. "Frank Lloyd Wright Receives National Institute's Medal." *Arch & Eng* CXCIV (Jy 1953), p. 5.
    Gold Medal for Architecture, National Institute of Arts and Letters.

939. "Frank Lloyd Wright's Concrete and Copper Skyscraper on the Prairie for H. C. Price Co." *Arch For* XCVIII (My 1953), pp. 98-105 and cover.
    Price Tower, Bartlesville.

940. "Frank Lloyd Wright Speaks Up." *House B* XCV (Jy 1953), pp. 86-8, 90.

"...Against the sterility and the totalitarian threat of the 'International Style'."

941. "Frank Lloyd Wright Talks to and with the Taliesin Fellowship." *Arch For* XCVIII (Ap 1953), pp. 194, 198.

Concerns three records issued by Caedmon. The same article appears in *House & Home* III (My 1953), pp. 200, 204.

942. "Frank Lloyd Wright: This New Desert House for His Son Is a Magnificent Coil of Concrete Block." *H & H* III (Je 1953), pp. 99-107 and cover.

David Wright house, Phoenix.

943. "Give Me Land, Lots of Land." *Life* XXXIV (15 Je 1953), p. 48.

Editorial which mentions Wright's contribution.

944. Gumpert, Martin. "Ten Who Know the Secret of Age." *NYTM* (27 D 1953), pp. 10-11.

Includes biographical sketch of Wright.

945. "Helio-Laboratory for Johnson Wax Co., Racine, Wisconsin." *Roy Arch Inst Can J* XXX (Ap 1953), pp. 104-7.

946. "Himself." *Harper* CCVII (D 1953), pp. 87-9.

947. Louchheim, Aline B. "Frank Lloyd Wright Talks of His Art." *NYTM* (4 O 1953), pp. 26-7, 47.

948. "Man of Culture." *Newsweek* XLII (2 N 1953), p. 64.

949. Manson, Grant Carpenter. "Frank Lloyd Wright and the Fair of '93." *Art Q* XVI (Su 1953), pp. 114-23.

950. Manson, Grant C. "Wright in the Nursery: The Influence of Froebel Education on the Work of Frank Lloyd Wright." *Arch R* CXIII (Je 1953), pp. 349-51.

951. "Modern Architecture: Mobocratic or Democratic?" *Art D* XXVII (Ag 1953), pp. 20-1.

Includes excerpts from Wright's 1953 pamphlet (see no. 2065) attacking the International Style, with a reply from René d'Harnoncourt.

952. Mumford, Lewis. "Sky Line: A Phoenix Too Infrequent." *New Yorker* XXIX (28 N, 12 D 1953), pp. 80-2, 85-7; 105-10, 113-15.

"Sixty Years of Living Architecture" exhibit, New York.

953. "Naughty Nautilus." *Time* LXII (10 Ag 1953), p. 70.

Guggenheim Museum, New York.

954. "A New House by Frank Lloyd Wright Opens Up a New Way of Life on the Old Site." *H & H* IV (N 1953), pp. 122-7.

Neils house, Minneapolis.

955. Nichols, Lewis. "Talk with Mr. Wright." *NYTBR* (1 N 1953), p. 24.

956. "Our New Crystal Towers." *Arch For* XCVIII (Fe 1953), pp. 142-5.

Includes S. C. Johnson and Son research tower, Racine.

957. "Outside the Profession." *New Yorker* XXIX (26 Se 1953), pp. 26-7.

Conversation with Wright.

958. Persitz, A. "Frank Lloyd Wright." *Arch d'Aujourd'hui* XXIV (D 1953), p. 10.

Illustrations of current work follow on pp. 11-25.

959. Portela, Francisco V. "Frank Lloyd Wright, arquitecto y creador." *La Prensa* (New York) (1 N 1953).

Not seen. From Karpel (see no. 1046).

960. [Portrait.] *Newsweek* XLII (10 Ag 1953), p. 43.

961. "Prairie Skyscraper." *Time* LXI (25 My 1953), p. 94.

Also: "Very Village Like," p. 25. Both articles concern the Price Tower, Bartlesville.

962. "Recordings by Frank Lloyd Wright." *RIBA J* LX (Ap 1953), p. 214.

963. Roth, Jack. "The Heritage of Lao-Tse." *Art D* XXVIII (1 N 1953), p. 17.

964. Samonà, Joseph. "Man, Matter and Space: On the Architecture of Frank Lloyd Wright." *Arch Yrbk* V (1953), pp. 110-22.
    Translated by Edgar Kaufmann, Jr., from *Metron* (no. 842). Reprinted as introduction to *Drawings for a Living Architecture* (no. 1265).

965. " 'Sixty Years of Living Architecture'—the Work of Frank Lloyd Wright." *Arch For* XCIX (N 1953), pp. 152-5.
    Exhibit in New York.

966. "Solomon R. Guggenheim Museum." *Museums Journal* LIII (D 1953), pp. 230-1.

967. "This New House by Frank Lloyd Wright Is a Rich Textbook of the Principles He Pioneered." *H & H* III (Mr 1953), pp. 106-13 and cover.
    Brown house, Kalamazoo.

968. Thomas, Mark Hartland. "F. L. W. Again." *Arch Design* (D 1953), pp. 347-9.
    David Wright house, Phoenix; Price Tower, Bartlesville.

969. Tselos, Dimitri. "Exotic Influences in the Architecture of Frank Lloyd Wright." *Mag Art* XLVI (Ap 1953), pp. 160-9, 184.

970. "Usonia Homes." *Journal of Housing* X (O 1953), pp. 318-20, 344-5.
    Usonia II: master plan, executed in part, Pleasantville.

971. Völckers, Otto. "Über die Baukunst Frank Lloyd Wright's." *Glas Forum* (no. 1, 1953), pp. 39-40.
    Reprinted in English translation, see no. 1195.

972. "Wright Awarded Brown Medal." *Arch & Eng* CXCV (O 1953), p. 33.

973. "Wright, Continued." *New Yorker* XXIX (31 O 1953), pp. 25-7.
   "Sixty Years of Living Architecture" exhibit, New York.

974. Wright, Frank Lloyd. "Against the Steamroller." *Arch R* CXIII (My 1953), pp. 283-5.
   Commentary by J. M. Richards.

975. Wright, Frank Lloyd. "Excerpts from the 'International Style'." *Arch Rec* CXIII (Je 1953), pp. 12, 332.
   An editorial which attacks the International Style. The complete text was published by the Taliesin Press (see no. 2066), and also appears in *House Beautiful* (July, 1953).

976. Wright, Frank Lloyd. "For a Democratic Architecture." *House B* XCV (O 1953), pp. 316-17.

977. Wright, Frank Lloyd. "Frank Lloyd Wright: Some Answers." *Art N* LII (O 1953), pp. 42-3.
   Excerpted from *The Future of Architecture* (no. 913).

978. Wright, Frank Lloyd. "L'architettura organiza guarda l'architettura moderna." *Metron* VIII (no. 48, 1953), pp. 7-10.

979. Wright, Frank Lloyd. "La palabra sobre diseño." *Revista de Arquitectura* XXXVIII (no. v-x, 1953), pp. 73-6.
   Excerpted from the 1939 London lectures (no. 463).

980. Wright, Frank Lloyd. [Letter to Talmadge C. Hughes.] *Monthly Bulletin, Michigan Society of Architects* XXVII (O 1953), p. 35.

981. Wright, Frank Lloyd. "Progress in Architectural Education." *Line Magazine* (1953), unpaged.
   Excerpts from a talk to the 84th Annual Convention of the American Institute of Architects.

982. Wright, Frank Lloyd. "The Future: Four Views." *NYTM* (1 Fe 1953), p. 64.

983. Wright, Frank Lloyd. "The Language of Organic Architecture." *Arch For* XCVIII (My 1953), pp. 106-7.
An explanation of Wright's buildings and writings on organic architecture. Also issued as *Taliesin Square-Paper.* No. 16 (see no. 2069).

984. Wright, Frank Lloyd. "To Espacios." *Espacios* (no. 13, 1953), unpaged.
Tribute to Mexico.

985. "Wright Is Right." *Newsweek* XLI (11 My 1953), pp. 97-8.
Note on speech to 23rd annual conference of Association of Western Hospitals in Salt Lake.

986. "Wright Makes New York!" *Arch Rec* CXIV (O 1953), p. 20.
"Sixty Years of Living Architecture" exhibit, New York.

987. "Wright's Might." *Time* LXII (9 N 1953), p. 74.
"Sixty Years of Living Architecture" exhibit, New York.

1954

Books

988. Amano, Tarō, ed. *Frank Lloyd Wright.* Tokyo: Shokokusha Publishing Co., Inc., 1954.
19.7 x 21 cm., 158 pp., 186 ills., cloth.
Japanese text. Includes statement by Prof. Wallace Baldinger. A softcover edition was also published.

989. Chicago. Art Institute. Burnham Library of Architecture. *Buildings by Frank Lloyd Wright in Six Middle Western States: Illinois, Indiana, Iowa, Michigan, Minnesota, Wisconsin.* Chicago: Art Institute of Chicago, 1954.
See no. 747.

990. Robsjohn-Gibbings, T. H. "Organic Architecture: Frank

Lloyd Wright." In *Homes of the Brave*. With Drawings by Mary
Petty. New York: Alfred A. Knopf, 1954. Pp. 7-16.

991.   Wright, Frank Lloyd. *Sixty Years of Living Architecture.*
Los Angeles: The Municipal Art Patrons and the Art Commission
of Los Angeles, [1954].
   21.4 x 21.4 cm., 36 pp., front., 50 ills.
   A catalogue for the traveling exhibit "Sixty Years of Living
Architecture."

992.   Wright, Frank Lloyd. *The Natural House*. New York:
Horizon Press, 1954.
   25.3 x 20.3 cm., 223 pp., front., 112 ills., cloth.
   The text is divided into two "books." "Book I: 1936-1953"
includes the following previously published articles: "Organic
Architecture" (from the *Architects' Journal,* 1936); "Building
the New House;" "In the Nature of Materials: A Philosophy;"
and "The Usonian House I" and "The Usonian House II"
(from *An Autobiography,* 1943). The final article, "Concerning
the Usonian House," was written in 1953. "Book II: 1954"
contains five chapters written for this book in 1954: "Integrity:
In a House as in an Individual;" "From the Ground Up;"
"Grammar: The House as a Work of Art;" "The Usonian Auto-
matic;" and "Organic Architecture and the Orient."
   □ An undated, less expensive edition was reissued by Bramhall
House, New York.
   □ A British edition was published by Pitman & Sons, Ltd., London, 1972.

REVIEWS of the 1954 edition
993. Andrews, Wayne. "Architect's Creed." *Sat R* XXXVII
     (18 D 1954), pp. 17, 41.
994. Brett, Lionel. "Wright's Houses." *Arts Digest* XXIX (1 Ja
     1955), p. 16.
995. Goble, Emerson. "FLlW Tells How to Build Your Own."
     Arch Rec CXVII (Ja 1955), p. 46.
996. Kennedy, Robert Woods. "The Natural House." *New
     Repub* CLXV (30 O 1971), pp. 30-2.
997. Mawn, Lawrence E. "Unrestrained as Usual." *Progress
     Arch* XXXVI (Mr 1955), pp. 216, 218.

998.   Zevi, Bruno. *Frank Lloyd Wright.* Milano: Il Balcone, 1954.
See no. 687.

Periodicals

999.   "Art on Olive Hill." *Art N* LIII (O 1954), p. 56.
Exhibition pavilion, Los Angeles.

1000.   Bayley, John Barrington. "Frank Lloyd Wright and the Grand Design." *Landscape* IV (Su 1954), pp. 30-3.
Letter to the editor, concerning the Masieri Memorial Building, Venice (project).

1001.   Bettini, Sergio. "Presentazione del Palazzo Masieri a Venezia." *Metron* IX no. 49-50 (Ja-Ap 1954), pp. 14-26.
Preceded by color reproductions of drawings for this building. English translation, pp. 27-30.

1002.   Brest, René. "A 84 ans, Frank Lloyd Wright est l'architecte le plus moderne." *Science et Vie* LXXXVI (Jy 1954), pp. 62-9.

1003.   Campo, Santiago del. "An Afternoon with Frank Lloyd Wright." *Américas* VI (Ap 1954), pp. 9-12, 44-6 and cover.

1004.   "Drawing for the Solomon R. Guggenheim Museum." *Art D* XXVIII (1 Ja 1954), p. 11.

1005.   "Early Wright." *Architects' J* CXIX (4 Fe 1954), pp. 145, 156.
Masieri Memorial Building, Venice (project).

1006.   "18-Story Tower Cantilever Structure of Concrete and Glass: Dramatic Frank Lloyd Wright Design." *Building Materials Digest* XIV (D 1954), p. 425.
Price Tower, Bartlesville.

1007.   "Frank Lloyd Wright Has Designed His First Synagogue..." *Arch Rec* CXVI (Jy 1954), p. 20.
Beth Sholom Synagogue, Elkins Park.

1008. "Frank Lloyd Wright Lecture." *Monthly Bulletin, Michigan Society of Architects* XXVIII (My 1954), p. 17.

1009. "Frank Lloyd Wright Says He'll Quit Wisconsin." *H & H* VI (D 1954), p. 53.
    In dispute over taxes.

1010. "Frank Lloyd Wright Talks about Photography." *Photography* XXXIV (Fe 1954), pp. 40-1, 118.

1011. "Glass-Towered Synagogue, Frank Lloyd Wright's First." *Arch For* C (Je 1954), p. 145.
    Beth Sholom Synagogue, Elkins Park. "Errata." CI (Se 1954), p. 86.

1012. Guerrero, Pedro E., and Robert H. Miller, photographers. "Frank Lloyd Wright." *Lincoln Mercury Times* VI (Mr-Ap 1954), pp. 5-7.
    Includes color photograph of two Lincoln Continental automobiles restyled by Wright for his own use.

1013. Henken, Priscilla J. "A 'Broad-Acre' Project: A Description by a Resident of a Co-operative House-Building Scheme, under the Influence of Frank Lloyd Wright." *Town and Country Planning* XXIII (Je 1954), pp. 294-300.
    Usonia II: master plan, executed in part, Pleasantville.

1014. "*House Beautiful* Dedicates This Exhibition to Frank Lloyd Wright." *House B* XCVI (O 1954), pp. 176-7.
    "The Arts of Daily Living," presented by *House Beautiful* magazine and the Los Angeles County Fair.

1015. Knapp, W. "Testament of Frank Lloyd Wright." *Reporter* X (19 Ja 1954), pp. 38-40.

1016. [Masieri Memorial Building, Venice (project).] *AIA J* XXII (Jy 1954), pp. 24-5.

1017. Michelucci, Giovanni. "Le ragioni di una polemica." *Nuova Città* no. 14-15 (Je 1954), pp. 48-52.

1018. "A New Debate in Old Venice." *NYTM* (21 Mr 1954),
pp. 8-9.
    Masieri Memorial Building (project). Includes statements by
Wright and Bernard Berenson.

1019. "A Planning Lesson from Frank Lloyd Wright... How
Big Can a Tiny House Be?" *H & H* V (Mr 1954), pp. 98-105 and
cover.
    Walker house, Carmel.

1020. [Portrait.] *Look* XVIII (7 Se 1954), p. 58.

1021. [Portrait.] *Newsweek* XLIII (14 Je 1954), p. 73.

1022. [Portrait.] *Newsweek* XLIV (22 N 1954), p. 63.

1023. "Presentation of the Frank P. Brown Medal." *Journal of
the Franklin Institute* CCLVIII (Se 1954), pp. 217-18.
    See also no. 1037.

1024. "Projekt Frank Lloyd Wrights für ein Studentenheim in
Venedig." *Werk* XLI (Mr 1954), sup. p. 43.
    Masieri Memorial Building (project).

1025. "Promised Hosanna." *Time* LXIII (31 My 1954), p. 54.
    Beth Sholom Synagogue, Elkins Park.

1026. "Question: Is Venice Ready for an FLLW Palazzo?" *Arch
For* C (My 1954), p. 39.
    Masieri Memorial Building, Venice (project).

1027. Ragghianti, Carlo L. "Letture di Wright, 1"; "Letture di
Wright, 2." *Critica d'Arte* no. 1 (Ja 1954), pp. 67-82; no. 4 (Jy
1954), pp. 355-383.

1028. Reed, Henry H. "Viollet-le-Duc and the USA: A Footnote
to History." *Liturg Art* XXIII (N 1954), pp. 26-8.

1029. Richards, J. M. "Venice Preserv'd." *Roy Arch Inst Can J*
XXXI (Ag 1954), pp. 281-3.
    Masieri Memorial Building, Venice (project).

1030.   Rogers, Ernesto N. "Polemica per una polemica." *Casabella* no. 201 (My-Je 1954), pp. 1-4.
Masieri Memorial Building, Venice (project).

1031.   Scully, Vincent J., Jr. "Wright vs. the International Style." *Art N* LIII (Mr 1954), pp. 32-5, 64-6.
Discussion of Wright's influence on European architects, and their later influence on him. Responses from Edgar Kaufmann, Jr., T. H. Robsjohn-Gibbings, and Elizabeth Gordon, with a rejoinder from Scully, were published in September, pp. 48-9.

1032.   "Seven Lessons from Frank Lloyd Wright." *H & H* VI (N 1954), pp. 98-105 and cover.
Anthony house, Benton Harbor.

1033.   Tunnard, Christopher. "The Future of Frank Lloyd Wright." *Landscape* III (Sp 1954), pp. 6-8.

1034.   Walker, Ralph. "Presentation to Frank Lloyd Wright of the Gold Medal for Architecture." *Proceedings of the American Academy of Arts and Letters and the National Institute of Arts and Letters*, second series (no. 4, 1954), pp. 14-15.
See also nos. 911 and 1036.

1035.   "Wright and Mies Open New York Offices." *Arch For* CI (D 1954), p. 41.

1036.   Wright, Frank Lloyd. "Acceptance." *Proceedings of the American Academy of Arts and Letters and the National Institute of Arts and Letters,* second series (no. 4, 1954), pp. 16-17.
Remarks at the time of the receipt of the Gold Medal for Architecture. See also nos. 911 and 1034.

1037.   Wright, Frank Lloyd. "American Architecture." *Journal of the Franklin Institute* CCLVIII (Se 1954), pp. 219-24.
Acceptance speech upon award of the Frank P. Brown Medal (see also no. 1023).

1038.   Wright, Frank Lloyd. "American Architecture." *United States Lines Paris Review* (Je 1954), unpaged.

1039. Wright, Frank Lloyd. "An Address under Auspices of American Institute of Architects, Detroit Chapter." *Monthly Bulletin, Michigan Society of Architects* XXVIII (Je 1954), pp. 9, 11, 13, 15, 17, 19-21, 23.

1040. Wright, Frank Lloyd. "Man." *Monthly Bulletin, Michigan Society of Architects* XXVIII (Ap 1954), pp. 33-48.
    Followed by illustrations of work.

1041. Wright, Frank Lloyd. "More Than the Turtle's Shell." *Phi Delta Kappan* XXXV (My 1954), pp. 297-9, 302.
    Based on "Some Aspects of the Past and Present of Architecture," published in *The Future of Architecture* (no. 913).

1042. "Wright in Venice." *Arch R* CXV (Ap 1954), p. 223.
    Masieri Memorial Building (project).

1043. "Wright or Wrong." *Time* LXIII (22 Mr 1954), p. 92.
    Masieri Memorial Building, Venice (project).

1044. "Wright Threatens to Forsake Wisconsin Because of Taxes." *Arch For* CI (D 1954), p. 45.

1045. "The Wright Word." *Time* LXIV (2 Ag 1954), p. 61.
    Conversation with Wright.

1955

Books

1046. Karpel, Bernard. *What Men Have Written about Frank Lloyd Wright: A Bibliography Arranged by Decades from 1900 to 1955.* [New York]: House Beautiful, 1955.
    27.7 x 21.4 cm., 34 pp., paper.
    Cover title. An annotated list of 330 books and periodicals, especially prepared to be used with the November, 1955 issue of *House Beautiful* devoted to Wright (see no. 1066). It was expanded in 1959 to include writings by Wright with additional references by others through 1959 (see no. 1264).

1047.   Scully, Vincent J., Jr. "Frank Lloyd Wright." In *The Shingle Style: Architectural Theory and Design from Richardson to the Origins of Wright.* New Haven and London: Yale University Press, [1955]. Chapter 9, pp. 155-64.

A chapter which views Wright's early, formative work as a continuing development of late nineteenth-century architecture.

REVIEW
1048.   Fitch, James M. *Society of Architectural Historians. Journal* XVII (Mr 1958), p. 36.

1049.   Tedeschi, Enrico. *Frank Lloyd Wright.* Buenos Aires: Editorial Nueva Visión, [1955].
19.5 x 14.2 cm., 87 pp., 35 ills., paper.
A study of Wright's life and work. Spanish text.

1050.   Wright, Frank Lloyd. *An American Architecture.* Edited by Edgar Kaufmann. New York: Horizon Press, 1955.
30.4 x 22.8 cm., 269 pp., front., 237 ills., cloth.
An anthology of Wright's statements dated between 1894 and 1954. Some unpublished material came from the Taliesin files; the rest had appeared in previous publications. A source list is included.
□ A British edition was published by the Architectural Press, London, 1956.

REVIEWS of 1955 and British editions
1051.   Banham, Reyner. "Wright Anthology." *Arch R* CXX (O 1956), p. 264. [1955]
1052.   Blake, Peter. "Our Elder Spaceman." *Sat R* XXXIX (4 Ag 1956), pp. 22-3. [1955]
1053.   Kramer, Hilton. "Architecture and Rhetoric." *New Repub* CXXXIII (26 D 1955), p. 20. [1955]
1054.   Pokorny, Elizabeth. "Use, Form and Art." *Nation* CLXXXII (14 Ja 1956), pp. 35-6. [1955]
1055.   Saarinen, Aline B. "Frank Lloyd Wright Discusses..." *Arch Rec* CXIX (Ap 1956), pp. 62, 66, 446. [1955]
1056.   Scully, Vincent J., Jr. "Architecture and Ancestor Worship." *Art N* LIV (Fe 1956), pp. 26, 56. [1955]

1057. Williams-Ellis, Clough. *RIBA J* LXIV (Se 1957), p. 468.
[British]

1058. Zucker, Paul. *Journal of Aesthetics and Art Criticism*
XV (Mr 1957), pp. 362-3. [1955]

1059. Wright, Frank Lloyd. *Mon Autobiographie.* Paris: Éditions
d'Histoire et d'Art, Librairie Plon, 1955.
See no. 303.

1060. Wright, Olgivanna Lloyd. *The Struggle Within.* New York,
Horizon Press, 1955.
21 x 13.5 cm., 176 pp., cloth.
A book of personal philosophy. The dust wrapper was de-
signed by Eugene Masselink.
□ The book was reprinted in [1971].

Periodicals

1061. Alford, John. "Modern Architecture and the Symbolism
of Creative Process." *Coll Art J* XIV (W 1955), pp. 102-23.

1062. "Approve Spiral-Ramp Museum." *Engin N R* CLV (29 D
1955), p. 24.
Guggenheim Museum, New York.

1063. "The Atomic Mr. Wright." *Newsweek* XLV (15 My 1955),
p. 98.
Note on speech at Institute of Contemporary Art, Boston.

1064. Bohrer, Florence Fifer. "The Unitarian Hillside Home
School." *Wis Mag Hist* XXXVIII (Sp 1955), pp. 151-5.
A description of a school run by Wright's aunts Jane and
Nell Lloyd-Jones.

1065. Carillo, René. "Two Very Different Houses." *Interiors*
CXIV (Fe 1955), p. 8.
A comparison of the Boomer house, Phoenix, with a design
by Joseph Salerno.

1066. "The Dramatic Story of Frank Lloyd Wright." *House B*

XCVIII (N 1955), pp. 233-90, 292, 294, 299-300, 302, 304, 306-14, 317-32, 335-58, 361-80 and cover.

Special issue devoted to Wright. Includes articles by Joseph A. Barry, John de Koven Hill, Robert Mosher, Bruno Zevi, James Marston Fitch, Frank Lloyd Wright, Elizabeth Gordon, Richard Williams, and Cecile Starr.

□ This issue was also offered in a specially bound, hard-cover edition. A bibliography of works about Wright was published concurrently (see no. 1046).

1067.   Edwards, Folke. "Frank Lloyd Wright." *Paletten* (no. 4, 1955), pp. 114-27.

Swedish text.

1068.   "FLLW'S Characteristic Double-Decker Flat Top." *H & H* VII (Ap 1955), pp. 116-21 and cover.

Miller house, Charles City.

1069.   "FLLW's Double-Decker Flat-Top Idea Was Adapted in Utah Builder House." *H & H* VII (Ap 1955), pp. 122-5.

1070.   "Frank Lloyd Wright and 'the Natural House'." *H & H* VII (Ja 1955), pp. 166-8.

1071.   "Frank Lloyd Wright Completes a Long, Low Industrial Arts Building for Florida Southern University...and Begins a Civic Center for the Capital of His Home State." *Arch For* CII (Ap 1955), pp. 114-21.

Monona Terrace Civic Center, Madison (project).

1072.   "Frank Lloyd Wright." *Design* LVI (Ja-Fe 1955), pp. 103-4.

Text reprinted from *Lincoln Mercury Times.*

1073.   "Frank Lloyd Wright Designs a Small Commercial Installation: A Showroom in New York for Sport Cars." *Arch For* CIII (Jy 1955), pp. 132-3.

Hoffman Jaguar auto showroom.

1074.   "Frank Lloyd Wright Discusses Taste, Inheritance, and

Creative Environment in an Exclusive Interview with I. Monte Radlovic, Editor." *Diplomat* VII (O 1955), pp. 24, 68.

1075. "Frank Lloyd Wright Projects." *Interiors* CXIV (Je 1955), p. 130.
  Fabrics and wallpapers for F. Schumacher and Co.

1076. Haverstick, John. "To Be or Not to Be." *Sat R* XXXVIII (21 My 1955), p. 13.
  Guggenheim Museum, New York.

1077. Howe, George. "Moses Turns Pharaoh." *USA Tomorrow* I (Ja 1955), p. 11.
  Reprinted from *T-Square* (see no. 341).

1078. Manson, Grant. "Sullivan and Wright, an Uneasy Union of Celts." *Arch R* CXVIII (N 1955), pp. 297-300.

1079. "A Master Architect Creates Fabric and Wall Paper Designs." *American Fabrics and Fashions* no. 35 (W 1955–56), pp. 50-1.
  For F. Schumacher and Co.

1080. Morassutti, Bruno. "Considerazioni sugli uffici Johnson, di Frank Lloyd Wright." *Domus* no. 305 (Ap 1955), pp. 2-6.
  S. C. Johnson and Son administration building and research tower, Racine.

1081. "New Era for Wright at 86: The Marketplace Redeemed?" *Arch Rec* CXVIII (O 1955), p. 20.
  Fabrics and wallpapers for F. Schumacher and Co., carpets for Karastan.

1082. Pieper, Iovanna Lloyd. "Contemporary Living." *Diplomat* VII (O 1955), pp. 25-7.

1083. [Portrait.] *Werk* XLII (D 1955), sup. pp. 241-2.

1084. Shear, John Knox. [Frank Lloyd Wright and the Design for the Air Force Academy.] *Arch Rec* CXVIII (Ag 1955), pp. 132a-b.

1085. "Taliesin to the Trade." *Interiors* CXV (O 1955), pp. 130-3.
    Fabrics and wallpapers for F. Schumacher and Co., furniture for Heritage-Henredon.

1086. "Wisconsin Makes Peace with Wright." *Arch Rec* CXVII (Ap 1955), p. 18.
    After dispute over taxes.

1087. "World's Greatest Architecture." *Arch For* CII (Je 1955), p. 139.
    "Excerpts from an address by Frank Lloyd Wright before the 1955 convention of Wisconsin Architects Assn."

1088. "Wright Architecture Rejected by Park Service." *National Parks Magazine* XXIX (Ja-Mr 1955), p. 4.
    Yosemite National Park Restaurant (project).

1089. Wright, Frank Lloyd. "Ein Dialog." *Der Aufbau* X (Ja 1955), p. 75.

1090. Wright, Frank Lloyd. "For All May Raise the Flowers Now for All Have Got the Seed." *USA Tomorrow* I (Ja 1955), pp. 8-10.
    Reprinted from *T-Square* (see no. 353).

1091. Wright, Frank Lloyd. "Future of the City." *Sat R* XXXVIII (21 My 1955), pp. 10-13 and cover.

1092. "Wright Stays in Wisconsin." *Arch For* CII (Mr 1955), p. 29.
    After dispute over taxes.

1956

Books

1093. *The Price Tower, Bartlesville, Oklahoma, February 9, 1956.*
    28 x 22.1 cm.

A promotional folder distributed in a specially printed envelope. It includes seven photographs of the Tower, six postal cards, personal commentary by Wright, a plan of a typical office floor, notes on the structure, and an advertisement for *The Story of the Tower* (no. 1095).

1094. Wright, Frank Lloyd. *Sixty Years of Living Architecture, Series Nine, Chicago: Early Chicago Buildings; Later Cantilever Structures Including Mile-High Illinois.* Chicago, 1956.
21.6 x 21.5 cm., 31 pp., front., 46 ills., paper.
Cover title. A catalogue for "Frank Lloyd Wright Day," 17 October 1956, in Chicago. It includes illustrations of work, a list of citations and gold medals, a list of material in an exhibition at the Hotel Sherman, and an insert which describes the mile-high skyscraper, "The Illinois" (project).

1095. Wright, Frank Lloyd. *The Story of the Tower: The Tree That Escaped the Crowded Forest.* New York, Horizon Press, 1956.
27.8 x 21.4 cm., 134 pp., front., 130 ills., 6 color pls., cloth.
A monograph on the Price Tower, Bartlesville. According to a publisher's note, it contains all of Wright's writings on the subject, revised and brought up to date for this book. Portions of it are based on material which originally appeared in *An Autobiography* (1932), *Architectural Forum* (1938, 1953), and *The New York Times* (1953). Photographs taken during construction and of the completed building are included.

Periodicals

1096. "Broadside from FLW." *Builder* CXCI (27 Jy 1956), p. 132.
In England to receive honorary degree of Doctor of Laws of University of Wales.

1097. "Bust of Wright." *Arch Rec* CXX (D 1956), p. 28.
Bust of Wright presented to him at convention of Architectural Woodwork Institute.

1098. "Cities: Medieval or Modern." *Arch For* CV (Ag 1956),

pp. 151, 168, 172.
"Excerpts from a discussion telecast by...the NBC network..."

1099. Eaton, Leonard K. "Louis Sullivan and Hendrik Berlage: A Centennial Tribute to Two Pioneers." *Progress Arch* XXXVII (N 1956), pp. 138-41, 202-4, 210, 216, 220, 222, 226, 230, 234.
Includes discussion of Berlage's visit to the U.S.A. where he saw Wright's work.

1100. "Famous Designers Disagree." *Engin N R* CLVI (3 My 1956), p. 27.
Wright and Italian engineer Pier Luigi Nervi.

1101. "FLLW Designs Home Furnishings." *H & H* IX (Ja 1956), p. 188.
Fabrics and wallpapers for F. Schumacher and Co., furniture for Heritage-Henredon.

1102. "Frank Lloyd Wright a Roma." *Architettura* II (O 1956), p. 456.

1103. "Frank Lloyd Wright: After 36 Years His Tower Is Completed." *Arch For* CIV (Fe 1956), pp. 106-13 and cover.
Price Tower, Bartlesville.

1104. "The Frank Lloyd Wright Campus." *Bulletin of Florida Southern College* LXXII (Ja 1956), pp. 1-17, 20 and cover.

1105. "Frank Lloyd Wright Day Proclaimed in Chicago; Taliesin Endowment Begun." *Arch For* CV (N 1956), p. 21.

1106. "Frank Lloyd Wright." *H & H* IX (My 1956), pp. 164-8.
Mossberg house, South Bend; Walker house, Carmel; Neils house, Minneapolis, David Wright house, Phoenix.

1107. "Frank Lloyd Wright: la 'Price Tower'." *Casabella Continuità* no. 211 (Je-Jy 1956), pp. 8-21.

1108. "Frank Lloyd Wright's Mile-High Office Tower." *Arch*

For CV (N 1956), pp. 106a-d.
"The Illinois" (project).

1109. "Gratte-ciel à Bartlesville, cité de 25,000 habitants,
U.S.A." *Arch d'Aujourd'hui* XXVII (O 1956), p. xxiii.
Price Tower.

1110. "Guggenheim Museum to Rise—Victory for Wright in 12-
Year Design Battle." *Arch For* CIV (Je 1956), p. 13.

1111. "The H. C. Price Tower." *Arch Rec* CXIX (Fe 1956), pp.
153-60 and cover. (Also issued as offprint.)
Includes essays by Wright, Harold C. Price, Joe D. Price,
and Edgar Kaufmann, Jr.

1112. "Here is Prefabrication's Biggest News for 1957." *H & H*
X (D 1956), pp. 117-21 and cover.
Pre-fab no. 1 (Van Tamelen), Madison.

1113. Hill, John de Koven. "A Fine Old Stable Becomes a Fine
New House." *House B* XCVIII (Fe 1956), pp. 104-7, 142.
Coonley stables, Riverside.

1114. Hill, John de Koven. "The Look of American Life at the
Top Level." *House B* XCVIII (N 1956), pp. 258-65.
Harold Price, Jr., house, Bartlesville; Harold Price house,
Paradise Valley.

1115. "How Fresh and Fitting Is the Furniture of Frank Lloyd
Wright in Traditional Rooms." *House B* XCVIII (Je 1956), pp.
114-17.

1116. "The Illinois." *Arch Rec* CXX (N 1956), p. 11.
Mile-high skyscraper, Chicago (project).

1117. Kennedy, Warnett. "Famous Living Architects: Frank
Lloyd Wright." *Roy Arch Inst Can J* XXXIII (My 1956), pp.
187-8.

1118. "Listen to…Frank Lloyd Wright." *Colliers* CXXXVIII
(3 Ag 1956), pp. 20-1.

1119. McCoy, Esther. "Roots of California Contemporary Architecture." *Arts & Arch* LXXIII (O 1956), pp. 14-17, 36-9.
Includes a note on Wright's block houses.

1120. "Merchandising." *H & H* IX (Ap 1956), pp. 140-1.
Zimmerman house, Manchester.

1121. "Milestones and Memoranda on the Work of Frank Lloyd Wright." *Land Economics* XXXII (N 1956), pp. 361-8.

1122. "A Modern House in the Old West." *Household* (Topeka) LVI (Je 1956), pp. 25-7, 70 and cover.
Blair house, Cody.

1123. "The New Guggenheim Museum." *Arts* XXX (Je 1956), p. 11.

1124. "One Hundred Years of Significant Building." *Arch Rec* CXX (D 1956), p. 180.
Includes Unity Temple, Oak Park. Comments by Alan Burnham and Buford Pickens.

1125. "One Hundred Years of Significant Building." *Arch Rec* CXX (O 1956), p. 194.
Includes Willits house, Highland Park. Comments by Edgar Kaufmann and John Knox Shear.

1126. Pellegrin, Luigi. "Alla ricerca del primo Wright." *Architettura* II (Je 1956), pp. 126-31.

1127. Pellegrin, Luigi. "La decorazione funzionale del primo Wright." *Architettura* II (Jy 1956), pp. 198-203.

1128. "Un peruano visita Taliesin en Arizona." *El Arquitecto Peruano* XX (Ja-Fe 1956), pp. 31-6.

1129. [Portrait.] *Architects' J* CXXIV (2 Ag 1956), p. 150.

1130. [Portrait.] *Time* LXVII (11 Je 1956), p. 69.

1131. [Portrait.] *Time* LXVIII (2 Jy 1956), p. 51.

1132. Robinson, Kenneth J. "From Taliesin to Shepherds Bush: The *Journal* Entertains—and Is Entertained by—Frank Lloyd Wright." *Architects' J* CXXIV (26 Jy 1956), pp. 109-11.

1133. "Roots of Contemporary California Architecture." *Pac Arch & Build* LXII (D 1956), pp. 10-11.
Discusses Wright's contribution to the development of California architecture.

1134. Rowe, Colin. "Chicago Frame." *Arch R* CXX (N 1956), pp. 285-9 and cover.
Includes discussion of Wright's large office and residential buildings and projects.
□ A revised version was published in 1970 (see no. 1838). The article was reprinted in Rowe's *The Mathematics of the Ideal Villa and Other Essays.* Cambridge, Massachusetts, and London, England: The MIT Press, [1976]. Pp. 89-117.

1135. Scully, Vincent J., Jr. "Architecture and Ancestor Worship." *Art N* LIV (Fe 1956), p. 26.

1136. "Skies Clearing for Wright's Ramp Museum, Synagogue." *Arch For* CIV (Fe 1956), p. 9.
Guggenheim Museum, New York; Beth Sholom Synagogue, Elkins Park.

1137. "Tall Tale." *Newsweek* XLVIII (10 Se 1956), p. 98.
Mile-high skyscraper, "The Illinois," Chicago (project).

1138. "This Rich and Rhythmic House Expresses 32 Simple and Basic Design Ideas." *H & H* X (Se 1956), pp. 136-41.
Zimmerman house, Manchester.

1139. Tselos, Dimitri. "Frank Lloyd Wright e a arquitetura mundial." *Habitat* VI (Fe 1956), pp. 11-15.

1140. Walker, Ralph A. "Frank Lloyd Wright: His Contribution to Our American Culture." *Land Economics* XXXII (N 1956), pp. 357-60.

1141. "Wright Completes Skyscraper." *Progress Arch* XXXVII
(Fe 1956), pp. 87-90.
       Price Tower, Bartlesville.

1142. Wright, Frank Lloyd. "Architecture: Organic Expression
of the Nature of Architecture." *Arizona Highways* XXXII (Fe
1956), pp. 12-29 and cover.
       List of honorary citations, degrees and medals; introduction
by Raymond Carlson, p. 1.

1143. Wright, Frank Lloyd. "Frank Lloyd Wright ai suoi critici."
Casabella Continuità no. 211 (Je-Jy 1956), front., pp. 6-7.

1144. Wright, Frank Lloyd. "The Shape of the City." American
Municipal Association. *Proceedings* (1956), pp. 30-4.
       Text of a speech read 26 November 1956.

1145. "Wright Proposes Mile-High Skyscraper." *Science Digest*
XL (N 1956), p. 77.
       "The Illinois" (project).

1146. "Wright Revisited." *New Yorker* XXXII (15 Je 1956),
pp. 26-7.

1147. "Wright Sketches 510-Story Office Tower; Round, Blue-
Roof Greek Orthodox Church." *Arch For* CV (O 1956), p. 17.
       Mile High skyscraper, "The Illinois," Chicago (project);
Annunciation Greek Orthodox Church, Wauwatosa.

1957

Books

1148. Schumacher, F. *Schumacher's Taliesin Line of Decorative
Fabrics and Wallpapers. Designed by Frank Lloyd Wright.* [Chi-
cago: E. W. Bredemeier & Co. Sample Books.]
       Cover title. 57.8 x 44.3 cm., 36 pp., 30 ills., cloth.
       A book distributed to retail outlets which contains samples
of fabric and wallpaper designed or chosen by Wright. There
are thirteen fabrics in one hundred forty-two colorways and

four wallpapers in twenty-three colorways. The wallpaper samples are not included in the collation above. The illustrations include photographs of Schumacher's "Taliesin" suite, located in the National Republican Club, New York, and decorated with the fabrics and wallpapers. There are also photographs of several of Wright's buildings from which many of the Schumacher designs derived. The book is undated and possibly appeared in 1955.

1149. Wright, Frank Lloyd. *A Testament.* New York: Horizon Press, [1957].
30 x 22.6 cm., 256 pp., 183 ills., cloth.

   The book is divided into two sections, the first one autobiographical, the second dealing with the new architecture. A section on the mile-high building, "The Illinois," Chicago (project), with a foldout illustration, is included.

□ An undated, less expensive edition was reissued by Bramhall House, New York.

□ A British edition was published by The Architectural Press, London, 1959.

□ An Italian edition was published by Editore Einaudi, Turin, 1963.

□ A German edition was published under the title *Ein Testament: Zur neuen Architektur.* Deutsche Ubertragung von Peter Jonas. Hrsg: Ernesto Grassi. Redaktion: Ursula Schwerin und Eginhard Hora. Reinbek bei Hamburg: Rowohlt, 1966.

□ A Japanese edition, translated by Masami and Yoshiko Tanigawa, was published by Shokokusha, Tokyo, 1966.

REVIEWS of the 1957, 1959, and 1963 editions
1150. Atkinson, Fello. *Arch R* CXXVIII (Ag 1960), p. 99. [1959]
1151. Byrne, Barry. "On Frank Lloyd Wright." *Liturg Art* XXVI (Fe 1958), p. 61. [1957]
1152. Hitchcock, Henry-Russell. "Architecture and the Architect." *NYTBR* (17 N 1957), p. 44. [1957]
1153. Kaufmann, Edgar, Jr. "Constructive Vision." *Progress Arch* XXXIX (Mr 1958), pp. 246, 248. [1957]
1154. La Farge, John. "The Master of Taliesin." *America* XCVIII (30 N 1957), pp. 297-8. [1957]

1155.   Martin, Bruce. *RIBA J* LXVII (Jy 1960), p. 340.
[1959]
1156.   Moholy-Nagy, Sibyl. "Frank Lloyd Wright's Testament." *Coll Art J* XVIII (Su 1959), pp. 319-29. [1957]
1157.   Moore, Charles W. "Gospel According to Wright." *Arch Rec* CXXIII (Fe 1958), pp. 58, 62. [1957]
1158.   Rossi, Sara. *Architettura* IX (D 1963), p. 647. [1963]

1159.   Wright, Frank Lloyd. *Oasis: Plan for Arizona State Capitol Submitted by Frank Lloyd Wright, Architect. February 15, 1957.*
31 x 20.3 cm., 5 folded pp., 3 ills.
A publicity announcement intended for distribution to enlist voters' support for Wright's design. The building remained a project.

Periodicals

1160.   Adams, Richard P. "Architecture and the Romantic Tradition: Coleridge to Wright." *Am Q* IX (Sp 1957), pp. 46-62.

1161.   "At 88, Frank Lloyd Wright Still Has a...Career on the Upgrade." *Engin N R* CLIX (5 D 1957), pp. 108, 110, 112, 114, 116 and cover.
Biographical information.

1162.   Boyd, Robin. "Two Ways with Modern Monuments." *Architects' J* CXXV (Ap 1957), pp. 523, 525.
Kaufmann house, "Fallingwater," Bear Run; Robie house, Chicago.

1163.   Buitenhuis, Peter. "Aesthetics of the Skyscraper: The Views of Sullivan, James and Wright." *Am Q* IX (Fa 1957), pp. 316-24.

1164.   "Chicagoans Rally to Save Wright's Robie House." *Arch For* CVI (Mr 1957), p. 9.

1165.   "La contraddizione che non c' è." *Architettura* II (Fe 1957), p. 740.

Mile-high skyscraper, "The Illinois," Chicago (project).

1166. "Una democrazia festosa e aderente alle tradizioni: il 'Capitol' dell'Arizona." *Architettura* III (Ag 1957), p. 250.
Arizona State Capitol, "Oasis," Phoenix (project).

1167. Elken, Ants. "Pilgrimage to the Midwest." *Roy Arch Inst Can J* XXXIV (N 1957), pp. 420-1.

1168. "FLLW Fighting to Design New Arizona Capitol." *Arch For* CVI (Ap 1957), pp. 7, 9.
"Oasis," Phoenix.

1169. "Frank Lloyd Wright: Architecture's Stormy Colossus." *Coronet* XLII (Ag 1957), pp. 83-93.

1170. "Frank Lloyd Wright will 1600 Meter hohen Wolken Kratzer in Chicago bauen." *Neue Heimat* no. 6 (1957), pp. 31-3.
Mile-high skyscraper, "The Illinois," Chicago (project).

1171. Gross, Martin L. "Master of the Broken Rule." *True* XXXVIII (My 1957), pp. 18-20, 22, 24, 26, 122-6.

1172. Huxtable, Ada Louise. "Progressive Architecture in America: Larkin Company Administration Building—1904, Buffalo, New York, Frank Lloyd Wright, Architect." *Progress Arch* XXXVIII (Mr 1957), pp. 141-2.

1173. Johnson, Philip, & Eero Saarinen. "Conversations Regarding the Future of Architecture." *Print* XI (Fe-Mr 1957), pp. 37-9.
Includes a discussion of Wright from the long playing record "Conversations Regarding the Future of Architecture."

1174. Johnson, Philip C. "100 Years, Frank Lloyd Wright and Us." *Pac Arch & Build* LXIII (Mr 1957), pp. 13, 35-6.
From a talk to the Washington State Chapter, AIA.

1175. Kaufmann, Edgar, Jr. "Frank Lloyd Wright: 3 New Churches." *Art in Am* XLV (Fa 1957), pp. 22-5.
Beth Sholom Synagogue, Elkins Park; Annunciation Greek

Orthodox Church, Wauwatosa; Christian Science Church, Bolinas (project).

1176. "Lunch Hour." *New Yorker* XXXIII (10 Ag 1957), pp. 17-18.
Guggenheim Museum, New York.

1177. "The Mile High Illinois." *Arch Rec* CXXI (Mr 1957), p. 250.

1178. "1900's: Birth of an Idea." *H & H* XI (My 1957), p. 116.
Robie house, Chicago.

1179. "One Hundred Years of Significant Building, 9: Houses Since 1907." *Arch Rec* CXXI (Fe 1957), pp. 199-206.
Includes: Robie house, Chicago; Coonley house, Riverside; Wright house, "Taliesin West," Scottsdale; and Kaufmann house, "Fallingwater," Bear Run.

1180. "Our Strongest Influence for Enrichment." *House B* XCIX (Ja 1957), pp. 40-7, 105-6.

1181. Pellegrin, Luigi. "L'ora 'classica' di Wright." *Architettura* II (Fe 1957), pp. 742-5.

1182. Pellegrin, Luigi. "La sintesi culturale del primo Wright." *Architettura* II (Ja 1957), pp. 666-71.

1183. "Perspectives." *Arch Rec* CXXI (Ap 1957), p. 9.
Robie house, Chicago.

1184. [Portrait.] *Time* LXX (11 N 1957), p. 47.

1185. "Proposed State Capitol for Arizona by Frank Lloyd Wright." *Arch For* CVI (Ap 1957), pp. 108a-d.
"Oasis," Phoenix (project).

1186. Ray, David. "Epitaph for a Landmark." *Nation* CLXXXV (28 Se 1957), p. 196 and inside cover.
Robie house, Chicago. A reply from Albert Guerard, "Move

the House," was published 26 October 1957, inside cover.

1187.   Saarinen, Aline B. "Tour with Mr. Wright." *NYTM* (22 Se 1957), pp. 22-3, 69-70.
Guggenheim Museum, New York.

1188.   Schall, James V. "An Architect in the Capital." *America* XCVIII (30 N 1957), p. 265.
Note concerning Wright's speech on architecture at the Washington Institute of Contemporary Arts, October 14.

1189.   "Spite Bill Hits at FLLW Madison Civic Center." *Arch For* CVII (Ag 1957), p. 7.
Monona Terrace (project).

1190.   Stengade, Erik. "Frank Lloyd Wright." *Arkitekten* LIX (no. 10, 1957), pp. 145-55.

1191.   "A Tradition to Preserve: Wright's Robie House." *Interiors* CXVI (My 1957), pp. 10, 12.

1192.   "The Value of Used Architecture: Robie House, Chicago." *Arch For* CVI (Ap 1957), pp. 107-8.

1193.   "View into Unboxed Space at Wright's Taliesin West." *Interiors* CXVII (Ag 1957), p. 101.

1194.   "A Visit with Frank Lloyd Wright." *Look* XXI (17 Se 1957), pp. 28-34, 37.

1195.   Völckers, Otto. "Save the Robie House!" *AIA J* XXVIII (Ag 1957), pp. 247-8.
Translated from *Glas Forum* (see no. 971) by Richard W. E. Perrin. A reply from Karl Kamrath was published in November, p. 420.

1196.   "Wedding Chapel by FLLW with Fountain Below." *Arch For* CVII (O 1957), p. 7.
For Hotel Claremont, Berkeley (project).

1197.   Wiener, Paul Lester. "Titan of Taliesin." *Sat R* XL (21 D 1957), pp. 18-19.

1198.   "Wisconsin Governor Signs Spite Bill That Kills Frank Lloyd Wright's Madison Civic Center." *Arch For* CVII (N 1957), pp. 7, 9.
    Monona Terrace (project).

1199.   Wright, Frank Lloyd. "Architecture and Music." *Sat R* XL (28 Se 1957), pp. 72-3.

1200.   Wright, Frank Lloyd. "The House of the Future." *National Real Estate and Building Journal* LVIII (O 1957), p. 43.
    First published in 1932 (see no. 357).

1201.   Wright, Frank Lloyd. "Frank Lloyd Wright Townhall Lecture, Ford Auditorium, Detroit, Oct. 21, 1957." *Monthly Bulletin, Michigan Society of Architects* XXXI (D 1957), pp. 23, 25, 27, 29, 31-2.

1202.   Wright, Frank Lloyd. "Organic." *Edge* no. 7 (Ag 1957), pp. 4-5.
    Extracted by Ralph Reid from *The Future of Architecture* (1953).

1203.   "Wright Picks a Fight in Arizona: Architect Scorns a Sky-scraper and Offers a Weird Substitute." *Life* XLII (13 My 1957), p. 59.
    Arizona State Capitol, "Oasis," Phoenix (project).

1204.   "Wright, Sandburg Steal Chicago Dynamic Show." *Arch For* CVII (D 1957), pp. 12, 14.

1205.   "Wright to Design Baghdad Opera." *Arch For* CVI (Mr 1957), p. 97.

Plate 1. Title page of *The Eve of St. Agnes,* 1896 (no. 22). Red and black on white paper. 20.3 x 12.4 cm. Courtesy of The Newberry Library, Chicago.

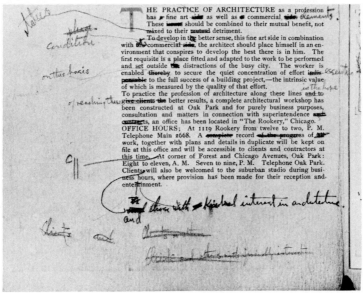

Plate 2. An announcement of Wright's practice of architecture, published ca. 1898 (no. 27). Cover of final version (top). Inside text of preliminary version (bottom) with revisions in the architect's hand, which were incorporated into the final printed text. Both versions are in Avery Library, Columbia University. Red and black on gray paper. 12.3 x 14.3 cm.

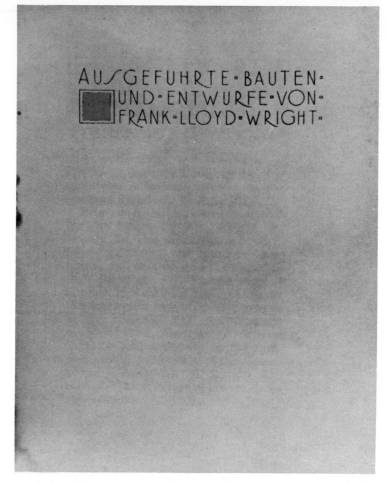

Plate 3. Cover of announcement ca. 1911 (no. 100) describing
the 1910 Wasmuth portfolio and offering it for sale in the
United States. Red and black on tan paper. 15.2 x 11.4 cm.

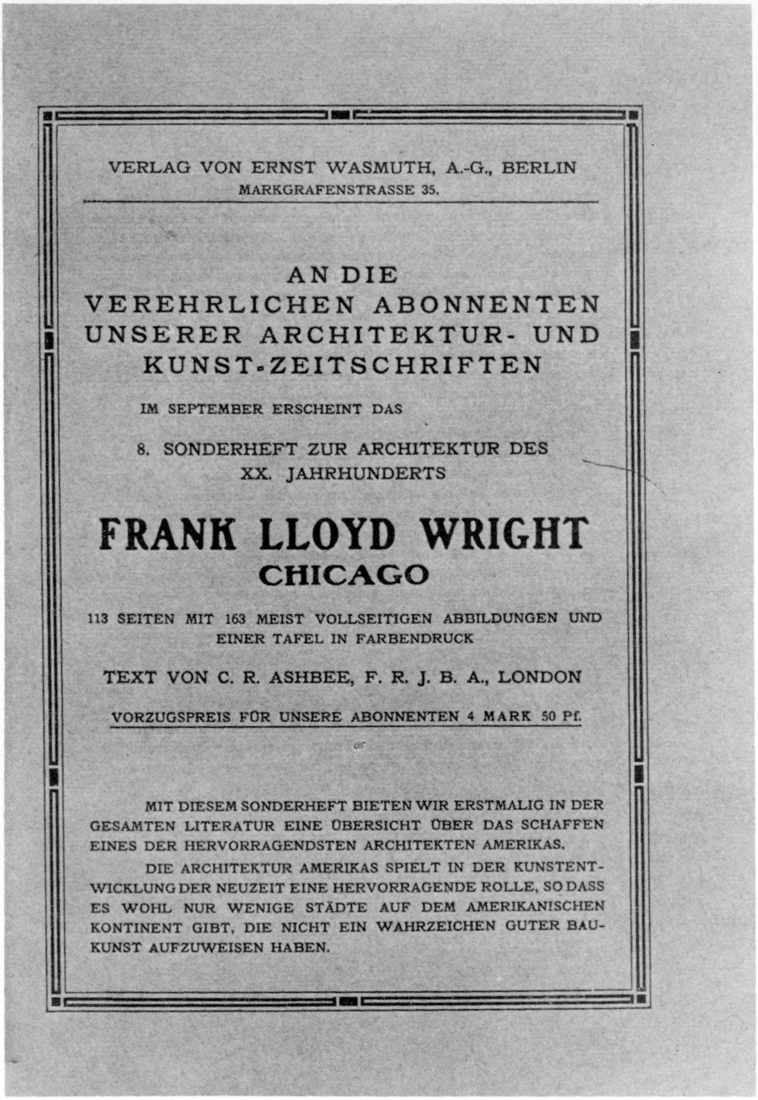

Plate 4. Advertisement for *Frank Lloyd Wright, Chicago,* 1911 (no. 101). This notice appeared in *Berliner Architekturwelt* XIV (1911/12), p. 504, and is not separately described in the bibliography.

THE JAPANESE PRINT

AN INTERPRETATION

BY FRANK LLOYD WRIGHT

THE RALPH FLETCHER SEYMOUR CO.

FINE ARTS BUILDING

CHICAGO MCMXII

Plate 5. Title page of *The Japanese Print: An Interpretation,* 1912 (no. 109). Black on tan paper. 20.8 x 13 cm.

Plate 6. Title page of *Wendingen* VII (no. 3, 1925; bibl. item
no. 168). Black, gray, and red on white paper. 33 x 32.2 cm.
Designed by H. Th. Wijdeveld

Plate 7. Cover of *Town and Country* XCII (July, 1937; bibl.
item no. 415). Red, yellow, blue, and black on white paper.
34.3 x 24.7 cm. Designed in 1926–27. The copy illustrated
is cropped about one-quarter inch at the left margin. Courtesy
of *Town and Country*.

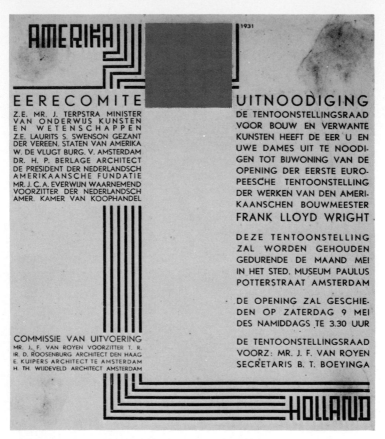

Plate 8. Invitation designed by H. Th. Wijdeveld for opening of Frank Lloyd Wright exhibition in Amsterdam, 9 May 1931. Gray type and red square on cream-colored paper. 22.3 x 19.7 cm. Not separately described in the bibliography.

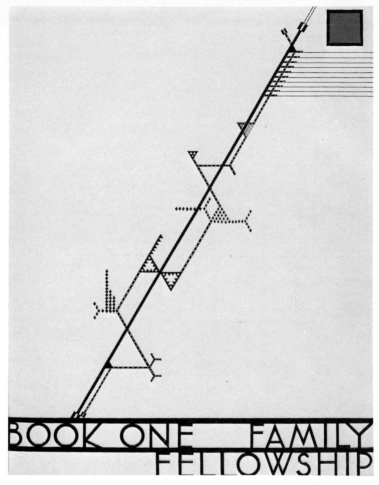

BOOK ONE FAMILY FELLOWSHIP

Plate 9. Title page of Book I of *An Autobiography,* 1932 (no. 303). Black type and design with red square. 22.6 x 18.1 cm.

"Taking the boy by the hand he...started straight across and up the sloping fields toward a point upon which he had fixed his keen blue eyes.

Neither to right nor to left...straight forward he walked...

But...the boy...ran first left, to gather beads on stems... Then right, to gather prettier ones." (Page 1)

Plate 10. Cover of *The Taliesin Fellowship*, December, 1933 (no. 2036). Red on white paper. 21.6 x 21.6 cm.

Plate 11. Internal title page (folded) of *Architectural Forum* LXVIII (January, 1938; bibl. item no. 457). Black and red on cream-colored paper. 30.2 x 22.2 cm.

Plate 12. Cover of *Taliesin* I, no. 1, October, 1940 (no. 2040).
Printed in red and black on white paper. 21.8 x 21.7 cm.

1958

Books

1206.   Manson, Grant Carpenter. *Frank Lloyd Wright to 1910: The First Golden Age.* With a foreword by Henry-Russell Hitchcock. New York: Reinhold Publishing Corporation, [1958].
   25.9 x 21 cm., x, 228 pp., front., 135 ills., buckram.

   An analysis and discussion of the architect's work up to his departure for Europe in 1909. This study was expanded from Manson's 1940 unpublished Ph.D. dissertation, Harvard University. Manson met Wright and was given access to the archives of photographs, drawings, and plans at Taliesin. Appendix A: program transcribed from the catalogue of the University of Wisconsin for the academic year 1885-86. Appendix B: list, transcribed from pertinent editions of The Lakeside City Directory of Chicago, of downtown offices occupied by Wright between 1890 and 1912. Appendix C: list of Japanese printmakers represented in Wright's collection at the time of forced sale at Anderson Galleries, New York, 1927. Appendix D: list of designs and objects exhibited by Wright in the Chicago Architectural Club Annual Exhibitions between 1894 and 1907. Appendix E: list of commissions in which Wright and Webster Tomlinson collaborated. Appendix F: list and discussion concerning the assistants employed at the Oak Park Studio. Bibliography of books and periodicals, pp. 219-22. A map of Oak Park and River Forest, Illinois showing the locations of buildings designed by Wright, appears on the endpapers. Although the many works of Wright discussed in this book are not listed individually in this description, entries for all of them appear in the building index. A statement printed on the dust wrapper indicates that two additional volumes of Mr. Manson's biography of Wright were to be forthcoming. These did not appear.
   □ The book was distributed in London by Chapman and Hall.
   □ An Italian edition was published as *Frank Lloyd Wright: la prima età d'oro.* Roma: Officina Edizioni, [1969].

REVIEWS of the 1958 and 1969 editions
1207.   Anonymous. *Arch For* CVIII (Ap 1958), p. 157. [1958]
1208.   Anonymous. *Werk* XLVI (O 1959), sup. pp. 222-3.
   [1958]

1209.   Brooks, H. A. "The Spontaneous Genius." *Progress Arch* XXXIX (Se 1958), pp. 226, 229-30. [1958]

1210.   Gebhard, David. *Coll Art J* XVIII (Sp 1959), pp. 277-9. [1958]

1211.   Jordy, William H. *Arts* XXXII (Se 1958), p. 16. [1958]

1212.   Kaufmann, Edgar, Jr. "Manson's Wright, Volume I." *Interiors* CXVII (Mr 1958), p. 20. [1958]

1213.   Morrison, Hugh. "Wright's Early Years Portrayed." *Arch Rec* CXXV (Ja 1959), pp. 60, 64. [1958]

1214.   Pica, Agnoldomenico. *Domus* no. 485 (Ap 1970), p. 10. [1969]

1215.   Tselos, Dimitri. *JSAH* XVII (W 1958), p. 39. [1958]

1216.   Nickel, Richard. *Frank Lloyd Wright Negatives at Chicago Architectural Photo Co.* 1958.
   An unpublished list in the Burnham Library, Chicago Art Institute.

1217.   Preston, Charles and Edward A. Hamilton, eds. "Frank Lloyd Wright." In *Mike Wallace Asks: Highlights from 46 Controversial Interviews.* New York: Simon and Schuster, 1958. Pp. 122-8.

1218.   Wright, Frank Lloyd. *The Living City.* New York: Horizon Press, 1958.
   25.3 x 20.2 cm., 222 pp., front., 51 ills. and a folded color map of Broadacre City, cloth.
   A rewritten version of *The Disappearing City* (no. 328) and *When Democracy Builds* (no. 609). It includes detailed plans for Broadacre City, completed in 1958.
   □ An undated, less expensive edition was reissued by Bramhall House, New York.
   □ A Japanese edition, translated by Masami and Yoshiko Tanigawa, was published by Shokokusha, Tokyo, 1968.

REVIEWS of the 1958 edition

1219.   Feiss, Carl. "Broadacre City Revisited: FLW's Restatement, with Embellishments." *Progress Arch* XL (Jy 1959), pp. 181-2, 188.

1220.   Thabit, Walter. *Am Inst Plan J* XXV (Ag 1959), pp. 163-4.

1221.   Weinberg, Robert C. *Am Inst Plan J* XXVII (N 1961), p. 354.

Periodicals

1222.   "Autoist Gets Eyeful for Tankful." *Engin N R* CLXI (30 O 1958), p. 28.
    Lindholm service station, Cloquet.

1223.   Bendiner, Alfred. "How Frank Lloyd Wright Got His Medal." *Harper* CCXVI (My 1958), pp. 30-5 and cover.
    Gold medal of the Philadelphia Chapter of the American Institute of Architects awarded to Wright.

1224.   Blake, Peter. "Frank Lloyd Wright: Master of Architectural Space." *Arch For* CIX (Se 1958), pp. 120-5, 196-7.

1225.   "Chicago Dynamic." *Am Inst Plan J* XXIX (Ja 1958), pp. 18-20.
    Excerpts from a conversation between Frank Lloyd Wright and Carl Sandburg, guided by Alistair Cooke.

1226.   Cohen, George N. "Frank Lloyd Wright's Guggenheim Museum." *Concrete Construction* III (Mr 1958), pp. 10-13 and cover.

1227.   "Commencement." *New Yorker* XXXIV (14 Je 1958), pp. 26-7.
    Note on Wright's appearance at Sarah Lawrence College.

1228.   "A Famous House Rescued." *Arch For* CVIII (Fe 1958), p. 69.
    Robie house, Chicago.

1229.   "Flat on Our Faces." *New Repub* CXXXIX (8 Se 1958), pp. 14-15.
    Interview edited by Henry Brandon.

1230.   "FLLW Has Friends, Foes in Civic Center Feud." *Pac Arch & Build* LXIV (My 1958), p. 8.
    Marin County Civic Center, San Rafael.

1231. "Four Current Projects in the News." *Arch Rec* CXXIV (Jy 1958), pp. 148-9.
Includes Juvenile Cultural Study Center, University of Wichita.

1232. "Frank Lloyd Wright and the Toronto City Hall." *Builder* CXCV (10 O 1958), p. 615.
Interview by Pierre Berton.

1233. "Frank Lloyd Wright: A Selection of Current Work." *Arch Rec* CXXIII (My 1958), pp. 167-90 and cover.
Includes: Dallas Theater Center; Monona Terrace Civic Center, Madison (project); Music Building, Florida Southern College (project); Bramlett Motor Hotel, Memphis (project); Christian Science Church, Bolinas (project); Annunciation Greek Orthodox Church, Wauwatosa; Beth Sholom Synagogue, Elkins Park; Guggenheim Museum, New York, and a statement by Wright, "The Solomon R. Guggenheim Memorial."

1234. "Frank Lloyd Wright Designs for Baghdad." *Arch For* CVIII (My 1958), pp. 89-101 and cover.
Plan for greater Baghdad. Text excerpted from Wright's submission to the Development Board of Iraq.

1235. "Frank Lloyd Wright on Restaurant Architecture." *Food Service Magazine* XX (N 1958), pp. 17-21, 32.
An interview. It includes illustrations of and comments on the Yosemite National Park Restaurant (project).

1236. "The Guggenheim Progresses." *Progress Arch* XXXIX (Ja 1958), p. 77.

1237. " 'House of the Century' Gets a Reprieve from Demolition." *H & H* XIII (Fe 1958), p. 68.
Robie house, Chicago.

1238. Kaufmann, Edgar, Jr. "The Form of Space for Art—Wright's Guggenheim Museum." *Art in Am* XLVI (W 1958–59), pp. 74-7.

1239. Kultermann, Udo. "Frank Lloyd Wright und seine Nach-
folge." *Bauen und Wohnen* XII (O 1958), pp. 253-4.

1240. "The Latter Days of Frank Lloyd Wright." *Esquire* XLIX
(Fe 1958), pp. 52-4.

1241. "A Master Builder's Philosophy—Excerpts from Frank
Lloyd Wright's *Testament*." *H & H* XIII (Ja 1958), pp. 135-41.

1242. "Meetings and Miscellany." *Arch Rec* CXXIII (My 1958),
p. 24.
     Note on Wright's receipt of a medal from the National Con-
crete Masonry Institute.

1243. Mitgang, Herbert. "Sidewalk Views of That Museum."
NYTM (12 O 1958), pp. 14, 73.
     Guggenheim Museum, New York.

1244. "New Art Form in Minnesota." *Fortune* LVIII (O 1958),
p. 71.
     Lindholm service station, Cloquet.

1245. "No Oscar for Wright." *Arch For* CVIII (My 1958), pp.
79, 81.
     Wright offered part in movie "A Farewell to Arms."

1246. Oboler, Arch. "He's Always Magnificently Wright."
Reader's Digest LXXII (Fe 1958), pp. 49-54.
     Oboler house, Malibu.

1247. "P/A News Bulletins." *Progress Arch* XXXIX (Jy 1958),
p. 45.
     Wright named architect for Juvenile Cultural Study Center,
University of Wichita.

1248. Robie, Fred C., and Fred C. Robie, Sr. "Mr. Robie Knew
What He Wanted." *Arch For* CIX (O 1958), pp. 126-7, 206, 210.
     Robie house, Chicago.

1249. "Robie House Saved." *Hist Pres* X (no. 1, 1958), p. 14.

1250.   "Three New Houses by Frank Lloyd Wright." *H & H* XIV
(Ag 1958), pp. 101-13 and cover.
 Harper house, St. Joseph; Thaxton house, Bunker Hill (Houston); Austin house, Greenville.

1251.   "Wright Designs an Elementary School 'Teaching Laboratory' for Wichita University." *Arch For* CIX (Jy 1958), p. 9.
 Juvenile Cultural Study Center.

1252.   Wright, Frank Lloyd. "Away with the Realtor." *Esquire*
L (O 1958), pp. 179-80.

1253.   Wright, Frank Lloyd. "Education and Art in Behalf of
Life." *Arts in Society* I (Ja 1958), pp. 5-10.
 From tape-recorded comments to the editors of *Arts in
Society.*

1254.   Wright, Frank Lloyd. "Frank Lloyd Wright Talks on Prefabrication." *H & H* XIII (Ap 1958), pp. 120-2.
 Extracted from a talk given in 1958.

1255.   Wright, Frank Lloyd. "Mr. Wright's Agronomy." *Arch For*
CVIII (Fe 1958), p. 150.
 Excerpts from remarks before the Chicago Dynamic Forum.

1256.   Wright, Frank Lloyd. "This Is American Architecture."
Design LIX (Ja-Fe 1958), pp. 112-13, 128.
 Text of a speech delivered to a group of high school students
in Chicago.

1257.   Wright, Frank Lloyd. "What Is Architecture?" *Arch For*
CVIII (My 1958), p. 102.
 From the London lectures (1939).

1258.   Wright, John Lloyd. "In My Father's Shadow." *Esquire*
XLIX (Fe 1958), pp. 55-7.

1259.   "Wright to Design Dome Theater for Mike Todd." *Arch
For* CVIII (Fe 1958), p. 61.
 Todd-AO Universal Theatres (project).

1959

Books

1260. The American Federation of Arts. "Frank Lloyd Wright."
In *Form Givers at Mid-Century.* N.p.: [Time, Inc., 1959]. Pp. 12-
17.

A catalogue for a traveling exhibition organized and sponsored by *Time* magazine. The section on Wright is illustrated
with some of his most frequently published buildings and includes quotations from *An American Architecture* (no. 1050),
and *A Testament* (no. 1149).

1261. Cohen, Mortimer J. *Beth Sholom Synagogue: A Description and Interpretation.* [Elkins Park, Pennsylvania: Beth Sholom
Synagogue], 1959.

25.4 x 17.5 cm., 34 pp., 18 ills. (part color), cloth.

A paperback edition was also published.

REVIEW
1262. Anonymous. *Prairie Sch R* II (no. 1, 1965), p. 26.

1263. Forsee, Aylesa. *Frank Lloyd Wright, Rebel in Concrete.*
Philadelphia: Macrae Smith Company, [1959].

22.8 x 15.1 cm., x, 182 pp., front., 20 ills., cloth.

A juvenile biography.

□ A Brazilian edition was published under the title *Frank Lloyd
Wright, vida e obra.* Tradução de Manuela Gerardi. Belo Horizonte: Editôra Itatiana Limitada, 1962. (Coleção o homen e a
obra 2)

1264. Karpel, Bernard. *Frank Lloyd Wright: Selected Works by
Wright.* [New York]: *House Beautiful,* 1959.

27.9 x 21.5 cm., 10 pp., paper.

An annotated list of seventy-nine citations by Wright, dating
from 1897 to 1959; a list of articles by others, 1955–59; and
general references, 1955–59. This publication supplements the
list compiled by Karpel and published in 1955 (no. 1046).
This supplement was issued in conjunction with the October
1959 *House Beautiful* (no. 1374).

1265.   Wright, Frank Lloyd. *Drawings for a Living Architecture.*
New York: Published for the Bear Run Foundation Inc. and the
Edgar J. Kaufmann Charitable Foundation by Horizon Press,
1959.
 29.1 x 34.4 cm., 255 pp., 200 ills. (part color), cloth.

 A collection of original sketches and presentation drawings
dating from 1885 to 1958, and chosen at Taliesin under the
architect's supervision. Although the many projects and buildings illustrated in this bock are not listed individually in this
description, entries for all of them will be found in the building index. The book includes two introductions: ''The Architecture of Frank Lloyd Wright,'' by Giuseppe Samonà (from
the *Architects' Year Book,* no. 964); and "Frank Lloyd
Wright's Drawings," by A. Hyatt Mayor.

REVIEWS
1266.   Anonymous. "FLLW's Drawings." *Arch For* III (D
     1959), pp. 119-26.
1267.   Atkinson, Fello. *Arch R* CXXVIII (Ag 1960), p. 99.
1268.   Gutheim, Frederick. "Wright's Creative Process Shown
     in Drawings." *Arch Rec* CXXVI (D 1959), pp. 66, 70.
1269.   Hitchcock, H.-R. *JSAH* XIX (O 1960), pp. 129-31.
1270.   Hurley, D. J. "Wrightian Triplet: Review of Three
     Recent Books." *Liturg Art* XXVIII (Ag 1960), pp. 114-15.
1271.   Jacobus, John M., Jr. *Art B* XLII (Je 1960), pp. 166-7.
1272.   Jordy, William H. *Arts* XXXIV (My 1960), pp. 19, 71.
1273.   Tafel, Edgar. *Progress Arch* XLI (D 1960), pp. 184,
     190.

1274.   Wright, Olgivanna Lloyd. *Our House.* New York: Horizon
Press, 1959.
 21.5 x 13.3 cm., 308 pp., front., cloth.

 Selections from Mrs. Wright's column which ran in the *Madison Capital Times.* The dust wrapper was designed by Eugene
Masselink.

REVIEW
1275.   Anonymous. *Arch For* CX (Je 1959), p. 193.

Periodicals

1276. "Art d'aujourd'hui, musée de demain." *L'Oeil* LX (D 1959), pp. 106-11.
Guggenheim Museum, New York.

1277. Atkinson, Fello. "Frank Lloyd Wright, 1869–1959." *Architects' J* CXXIX (16 Ap 1959), pp. 571-3.

1278. Banham, Reyner. "Master of Freedom." *New Statesman* LVII (18 Ap 1959), pp. 543-4.
Eulogy.

1279. Blake, Peter. "The Guggenheim: Museum or Monument?" *Arch For* CXI (D 1959), pp. 86-93, 180, 184.
Also in *Kokusai Kentiku* (Mr 1960).

1280. Bloc, André, and others. "Frank Llyod [sic] Wright 1869–1959." *Arch d'Aujourd'hui* XXX (Ap 1959), pp. 2-3.
Obituaries; also by Marcel Lods and Alexandre Persitz.

1281. Bloc, André. "Depuis Wright, quoi de neuf?" *Arts* (Paris), no. 719 (22-29 Ap 1959), pp. 1, 9.

1282. "Buildings in the News." *Arch Rec* CXXVI (D 1959), p. 12.
Guggenheim Museum, New York.

1283. Bush-Brown, Albert. "The Honest Arrogance of Frank Lloyd Wright." *Atlantic* CCIV (Ag 1959), pp. 23-6.
A reply from Robert L. Wright was published in October, pp. 32-3.

1284. Carlos, John James. "Frank Lloyd Wright: Michelangelo of the 20th Century." *Architectural and Engineering News* I (My 1959), p. 7.
Eulogy.

1285. "Christmas Present for Dallas: A Theater by Wright." *Progress Arch* XL (D 1959), p. 79.
Dallas Theater Center.

1286.   Cooke, Alistair. "Memories of Frank Lloyd Wright."
AIA J XXXII (O 1959), pp. 42-4.
Reprinted from *Manchester Guardian Weekly,* 16 Ap 1959.

1287.   De Reus, Jim. "What We Learned from Frank Lloyd
Wright." *H & H* XV (Fe 1959), pp. 126-33.

1288.   Dudok, W. M. "Bij het overlijden van Frank Lloyd
Wright." *Bouwkundig Weekblad* LXXVII (7 N 1959), pp. 532-4.

1289.   Eaton, Leonard K. "Frame of Steel." *Arch R* CXXVI (N
1959), p. 289.
Includes note on E Z Polish Factory, Chicago.

1290.   "An Exhibition, Midland, Michigan, January 11th through
31st, 1959." *Monthly Bulletin, Michigan Society of Architects*
XXXIII (Ja 1959), pp. 34-5.

1291.   Ferraz, Geraldo. "Posicão de Frank Lloyd Wright." *Habitat* IX (Mr 1959), p. 1.

1292.   "The Finale at 89 for a Fiery Genius: Death Ends Wright's
Flamboyant Career." *Life* XLVI (27 Ap 1959), p. 53.

1293.   "First View of the Guggenheim." *Art N* LVIII (N 1959),
pp. 46-7.

1294.   Fitch, James Marston. "Frank Lloyd Wright, 1869–1959."
Arch For CX (My 1959), pp. 108-15.
Includes statements from numerous architects, critics, and
others.

1295.   "FLLW's Drawings." *Arch For* CXI (D 1959), pp. 119-
26.
Illustrations from *Drawings for a Living Architecture* (no.
1265), reproduced in color.

1296.   "Franck Lloyd Wright est mort." *Arts* (Paris) no. 719
(22-29 Ap 1959), p. 1.

1297. "Frank Lloyd Wright." *Arch & Build N* CCXV (15 Ap 1959), p. 467.

Note on Wright's death.

1298. "Frank Lloyd Wright." *Arch For* CX (Je 1959), pp. 115-46 and cover. (Also issued as offprint.)

Special portfolio reviewing Wright's career.

1299. "Frank Lloyd Wright." *Casabella* no. 227 (My 1959), pp. 1-28 and cover.

Includes articles by Ernesto N. Rogers, Enzo Paci, Sibyl Moholy-Nagy, Edoardo Persico, Gillo Dorfles, and Filippo Sacchi.

1300. "Frank Lloyd Wright." *Der Aufbau* XIV (Ag 1959), pp. 303-6.

1301. "Frank Lloyd Wright Designed This Big 'One-Space' Pre-fab." *H & H* XVI (Ag 1959), pp. 176-7.

Pre-fab no. 2 (Rudin), Madison.

1302. "Frank Lloyd Wright, 1869–1959." *Arch Rec* CXXV (My 1959), p. 9.

1303. "Frank Lloyd Wright (1869–1959)." *H & H* XV (My 1959), pp. 95, 98.

1304. "Frank Lloyd Wright 1869–1959." *Progress Arch* XL (My 1959), p. 135.

1305. "Frank Lloyd Wright: Ein Testament." *Werk* XLVI (D 1959), pp. 427-8.

Excerpts from *A Testament* (no. 1149).

1306. "Frank Lloyd Wright in Michigan." *AIA Monthly Bulletin, Michigan Society of Architects* XXXIII (D 1959), pp. 17-32 and cover. (Also issued as offprint without advertising; offprint reprinted, March, 1969.)

Special issue prepared by the Saginaw Valley Chapter of the American Institute of Architects. Includes: photographs of the

Anthony house, Benton Harbor; Affleck house, Bloomfield
Hills; Palmer house, Ann Arbor; Wall house, Plymouth;
Goetsch-Winkler house, Okemos; Meyer house, Galesburg;
McCartney house, Kalamazoo; Smith house, Bloomfield Hills;
and Meyer [sic] (should be May) house, Grand Rapids. Also
contains a complete list of homes constructed in Michigan.
Cover and frontispiece designed by Phil H. Feddersen.

1307.   "Frank Lloyd Wright." *AIA J* XXXI (My 1959), pp. 42-3.
   Obituary.

1308.   "Frank Lloyd Wright." *Nation's Schools* LXIII (Je 1959),
pp. 47-8.
   Discussion concerning his influence on school architecture.

1309.   "Frank Lloyd Wright." *New Repub* CXL (20 Ap 1959),
p. 4.
   Obituary.

1310.   "Frank Lloyd Wright." *Pacific Arts Association Bulletin*
(Su 1959), pp. 2-19, 21-7 and cover.
   Special issue on Wright. Includes articles by Walter R. Bim-
   son, Eugene Masselink, and Dr. Harry Wood.

1311.   "Frank Lloyd Wright." *Sele Arte* VII (Jy-Ag 1959), p.
3-14.
   Italian text. Includes photographs of models for several
   projects of the 1940's.

1312.   "Frank Lloyd Wright's Own Home in the Desert." *H & H*
XV (Je 1959), pp. 88-98.
   "Taliesin West," Scottsdale.

1313.   "Frank Lloyd Wright's Sole Legacy to New York." *Interiors* CXIX (D 1959), pp. 88-95.
   Guggenheim Museum.

1314.   Gebhard, David. "A Note on the Chicago Fair of 1893
and Frank Lloyd Wright." *JSAH* XVIII (My 1959), pp. 63-5.
   Includes a photograph of Cummings Real Estate office,
   River Forest.

1315.   Gill, Brendon [sic]. "Eine Begegnung mit Frank Lloyd Wright." *Bauen und Wohnen* XIII (Je 1959), pp. VI 6, VI 8.
　　Obituary. Translated from an unsigned article in the *New Yorker* (see no. 1343).

1316.   "The Great Dissenter." *Newsweek* LIII (20 Ap 1959), pp. 98-9.
　　Obituary.

1317.   "Guggenheim Museum Spirals toward Completion: Photographs Reveal Interiors at Last." *Progress Arch* XL (Jy 1959), pp. 75-7.

1318.   Hitchcock, Henry-Russell. "Frank Lloyd Wright, 1869–1959." *RIBA J* LXVI (Ag 1959), pp. 341-2 and cover.

1319.   Hitchcock, Henry-Russell. "Frank Lloyd Wright, 1867(?)–1959." *Art N* LVIII (My 1959), p. 25.

1320.   Holden, A. C. "Is this Death? For Frank Lloyd Wright." *AIA J* XXXI (Je 1959), p. 33.

1321.   "The House One Man Built." *Life* XLVII (28 D 1959), p. 92.
　　Berger house, San Anselmo.

1322.   Huxtable, Ada Louise. "Triple Legacy of Mr. Wright." *NYTM* (15 N 1959), pp. 18-19.
　　Review of buildings and projects.

1323.   Jones, Cranston. "Pride and Prejudices of the Master." *Life* XLVI (27 Ap 1959), pp. 54-6.

1324.   Jordan, R. Furneaux. "Frank Lloyd Wright: A Personal Impression." *Arch & Build N* CCXV (15 Ap 1959), pp. 464-7.

1325.   Jordy, William H. "Frank Lloyd Wright, 1869–1959." *Arts* XXXIII (My 1959), pp. 15, 68.

1326.   Kellogg, Cynthia. "Wright Ready-made." *NYTM* (25 O

1959), pp. 62-4.
Pre-fab no. 2 (Rudin), Madison.

1327. Kiesler, Frederick J. "Frank Lloyd Wright." *It Is* no. 4 (Au 1959), p. 27.
Obituary.

1328. Kramer, Hilton. "Month in Review." *Arts* XXXIV (D 1959), pp. 48-51.
Guggenheim Museum, New York.

1329. "Last Monument." *Time* LXXIV (2 N 1959), p. 67.
Guggenheim Museum, New York.

1330. Levin, E. A. "Frank Lloyd Wright: An Appreciation." *Habitat* II (My-Je 1959), pp. 21-4.
Eulogy.

1331. Lynes, Russell. "Mr. Wright's Museum." *Harper* CCXIX (N 1959), pp. 96, 98-100.
Guggenheim Museum, New York.

1332. Maluquer, J. M. Sostres. "Frank Lloyd Wright, el genio de la transición." *Cuadernos de Arquitectura* no. 35 (1959), pp. 2-4.

1333. McAuliffe, George. "The Guggenheim: Great Architecture, Difficult Installation." *Industrial Design* VI (N 1959), pp. 66-9.

1334. Moholy-Nagy, Sibyl. "F. Ll. W. and Ageing of Modern Architecture." *Progress Arch* XL (My 1959), pp. 136-42.
Also in *Perspective* (1959), pp. 40-5 (not seen).

1335. Morassutti, Bruno. "Ricordo di Frank Lloyd Wright." *Domus* no. 356 (Jy 1959), pp. 25-6.

1336. Moser, Werner M. "Die Bedeutung Frank Lloyd Wrights für die Entwicklung der Gegenwartsarchitektur." *Werk* XLVI (D 1959), pp. 423-7.

1337.   Moser, Werner M. "Frank Lloyd Wright." *Bouwkundig Weekblad* LXXVII (7 N 1959), pp. 535-43.

1338.   Moser, Werner M. "Hommage à Frank Lloyd Wright, 1869-1959." *Architecture, Formes et Fonctions* VI (1959), p. 115.

1339.   Mumford, Lewis. "The Skyline: What Wright Hath Wrought." *New Yorker* XXXV (5 D 1959), pp. 105-6, 108, 110, 112, 115-16, 118, 120, 122, 127-8, 130.

1340.   "Il Museo Guggenheim si è aperto al pubblico." *Casabella* no. 234 (D 1959), p. 50.

1341.   "Native Genius." *Time* LXXIII (20 Ap 1959), pp. 80, 83.
   Obituary.

1342.   "News and Comment." *JA* XXXIV (Jy 1959), p. 3.
   Comment on Wright's death.

1343.   "Notes and Comment." *New Yorker* XXXV (18 Ap 1959), pp. 33-4.
   Obituary. Also in *Bauen und Wohnen* (see no. 1315).

1344.   [Obituary.] *Arch R* CXXV (Je 1959), p. 373.

1345.   [Obituary.] *Arts & Arch* LXXVI (My 1959), p. 12.

1346.   [Obituary.] *Builder* CXCVI (17 Ap 1959), p. 735.

1347.   [Obituary.] *Commonwealth* LXX (24 Ap 1959), p. 94.

1348.   [Obituary.] *Architettura* V (My 1959), pp. 4-5.

1349.   [Obituary.] *RIBA J* s3 LXVI (Ag 1959), p. 369.

1350.   "P/A News Report." *Progress Arch* XL (Ag 1959), p. 79.
   Pre-fab no. 1 (Cass), Staten Island.

1351.   Peters, Matthew. "Two Domes." *Arch For* CXI (D 1959), p. 205.

Letter comparing the dome of the Guggenheim Museum
with one at the Vatican.

1352.   [Portrait.] *Architettura* V (Ag 1959), p. 282.

1353.   Rago, Louise Elliott, ed. "Frank Lloyd Wright's Last
Interview." *School Arts* LVIII (Je 1959), pp. 27-30.

1354.   Richards, John Noble. "Frank Lloyd Wright's Funeral,
April 12, 1959: Impressions Written on an Airplane." *AIA J*
XXXI (My 1959), p. 44.

1355.   Roth, Alfred. "Frank Lloyd Wright 8. Juni 1869 bis 9.
April 1959." *Werk* XLVI (My 1959), front.

1356.   Samton, Claude. "Frank Lloyd Wright." *Cuadernos de
Arquitectura* no. 36 (1959), pp. 61-4.

1357.   Seaux, J. "Frank Lloyd Wright." *Habiter* X (N 1959),
pp. 389-90.

1358.   Sekler, Eduard F. "Frank Lloyd Wright zum Gedächtnis."
Der Aufbau XIV (Ag 1959), pp. 299-302.

1359.   Shand, P. Morton. "Holland and Frank Lloyd Wright."
Arch Assn J LXXV (Ja 1959), pp. 179-83.
    Reprinted from *Architectural Review* (see no. 391).

1360.   *South African Architectural Record.* XLIV (Se 1959),
pp. 18-40 and cover.
    Special issue on Wright. Includes articles by John Fassler,
Richard Neutra, Gilbert Herbert, and Montie Simon.

1361.   Stone, Edward Durell. "Hero, Prophet, Adventurer."
Sat R XLII (7 N 1959), pp. 15-17, 43.

1362.   Strutt, J. W., and others. "Frank Lloyd Wright, 1869–
1959." *Roy Arch Inst Can J* XXXVI (Je 1959), pp. 202-4.
    Additional essays by H. Allen Brooks, Jr., and Inigo Adam-
son.

1363. "Taliesen [sic] Workshops." *Architectural and Engineering News* I (My 1959), pp. 4-5.

Note that Wright's work will be carried on by the Frank Lloyd Wright Foundation.

1364. "Tributes to Frank Lloyd Wright—1869–1959." *Arch For* CX (Je 1959), pp. 234, 238, 242, 246.

1365. "Two Projects in California's Marin County, One in Montana among Frank Lloyd Wright's Last." *Pac Arch & Build* LXV (Je 1959), pp. 12-13.

Marin County Civic Center, San Rafael; Christian Science Church, Bolinas (project); Lockridge Medical Clinic, Whitefish.

1366. "Le ultime creazioni di Frank Lloyd Wright." *L'Architettura* V (N 1959), pp. 472-83.

Jones chapel, Norman (project); Lenkurt Electric administration building and factory, San Mateo (project); Donahoe house, Paradise Valley (project).

1367. "Watch on Wright Landmarks." *Arch Rec* CXXVI (Se 1959), p. 9.

Sixteen buildings selected by the American Institute of Architects and the National Trust for Historic Preservation for recommendation as landmarks.

1368. "A Westerner Views the Museum." *Pac Arch & Build* LXV (D 1959), p. 50.

Guggenheim Museum, New York.

1369. "Who's W(right) in Montana?" *Pac Arch & Build* LXV (Ag 1959), p. 48.

Inquiry from a reader concerning a house in Billings with certain Wrightian characteristics but which was not in fact designed by him.

1370. "Wright Dies at 89." *Arch For* CX (My 1959), p. 5.

1371. Wright, Frank Lloyd. "A Culture of Our Own." *Progressive* XXIII (Ja 1959), pp. 70-2.

1372.   "Wright's Imperial Hotel." *Arch For* CX (Je 1959), p. 11.

1373.   "Wright's Legacy: Culture in the Southwest." *Arch For* CXI (Ag 1959), p. 9.
   Grady Gammage Memorial Auditorium, Tempe; Dallas Theater Center.

1374.   "Your Heritage from Frank Lloyd Wright." *House B* CI (O 1959), pp. 207-58, 260, 262, 266, 268-72, 275-82, 285-92, 295-302, 305-9, 313-20, 326-32, 334-6 and cover.
   The second special issue of *House Beautiful* devoted to Frank Lloyd Wright; the first was published in November, 1955 (see no. 1066). Also offered in a hard-cover edition. Includes: "How Frank Lloyd Wright Used Music," and "Shelter that Encloses Without Confining," by Curtis Besinger; "The Essence of Frank Lloyd Wright's Contribution," "Wright's Way with Little Things," and "Exploding the Box to Gain Spaciousness," by Elizabeth Gordon; "The Open Plan—a Way to Gain Spaciousness," by Guy Henle; and "Interior Space as Architectural Poetry," by John deKoven Hill. A bibliography of writings by and about Wright was prepared concurrently with this issue (no. 1264).

1375.   Zevi, Bruno. "Taliesin continua." *Architettura* V (O 1959), pp. 366-7.

1376.   "Zum Tode Frank Lloyd Wrights." *Baukunst und Werkform* XII (Je 1959), p. 330.
   Obituary.

1377.   "Zum Tod von Frank Lloyd Wright." *Baumeister* LVI (Je 1959), pp. 410-11.

1960

Books

1378.   Andrews, Leonard E. B., ed. *Dallas Theater Center.*
   21 x 25.3 cm., 38 pp., 27 ills. (part color), cloth.
   A book describing the theater and its uses. It includes

articles by Robert D. Stecker, Paul Baker, Jane Scholl, Eliot Elisofon, Allen R. Bromberg, Lon Tinkle, John Rosenfield, Virgil Miers, Harwell Hamilton Harris, W. Kelly Oliver, Gene McKinney, Aline de Grandchamp, and Ramsey Yelvington. A paperback edition also was published.

1379.   Blake, Peter. *The Master Builders: Le Corbusier, Mies van der Rohe, Frank Lloyd Wright.* New York: Alfred A. Knopf, 1960.

24.1 x 17 cm., xiii, 399 pp., 135 ills., cloth.

A biography; each architect is treated in a separate section.
□ A British edition was published by Gollancz, London, 1960.
□ The section on Wright was published separately in a paperback edition entitled *Frank Lloyd Wright: Architecture and Space.* Baltimore and Harmondsworth, Middlesex: Penguin, [1964].
□ A South American edition was published under the title *Maestros de la arquitectura.* Buenos Aires: Editorial Víctor Lerú S.R.L.
□ A new paperback edition with additional material was published by W. W. Norton & Company, New York, [1976].

REVIEWS of the 1960, 1964 and British editions
1380.   Anonymous. *AIA J* XXXIV (N 1960), p. 84. [1960]
1381.   Anonymous. *Prairie Sch R* II (no. 1, 1965), p. 25. [1964]
1382.   Barry, Gerald. "Holy Trinity." *Arch R* CXXIX (Ap 1961), p. 227. [British]
1383.   Brown, Theodore M. *JSAH* XX (D 1961), pp. 200-1. [1960]
1384.   Fitch, George H. "Hero of the Future: The City." *Progress Arch* XLII (Ap 1961), pp. 204, 210. [1960]
1385.   Hurley, David Jeremiah. *Liturg Art* XXIX (My 1961), pp. 82-3. [1960]
1386.   Semerani, Luciano. *Casabella* no. 268 (O 1962), p. 56. [1960]
1387.   Weinberg, Robert C. *Am Inst Plan J* XXVII (N 1961), pp. 352-3. [1960]

1388.   Caronia, Giuseppe. *L'opera e il messaggio di Frank Lloyd*

Wright. [Palermo: 1960.]
    23.7 x 16.9 cm., 20 pp., 20 ills. (Quaderni della Facoltà di
Architettura dell Università di Palermo.)
    Published in conjunction with a conference held 26 March
1960 to coincide with the first anniversary of Wright's death.
Italian text.

1389. Johnson & Son, Inc. *Frank Lloyd Wright: una mostra
della sua opera nell'ultimo decennio presentata dagli Stati Uniti
D'America alla XII Triennale di Milano—1960.* [Milano: 1960.]
    20.9 x 20.8 cm., 36 pp., 63 ills., paper.
    Cover title. A catalogue prepared in collaboration with the
United States Information Agency on the occasion of an exhibition at the XII Triennale of Milan. The text is in Italian.

1390. Linder, Paul; Luis Mior Quesada G.; and Hector Velarde.
Frank Lloyd Wright: un homenaje. [Lima]: Sociedad de Arquitectos del Peru, [1960].
    115 pp., 114 ills., paper.

1391. Rio de Janeiro. Museu de Arte Moderna. *Arquitetura de
Frank Lloyd Wright.*
    20.8 x 19.6 cm., 12 pp., 3 ills.
    Pamphlet for an exhibition held in February and March,
1960. Portuguese text.

1392. Robbins, I. D. *The Lighting of a Great Museum.* Hacken-
sack, New Jersey: American Lighting Corporation, 1960.
    24.9 x 21.7 cm., 16 pp., 14 ills., paper.
    A pamphlet which explains the adjustments made to Wright's
plan for lighting the Guggenheim Museum. The modifications
were carried out by the American Lighting Corporation.

1393. Sacriste, Eduardo. *"Usonia" aspectos de la obra de Wright.*
Buenos Aires: Ediciones Infinito, [1960].
    22.7 x 15.3 cm., 95 pp., front., 40 pls., 17 drawings. (Biblioteca
de arquitectura, volumen II.)

1394. Scully, Vincent, Jr. *Frank Lloyd Wright.* New York:
George Braziller, Inc., [1960].

25.4 x 18.5 cm., 125 pp., 127 ills., cloth. (Masters of World Architecture)

A study of the principles governing Wright's designs, with discussion of representative buildings. A paperback edition also was published.

□ A British edition was published by Mayflower, London, 1960.

REVIEWS

1395. Banham, Reyner. *Arts* XXXIV (Je 1960), pp. 12-13, 65.
1396. Gebhard, David. *Art J* XX (W 1960–61), pp. 118, 120.
1397. Hurley, D. J. "Wrightian Triplet: Review of Three Recent Books." *Liturg Art* XXVIII (Ag 1960), pp. 114-15.
1398. Manson, Grant C. *JSAH* XIX (D 1960), pp. 182-3.

1399. [Washington, D. C. United States Information Service.] *Frank Lloyd Wright, Master Architect.* [1960.]

26.7 x 21 cm., 32 pp., front., 14 ills.

A book published for foreign distribution, it includes excerpts from Wright's writings and tributes to him. USIA materials are not available in the United States.

1400. Wright, Frank Lloyd. *Budushchee arkhitektury.* 1960. See no. 913.

1401. Wright, Frank Lloyd. *Frank Lloyd Wright: Writings and Buildings.* Selected by Edgar Kaufmann and Ben Raeburn. New York: Horizon Press, [1960].

20.2 x 13.4 cm., 347 pp., 150 ills., cloth.

An anthology of Wright's writings grouped into seven sections, each preceded by an introduction by the editors. The book also contains the first comprehensive list of Wright's buildings extant in 1960. The list was compiled by Bruce F. Radde and arranged geographically with street addresses. A paperback edition was also published.

□ A British edition was published by Meridian Books: Mayflower.

□ A South American edition was published under the title *Frank Lloyd Wright: sus ideas y sus realizaciones.* Seleccionadas por Edgar Kaufmann y Ben Raeburn. Buenos Aires: Editorial Víctor Lerú S.R.L., [1962].

□ A German edition was published under the title *Schriften und Bauten.* München, Wien: Albert Langen, Georg Müller, [1963].

REVIEWS of the 1960 edition

1402. Hurley, D. J. "Wrightian Triplet; Review of Three Recent Books." *Liturg Art* XXVIII (Ag 1960), pp. 114-15.

1403. Schmertz, Mildred F. "A Wright Anthology." *Arch Rec* CXXIX (Ag 1960), p. 84.

1404. Weinberg, Robert C. *Am Inst Plan J* XXVII (N 1961), p. 354.

1405. Wright, Frank Lloyd. *The Solomon R. Guggenheim Museum. Architect: Frank Lloyd Wright.* New York: The Solomon R. Guggenheim Foundation and Horizon Press, [1960].
25.4 x 20.4 cm., 72 pp., front., 49 ills., cloth.

Includes an introduction by Harry F. Guggenheim, statements by Wright on the museum, a photographic tour of the building, and illustrations of a few works of art from the collection.

□ A paperback edition was also published. It varies from the hardcover edition in having a list of trustees on page five, a different view of the building in the photograph following page 48, and a revised list on page 72.

1406. Wright, Olgivanna Lloyd. *The Shining Brow: Frank Lloyd Wright.* New York: Horizon Press, 1960.
21.5 x 13.3 cm., 300 pp., front., 18 ills., cloth.

A volume of biographical reminiscences by the architect's widow. The dust wrapper was designed by Eugene Masselink.

REVIEW

1407. "Paean Sung Too Soon." *Progress Arch* XLI (Je 1960), pp. 250, 256.

Periodicals

1408. "Airhouse." *Domus* no. 364 (Mr 1960), pp. 17-18.

Air-inflated structure designed by Wright (?), exhibited at the International Home Exhibition, New York.

1409. "Architects as Wallpaper Designers." *Arch R* CXXVIII (Ag 1960), p. 140.
Includes two designs by Wright for F. Schumacher and Co.

1410. Blake, Peter. "The Guggenheim: Museum or Monument?" *Kokusai Kentiku* XXVII (Mr 1960), pp. 48-54.
Translated by Hiroshi Sasaki from the *Architectural Forum* (December 1959).

1411. Brooks, H. Allen, Jr. "The Early Work of the Prairie Architects." *JSAH* XIX (Mr 1960), pp. 2-10.
Includes references to Wright.

1412. "Carlo Levi e Frank Lloyd Wright." *Architettura* VI (Se 1960), pp. 292-3.

1413. Cole, Wendell. "The Theatre Projects of Frank Lloyd Wright." *Educational Theater Journal* XII (My 1960), pp. 86-93.

1414. Eaton, Leonard K. "Jens Jensen and the Chicago School." *Progress Arch* XLI (D 1960), pp. 144-50.
Includes discussion of the relationship of Jensen and Wright.

1415. Fitch, James Marston. "Frank Lloyd Wright's War on the Fine Arts." *Horizon* III (Se 1960), pp. 96-103, 127-28.

1416. "FLLW's Dallas Theater." *Arch For* CXII (Mr 1960), pp. 130-5.
Dallas Theater Center.

1417. "Frank Lloyd Wright." *Aujourd'hui* V (Fe 1960), pp. 56-9.
Annunciation Greek Orthodox Church, Wauwatosa; Art Museum, Baghdad (project); Arizona State Capitol, "Oasis," Phoenix (project); mile-high skyscraper, "The Illinois," Chicago (project); Guggenheim Museum, New York.

1418. Giedion-Welcker, Carola. "Zum neuen Guggenheim-Museum in New York." *Werk* XLVII (My 1960), pp. 178-81.

1419. "Ground is Broken for Wright's Marin County Center."
Progress Arch XLI (Ap 1960), p. 82.

1420. "The Guggenheim Museum." *Arch & Build N* CCXVIII
(27 Jy 1960), pp. 105-10 and cover.

1421. "The Guggenheim Museum." *AIA J* XXXIII (Ja 1960),
p. 124.

1422. Gutheim, Frederick. "The Wright Legacy Evaluated."
Arch Rec CXXVIII (O 1960), pp. 147-86 and cover.
    Reprinted, see no. 1971.

1423. Hitchcock, Henry-Russell. "Notes of a Traveller: Wright
and Kahn." *Zodiac* (no. 6, 1960), pp. 14-21.
    Guggenheim Museum, New York.

1424. "The House Beautiful." *AIA J* XXXIV (Ag 1960), p. 60.
    Information on the book printed by William H. Winslow
    and Wright in 1896 (see no. 18).

1425. "In Memoriam Frank Lloyd Wright." *Arch d'Aujourd'hui*
XXXI (Se 1960), pp. 11-19.

1426. "Il Museo Guggenheim a New York." *Edilizia Moderna*
LXIX (Ap 1960), pp. 39-46 and cover.

1427. Jennings, Michael. "The Guggenheim Museum: Frank
Lloyd Wright's Legacy to New York." *Light and Lighting* LIII
(Fe 1960), pp. 34-7 and cover.

1428. "Kalita Humphreys Theater, Dallas, Texas." *Arch Design*
XXX (Se 1960), p. 367.
    Dallas Theater Center.

1429. "Das Kalita-Humphreys-Theater in Dallas, Texas." *Baukunst und Werkform* XIII (no. 6, 1960), pp. 314-15.
    Dallas Theater Center.

1430. "Kalita Humphrey's Theater in Dallas, Texas." *Werk*

XLVII (Se 1960), pp. 301-3.
Dallas Theater Center.

1431. Kaufmann, Edgar, Jr. "Centrality and Symmetry in Wright's Architecture." *Arch Yrbk* IX (1960), pp. 120-31.

1432. Kjoer, Bodil. "Frank Lloyd Wright's Guggenheim-Bygning." *Arkitekten* LXII (20 Jy 1960), pp. 255-7.

1433. "Il laisse son oeuvre." *Zodiac* no. 5 (1960), pp. 28-37.
A photographic survey of Wright's work and a short statement by Le Corbusier.

1434. Lavagnino, Emilio. "Conferma la condanna a Sweeney." *Architettura* VI (Ag 1960), pp. 262-3.
Guggenheim Museum, New York.

1435. "Museu Guggenheim, Nova York." *Habitat* XI (Jy-Ag 1960), pp. 12-17.

1436. Norberg-Schulz, Chr. "Wright or Wrong?" *Byggekunst* XLII (no. 3, 1960), pp. 80-4.
Guggenheim Museum, New York.

1437. "Un'opera postuma di Frank Lloyd Wright: l'auditorium Kalila [sic] Humphreys a Dallas nel Texas." *Casabella* no. 239 (My 1960), pp. 52-4 and cover.
Dallas Theater Center.

1438. Pellegrin, Luigi. "Wright in Norvegia; Disegni di F. Ll. Wright." *Architettura* VI (My 1960), pp. 39-40.

1439. "A Portfolio of Houses by Frank Lloyd Wright." *H & H* XVIII (Se 1960), pp. 113-23.
Davis house, Marion; Palmer house, Ann Arbor; Hagan house, Uniontown; Sander house, Stamford.

1440. "A Prefabricated House by Frank Lloyd Wright." *Builder* CXCIX (19 Ag 1960), p. 313.
Pre-fab no. 1 (Cass), Staten Island.

1441.   Ragon, Michel. "L'Architecture américaine." *XXe Siécle* n. s. XXII (Je 1960), sup. pp. 1-3.
Includes English summary.

1442.   Rannit, A. "Das neue Museum der ungegenständlichen Kunst in New York." *Das Kunstwerk* XIII (Ja 1960), p. 24 (ills. follow).

1443.   "Das Salomon-R.-Guggenheim-Museum [sic]." *Baukunst und Werkform* XIII (no. 1, 1960), pp. 6-7.

1444.   "The Solomon R. Guggenheim Museum, New York; Frank Lliyd [sic] Wright, Architect." *Kokusai Kentiku* XXVII (Ja 1960), pp. 22-31.
From *Casabella* (no. 1299) and *Architectural Forum* (no. 1298).

1445.   Steegmuller, Francis. "Battle of the Guggenheim." *Holiday* XXVIII (Se 1960), pp. 60-1, 105-6.

1446.   Stone, Edward D. "A Tribute to a Personal Hero." *Pac Arch & Build* LXVI (Mr 1960), p. 20.
Remarks presented at the groundbreaking of the Marin County Civic Center.

1447.   Sweeney, James Johnson. "Chambered Nautilus on Fifth Avenue." *Museum News* XXXVIII (Ja 1960), pp. 14-15 and cover.
Guggenheim Museum, New York. With critical opinions by Lewis Mumford from the *New Yorker* (no. 1339), Peter Blake from *Architectural Forum* (no. 1279), and Alfred Frankenstein from *San Francisco Chronicle* (29 N 1959).

1448.   "Synagogue for the Beth Sholom Congregation, Pennsylvania; Frank Lloyd Wright, Architect." *Kokusai Kentiku* XXVII (Ja 1960), pp. 32-3.
From *Architectural Forum* (no. 1298).

1449.   "Il teatro di Wright: gli spettatori agganciati." *Architettura* VI (Jy 1960), p. 185.
Dallas Theater Center.

1450. "A Theater by Wright." *Arch Rec* CXXVII (Mr 1960), pp. 161-6.
Dallas Theater Center.

1451. Weinberg, Robert C. "A Distillation of FLLW....and the Genial Professor from Copenhagen." *AIA J* XXXIV (N 1960), pp. 62-4.

1452. Wheeler, Robert C. "Frank Lloyd Wright Filling Station, 1958." *JSAH* XIX (D 1960), pp. 174-5.
Lindholm service station, Cloquet.

1453. Whelan, Dennis. "Mr. Wright Makes Himself Clear: A Recollection." *Horizon* III (Se 1960), p. 128.

1454. "Wright Eulogized at Marin County Groundbreaking." *Pac Arch & Build* LXVI (Mr 1960), p. 13.

1455. Wright, F. Ll. "La memoria, l'abuso e l'apostasia." *Architettura* VI (D 1960), p. 551.

1456. Wright, John Lloyd. "Appreciation of Frank Lloyd Wright." *Arch Design* XXX (Ja 1960), pp. 1-34.
The author was Wright's son.

1457. "Wright Still Builds with California Church." *Progress Arch* XLI (N 1960), p. 70.
Pilgrim Congregational Church, Redding.

1458. Zevi, Bruno. "L'incessante polemica sul Museo Guggenheim." *Architettura* V (Ap 1960), pp. 798-9.

1961

Books

1459. Farr, Finis. *Frank Lloyd Wright: A Biography.* New York: Charles Scribner's Sons, [1961].
20.8 x 13.9 cm., xvii, 293 pp., front., 48 ills., cloth.
The first full-length biography of Wright. Also published in

slightly different form in *The Saturday Evening Post* (see no. 1469).

□ A British edition was published by Cape Ltd., London, 1962.

REVIEWS of the 1961 and 1962 editions

1460.   Kenny, Sean. "A Master Builder." *Spectator* CCVIII (23 Mr 1962), pp. 358-9. [1962]

1461.   Manson, Grant. "The Unvarnished Truth." *Progress Arch* XLIII (Ap 1962), pp. 206, 210, 216, 222. [1961]

1462.   Matthews, Peter. "Honest Vulgarity." *Time and Tide* XLIII (29 Mr 1962), p. 45. [1962]

1463.   Johonnot, Rodney F. *The New Edifice of Unity Church, Oak Park, Illinois. Frank Lloyd Wright, Architect.* Descriptive and Historical Matter by Dr. Rodney F. Johonnot, Pastor. Published by the New Unity Church Club, June, Nineteen Hundred and Six. [Oak Park: The Unitarian Universalist Church, 1961.]
    See no. 59.

1464.   University of Chicago. College Humanities Staff. *The Midway Gardens, 1914–1929: An Exhibition of the Building by Frank Lloyd Wright, and the Sculpture by Alfonso Iannelli.* April 24 to May 20, 1961. Lexington Hall Gallery, 5831 University Avenue. Chicago: University of Chicago, 1961.
    28 x 21.6 cm., iv, 10 pp., 9 ills., paper.
    A pamphlet to accompany the exhibition. It includes "The Midway Gardens," by Alan M. Fern and "Architect and Sculptor in the Making of Midway Gardens," by Alfonso Iannelli.

Periodicals

1465.   Bancroft, Dick. "From the Publisher's Desk." *Building Construction* XXXI (Se 1961), p. 5.
    S. C. Johnson and Son research tower, Racine. Additional comment, November, p. 5.

1466.   Byrne, Barry. "Wright and Iannelli." *Arch Rec* CXXIX (Ja 1961), pp. 242, 246.

1467.   Cooke, Alistair. "A Letter from Bath: The City and

Frank Lloyd Wright." *Listener* LXVI (6 Jy 1961), pp. 26-7.
Comment on Wright's opinion of historic architecture.

1468. Elmslie, G. G. [Letter.] *JSAH* XX (O 1961), pp. 140-2.
A response written in 1936 to Wright's review of Morrison's
biography of Louis Sullivan (see no. 394), together with a re-
printing of the original review.

1469. Farr, Finis. "Frank Lloyd Wright: Defiant Genius." *Saturday Evening Post* CCXXXIV (7 Ja 1961), pp. 17-21, 83, 85-6;
(14 Ja), pp. 32-3, 76-8; (21 Ja), pp. 24, 60-2; (28 Ja), pp. 32, 89,
91-2; (4 Fe), pp. 38, 93, 95-6.
A serialized version of Farr's biography on Wright (see no.
1459).

1470. "FLLW Job Resumed After Halt; Another Advancing."
Arch For CXIV (Fe 1961), pp. 9, 11.
Marin County Civic Center, San Rafael; Monona Terrace,
Madison (project).

1471. "F. L. Wright und der Begriff der organischen Architektur."
Bauen und Wohnen XV (O 1961), pp. 364-5.

1472. "Frank Lloyd Wright in Posthumous Recording." *Arch
Rec* CXXX (O 1961), p. 24.
"Frank Lloyd Wright on Record" issued by Caedmon Re-
cords, Inc.

1473. "Frank Lloyd Wright's Johnson Wax Building Finally
Made Dry." *Building Construction* XXXI (N 1961), pp. 20-3.

1474. "Half a Wright Project May Be Better Than None." *Arch
For* CXV (D 1961), p. 10.
Marin County Civic Center, San Rafael.

1475. Jacobs, Herbert. "A Light Look at Frank Lloyd Wright."
Wis Mag Hist XLIV (Sp 1961), pp. 163-76.

1476. "Mr. Wright and His Successors." *Western Architect and
Engineer* CCXXI (Mr 1961), pp. 20-33.

Fawcett house, Los Banos; Walton house, Modesto; Ablin house, Bakersfield; Marin County Civic Center, San Rafael; Pilgrim Congregational Church, Redding; Grady Gammage Memorial Auditorium, Tempe; Donahoe Triptych, Phoenix (project).

1477.   Pyron, Bernard. "Wright's Diamond Module Houses." *Art J* XXI (W 1961–62), pp. 92-6.

1478.   Scully, Vincent. "The Heritage of Wright." *Zodiac* (no. 8, 1961), pp. 8-13.

1479.   "Spirit of Byzantium: FLLW's Last Church." *Arch For* CXV (D 1961), pp. 82-7.
        Annunciation Greek Orthodox Church, Wauwatosa.

1480.   "Taliesin Continua." *Architettura* VI (Mr 1961), pp. 732-3.

1481.   "Teacup Dome." *Time* LXXVIII (18 Ag 1961), p. 50.
        Annunciation Greek Orthodox Church, Wauwatosa.

1482.   "Theater in Dallas, Texas." *Architektur und Wohnform* LXIX (Ap 1961), pp. 83-6 and cover.
        Dallas Theater Center.

1483.   "Vorfabriziertes Haus, von unserem New Yorker Korrespondenten." *Bauen und Wohnen* XV (D 1961), p. XII 22.
        Pre-fab no. 1 (Van Tamelen), Madison.

1962

Books

1484.   Forsee, Aylesa. *Frank Lloyd Wright, vida e obra.* Belo Horizonte: Editôra Itatiana Limitada, 1962.
        See no. 1263.

1485.   [Marin County, California. Board of Supervisors.] *Marin County Civic Center.* [San Rafael, California: Board of Supervisors, 1962.]

20.3 x 26.9 cm., 28 pp., 25 ills. (part color), paper.
Cover title. A pamphlet with photographs and plans, pub-
lished on the occasion of the dedication of the building in
October, 1962.

1486.   Ransohoff, Doris. *Living Architecture: Frank Lloyd
Wright.* Chicago: Britannica Books, [1962].
20.9 x 13.9 cm., 191 pp., 19 ills., cloth. (Britannica Book-
shelf—Great Lives for Young Americans)
A juvenile biography.

1487.   White, Morton, and Lucia White. "Architecture against
the City: Frank Lloyd Wright." In *The Intellectual Versus the
City: From Thomas Jefferson to Frank Lloyd Wright.* Cambridge,
Massachusetts: Harvard University Press and the M. I. T. Press,
1962. Pp. 189-99.

1488.   Wright, Frank Lloyd. *Frank Lloyd Wright: sus ideas y sus
realizaciones.* Buenos Aires: Editorial Víctor Lerú S.R.L., [1962].
See no. 1401.

1489.   Wright, Frank Lloyd. *The Drawings of Frank Lloyd
Wright.* [Selected by] Arthur Drexler. New York: Horizon Press
for the Museum of Modern Art, [1962].
29 x 22.1 cm., 320 pp., 303 ills., cloth.
A catalogue of original drawings exhibited at the Museum of
Modern Art in 1962. The introduction and explanatory comments for the plates are by Arthur Drexler, Director of the
Architecture and Design Department. The drawings range from
1895 through 1959 and also represent the work of Wright's
successor firm, Taliesin Associated Architects. Although the
many buildings and projects covered in this book are not listed
individually in this description, entries for all of them will be
found in the building index.
□ A British edition was published by Thames & Hudson, Ltd.,
London.
□ An undated, less expensive edition was reissued by Bramhall
House, New York.

REVIEWS of the 1962 and British editions

1490. Anonymous. "Drawings of a Master Designer." *Industrial Design* IX (Ap 1962), p. 12. [1962]

1491. Byrne, Barry. *JSAH* XXII (My 1963), pp. 108-9. [1962]

1492. Casson, Hugh. *Arch R* CXXXIII (Je 1963), pp. 386-7. [British]

1493. Schmertz, Mildred F. "FLW, Draftsman." *Arch Rec* CXXXI (Je 1962), pp. 42, 48. [1962]

1494. Tafel, Edgar A. *Progress Arch* XLIV (My 1963), p. 192. [1962]

1495. Wright, Frank Lloyd. *Japanese Prints Exhibition.* [Los Angeles]: Municipal Art Gallery, 1962.
21.4 x 21.4 cm., 16 pp., 11 ills., paper.
A catalogue for an exhibition of Wright's prints held at the Municipal Art Gallery from 10 January through 4 February 1962. It includes a reprint of the introduction from the 1917 Arts Club of Chicago exhibition catalogue (see no. 137), a list of terminology, and a chronological graph.

1496. Wright, Iovanna Lloyd. *Architecture: Man in Possession of His Earth. Frank Lloyd Wright.* Patricia Coyle Nicholson, designer and editor. Garden City, New York: Doubleday & Company, Inc., 1962.
31.6 x 23.8 cm., 128 pp., 241 ills. (part color), cloth.
A biography by Wright's daughter. It includes a discussion of materials in the format of the architect's 1928 series, "In the Cause of Architecture."
□ A British edition was published by MacDonald, London, 1963.

REVIEW of the 1962 edition

1497. Storrer, Bradley Ray. *Progress Arch* XLIV (Je 1963), pp. 185-6, 191.

Periodicals

1498. "Architecture of Ideas." *H & H* XXI (Mr 1962), pp. 116-27.

Includes a portrait of Wright and a photograph of the Zimmerman house, Manchester.

1499.   Armitage, Merle. "Frank Lloyd Wright: An American Original." *Texas Quarterly* V (Sp 1962), pp. 85-90. (Also issued as offprint.)

1500.   Brooks, H. Allen. "Architectural Drawings by Frank Lloyd Wright." *Burlington Magazine* CIV (My 1962), pp. 210-12.
      Exhibit at Museum of Modern Art, New York.

1501.   "La Casa de la Cascada: historia de una epopeya." *Nuestra Arquitectura* no. 397 (D 1962), pp. 8, 10.
      Kaufmann house, "Fallingwater," Bear Run.

1502.   Farr, Finis. "The Countenance of Principle." *Arts in Virginia* III (Fa 1962), pp. 2-9.

1503.   "First Building in Wright's Marin Center to Be Completed this Month." *Arch Rec* CXXXI (Je 1962), sup. pp. 4-5.
      Administration Building, Marin County Civic Center, San Rafael.

1504.   "First Phase of Marin County Center Is Completed." *Arch Rec* CXXXII (N 1962), p. 12.
      Administration Building, Marin County Civic Center, San Rafael.

1505.   "FLLW's Legacy: Projects and Sketches." *Arch For* CXVII (Jy 1962), p. 9.
      Grady Gammage Memorial Auditorium, Tempe; International Village and Court of Seven Seas, Santa Cruz (Taliesin Associated Architects).

1506.   "Frank Lloyd Wright et son école, une exposition du Musée d'Art Moderne de New York." *Arch d'Aujourd'hui* XXXIII (Je 1962), pp. 14-15.

1507.   "The Good Building Is One That Makes the Landscape More Beautiful Than It Was Before." *Arch For* CXVII (N 1962), pp. 122-9.

Marin County Civic Center, San Rafael.

1508. Huxtable, Ada Louise. "Drawings and Dreams of Frank
Lloyd Wright." *NYTM* (11 Mr 1962), pp. 24-5.
    Exhibit of Wright's drawings at the Museum of Modern Art,
New York.

1509. "Important Show at the Museum of Modern Art." *Apollo*
LXXVI (Ap 1962), p. 148.
    Frank Lloyd Wright drawings.

1510. Kaufmann, Edgar, Jr. "Frank Lloyd Wright's Fallingwater
25 Years After." *Architettura* VIII (Ag 1962), pp. 222-80.
    Kaufmann house, "Fallingwater," Bear Run. Reprinted, see
no. 1537.

1511. "The Master Builder." *Cue* XXXI (24 Mr 1962), p. 10.
    Exhibit of Wright's drawings at the Museum of Modern Art,
New York.

1512. McQuade, Walter. "Architecture." *Nation* CXCIV (14 Ap
1962), pp. 338-9.
    Exhibit at the Museum of Modern Art, New York.

1513. Mumford, Lewis. "Megalopolis as Anti-City." *Arch Rec*
CXXXII (D 1962), pp. 101-8.
    Includes discussion of Broadacre City (project).

1514. "On the Rolling Prairie, Oskaloosa, Iowa." *H & H* XXI
(Mr 1962), pp. 130-3.
    Alsop and Lamberson houses, Oskaloosa.

1515. "Rolling Shapes for Rolling Marin Hills." *Architecture
West* LXVIII (O 1962), pp. 6-7.
    Administration Building, Marin County Civic Center, San
Rafael.

1516. Scully, Vincent, Jr. "Wright, International Style and
Kahn." *Arts Magazine* XXXVI (Mr 1962), pp. 67-71, 77.
    Abridged form of a paper published in *Acts* of the Twen-

tieth International Congress of the History of Art, 1963. (See no. 1529.)

1517. Smith, C. Ray. "Rehousing the Drama." *Progress Arch* XLIII (Fe 1962), pp. 96-109.
Includes auditorium of Guggenheim Museum, New York.

1518. "Taliesin Revisited." *Let's See* (My 1962), pp. 21-5, 43-4.

1519. "Unity Restored." *Arch R* CXXXI (Ja 1962), pp. 5-6.
Unity Temple, Oak Park.

1520. Weisse, Rolf. "1935, F. L. Wright, Broadacre City." *Harvard University. Graduate School of Design. Intercity* (My 1962), pp. 7-1 through 7-3.

1521. "Wright and the Organic Tradition." *Industrial Design* IX (Ap 1962), p. 39.

1522. "Wright Drawings at the Modern." *Arts Magazine* XXXVI (Mr 1962), p. 69.
Exhibit at Museum of Modern Art, New York.

1523. Wright, Olgivanna Lloyd. "The Living Heritage of Frank Lloyd Wright." *Arizona Highways* XXXVIII (Ap 1962), pp. 2-3.

1524. Wright, Olgivanna. "The Ideas of Education." *Architecture Plus* no. 5 (1962-1963), unpaged.

1525. "Wright Post Office." *Progress Arch* XLIII (Se 1962), p. 76.
Marin County Civic Center, San Rafael.

1526. Zevi, Bruno. "Il vaticinio del Riegl e la Casa sulla Cascata." *Architettura* VIII (Ag 1962), pp. 218-21.
Kaufmann house, "Fallingwater," Bear Run. Reprinted, see no. 1537.

1963

Books

1527.   Chicago. Art Institute. Burnham Library of Architecture.
Guide to Chicago & Midwestern Architecture. Chicago: Art Institute of Chicago, 1963.
    See no. 747.

1528.   Columbia University. School of Architecture. *Four Great Makers of Modern Architecture: Gropius, Le Corbusier, Mies van der Rohe, Wright.* The Verbatim Record of a Symposium Held at the School of Architecture, Columbia University, from March to May, 1961. [New York: Trustees of Columbia University, 1963.]
    27.6 x 21.5 cm., vii, 296 pp., paper.
    Includes: "Broadacre City: Wright's Utopia Reconsidered," by George R. Collins; "The Social Implications of the Skyscraper," by Henry S. Churchill; "The Continuity of Idea and Form," by Alden B. Dow; "Wright and the Spirit of Democracy," by James Marston Fitch; "The Fine Arts and Frank Lloyd Wright," by Edgar Kaufmann, Jr.; "Frank Lloyd Wright and the Tall Building," by Grant Manson; and "The Domestic Architecture of Frank Lloyd Wright," by Norris Smith. Reproduced from typescript.
    □ Reprinted by Da Capo Press, New York, 1970. (Da Capo Press Series in Architecture and Decorative Art. General Editor: Adolf K. Placzek, Avery Librarian, Columbia University. Volume 37)

1529.   "Frank Lloyd Wright and Architecture around 1900." *In* International Congress of the History of Art, *Problems of the 19th & 20th Centuries.* Princeton, New Jersey: Princeton University Press, 1963.
    Includes: an introduction by Henry-Russell Hitchcock; "Frank Lloyd Wright and Twentieth Century Style," by Vincent Scully, Jr.; "The Prairie School, The Midwest Contemporaries of Frank Lloyd Wright," by H. Allen Brooks; "California Contemporaries of Frank Lloyd Wright, 1885–1915," by Stephen W. Jacobs; "Wright's Eastern-Seaboard Contemporaries: Creative Eclecticism in the United States Around 1900," by Carroll L. V. Meeks; and "The British Contemporaries of

Frank Lloyd Wright," by John Summerson.

1530. Gannett, William C. *The House Beautiful.* In a Setting Designed by Frank Lloyd Wright and Printed by Hand at the Auvergne Press in River Forest by William Herman Winslow and Frank Lloyd Wright during the Winter Months of the Year Eighteen Hundred Ninety Six and Seven. [Park Forest, Illinois: W. R. Hasbrouck, 1963.]
See no. 18.

1531. [Gebhard, David.] *Four Santa Barbara Houses: 1904–1917.* Santa Barbara: University of California, 1963.
21.5 x 27.9 cm., 3 pp., 4 ills., paper.
A pamphlet for an exhibition held from 17 September through 12 November 1963 at the University of California, Santa Barbara. It includes a description and photograph of the Stewart house, Montecito. The elevation of the house published in *Ausgeführte Bauten und Entwürfe* (see no. 87) and there identified as a summer house in Fresno is reproduced on the cover.

1532. Hitchcock, Henry-Russell. "Frank Lloyd Wright and His California Contemporaries." In *Architecture: Nineteenth and Twentieth Centuries.* Baltimore, Maryland: Penguin Books, [1963]. (The Pelican History of Art, edited by Nikolaus Pevsner.) Pp. 320-35.
Partially reprinted, see no. 573.

1533. Mumford, Lewis. "What Wright Hath Wrought." In *The Highway and the City.* New York: Harcourt, Brace & World, Inc., 1963. Pp. 124-38.
Also "Postscript: In Memoriam: 1869–1959." Pp. 139-42.

1534. Wright, Frank Lloyd. *Buildings, Plans and Designs.* New York: Horizon Press, [1963].
See no. 87.

1535. Wright, Frank Lloyd. *Schriften und Bauten.* Munchen, Wien: Albert Langen, Georg Muller, [1963].
See no. 1401.

1536.   Wright, Olgivanna Lloyd. *The Roots of Life.* New York: Horizon Press, 1963.
    21.6 x 13.3 cm., 256 pp., cloth.
    An anthology of Wright's writings and Mrs. Wright's lectures. Also combined with *Our House* (no. 1274) and *The Shining Brow* (no. 1406) into a boxed set entitled *When Past Is Future.*

1537.   Zevi, Bruno, and Edgar Kaufmann, Jr. *La Casa sulla Cascata di F. Ll. Wright: F. Lloyd Wright's Fallingwater.* [Milano, Italy]: ET/AS Kompass, [1963].
    31.7 x 23.1 cm., 80 pp., 123 ills. (part color), cloth.
    A book which first appeared as two articles in a special issue of *Architettura* (see nos. 1510 & 1526). The text is in Italian and English. It was also published in a soft cover edition.

REVIEW
1538.   Kostka, Robert. *Prairie Sch R* I (no. 3, 1964), p. 17.

Periodicals

1539.   Brooks, H. Allen. "Steinway Hall, Architects and Dreams." *JSAH* XXII (O 1963), pp. 171-5.

1540.   Byrne, Barry. "On Frank Lloyd Wright and His Atelier." *AIA J* XXXIX (Je 1963), pp. 109-12.
    Also in *Journal of Architectural Education* XVIII (Je 1963), pp. 3-6.

1541.   "Centre civique de Marin County, Californie, États-Unis." *Arch d'Aujourd'hui* XXXIV (Fe-Mr 1963), pp. 10-17.

1542.   "Committee Plans Restoration of Robie House." *Arch Rec* CXXXIII (Ap 1963), p. 29.

1543.   "Continuadora da obra de Frank Lloyd Wright." *Habitat* XIII (Mr 1963), p. 61.

1544.   "Editorial." *Arts & Arch* LXXX (Jy 1963), p. 6.
    Robie house, Chicago.

1545. "Fallingwater Saved Before It Is Imperiled: Kaufmann Makes a Gift of House at Bear Run." *Arch Rec* CXXXIV (O 1963), p. 24.

1546. Fern, Alan M. "Midway Gardens of Frank Lloyd Wright." *Arch R* CXXXIV (Ag 1963), pp. 113-16.

1547. Geiger, Martin. "Marin-Center, ein Beispiel Wrightscher Architektur, ausgeführt nach seinem Tode." *Werk* L (O 1963), sup. p. 224.

1548. "A Great Frank Lloyd Wright House." *House B* CV (Ja 1963), pp. 6, 8, 53-113, 117-20 and cover.
     A special issue devoted to the Hanna house, Palo Alto. It includes articles by Dr. Paul and Jean Hanna, and Curtis Besinger. It was also offered in a specially bound, hard-cover edition.

1549. Griswold, Ralph E. "Wright Was Wrong." *Landscape Arch* LIII (Ap 1963), pp. 209-14.
     Discussion of Pittsburgh's parks, with brief references to Wright.

1550. "A House Stays in Chicago." *Interiors* CXXII (Ap 1963), p. 10.
     Robie house.

1551. Huxtable, Ada Louise. " 'Natural Houses' of Frank Lloyd Wright." *NYTM* (17 N 1963), pp. 78-9.

1552. Kaufmann, Edgar, Jr. "Frank Lloyd Wright and the Fine Arts." *Perspecta* no. 8 (1963), pp. 40-2.

1553. "La Maison Robie de F. L. Wright sera sauvée." *Arch d'Aujourd'hui* XXXIV (Fe 1963), p. xi.

1554. "Marin Centre: Frank Lloyd Wright's Last Work?" *Arch R* CXXXIII (Fe 1963), p. 83.

1555. "Marin County Civic Center—A Monument to a Great

Architect." *Expanded Shale Concrete Facts* IX (no. 3, n. d.), pp. 2-3 and cover.

1556.   "News." *AIA J* XL (Ag 1963), p. 114.
Robie house, Chicago.

1557.   Pedio, Renato. "L'ultima opera di F. Ll. Wright riletta: il tempio di Filadelfia." *Architettura* IX (Je 1963), pp. 90-102.
Beth Sholom Synagogue, Elkins Park.

1558.   Pyron, Bernard. "Wright's Small Rectangular Houses: His Structures of the Forties and Fifties." *Art J* XXIII (Fa 1963), pp. 20-4.

1559.   "Die Rettung des 'Robie House' in Chicago." *Werk* L (My 1963), sup. p. 101.

1560.   "The Ship." *Point West* V (Ap 1963), p. 11.
Pauson house (ruin), Phoenix.

1561.   Tentori, Francesco. "Wrightiana." *Casabella* no. 274 (Ap 1963), pp. 38, 43.

1562.   "Uffici amministrativi e biblioteca di Marin County, San Rafael, California, 1959–62." *Casabella* no. 274 (Ap 1963), pp. 44-55.

1563.   "L'ultima opera di Wright costruita negli Stati Uniti." *Domus* no. 406 (Se 1963), pp. 1-6.
Marin County Civic Center, San Rafael.

1564.   Wright, Iovanna. "Masselink." *Point West* V (Ap 1963), pp. 30-2 and cover.

1565.   "Wright Masterpiece Preserved." *Interiors* CXXIII (O 1963), p. 12.
Kaufmann house, "Fallingwater," Bear Run.

1964

Books

1566. Blake, Peter. *Frank Lloyd Wright: Architecture and Space.* Baltimore and Harmondsworth, Middlesex: Penguin, [1964].
See no. 1379.

1567. Peisch, Mark L. *The Chicago School of Architecture: Early Followers of Sullivan and Wright.* New York: Random House, [1964]. (Columbia University Studies in Art History and Archaeology Number 5)
A study of the period between 1893 and 1914. It includes a chapter on the Oak Park studio, 1900–09, and numerous other references to Wright.

REVIEW
1568. Eaton, Leonard K. *Prairie Sch R* II (no. 3, 1965), p. 20.

1569. [Smith, Dean, ed.] *Grady Gammage Memorial Auditorium, Designed by Frank Lloyd Wright.* [Tempe, Arizona: Arizona State University, 1964.]
29.1 x 27.9 cm., 32 pp., 66 ills. (part color), paper.
A descriptive pamphlet including text, photographs, plans, and sections.
□ A new edition was published in June, 1970.

REVIEW of the 1964 edition
1570. Anonymous. *Prairie Sch R* II (no. 1, 1965), p. 26.

1571. Spencer, Robert C., Jr. *The Work of Frank Lloyd Wright from 1893 to 1900.* [Park Forest, Illinois: Prairie School Press, 1964.]
35 x 27.3 cm., 13 pp., 86 ills., paper. (A Prairie School Press Reissue)
A reprint of the first review of Wright's work, originally published in the *Architectural Review* (Boston), June, 1900 (see no. 41).

REVIEWS
1572. Brooks, H. Allen. *JSAH* XXIV (D 1965), pp. 330-1.

1573.   Hobson, L. H. *Prairie Sch R* I (no. 4, 1964), p. 24.

Periodicals

1574.   "Another Wrightean Farewell Performance." *Progress Arch* XLV (N 1964), pp. 54-5.
Grady Gammage Memorial Auditorium, Tempe.

1575.   Byrne, Barry. "Frank Lloyd Wright e il suo studio." *Architettura* X (My 1964), pp. 48-9.

1576.   Champion, Roberto A. "Acerca de la significación de la obra de Wright." *Nuestra Arquitectura* no. 412 (Mr 1964), pp. 25-8.

1577.   Cuscaden, R. R. "FLlW's Drawings Preserved." *Prairie Sch R* I (no. 1, 1964), p. 18.
Photostatic reproduction of original working drawings of seventeen Wright buildings, deposited in the A.I.A. archives, Washington, D. C.

1578.   Engel, Martin. "The Ambiguity of Frank Lloyd Wright: Fallingwater." *Charette* XLIV (Ap 1964), pp. 17-18.

1579.   "Frank Lloyd Wright in Western Pennsylvania." *Charette* XLIV (Ap 1964), p. 12.

1580.   "Frank Lloyd Wright: l'architecture organique." *Architecture de Lumière* (no. 11, 1964), pp. 2-24 and cover.

1581.   "Frank Lloyd Wright's Architectural Legacy." *Builder* CCVI (22 My 1964), p. 1058.
Work of Taliesin Associated Architects after Wright's death.

1582.   "Frank Lloyd Wright's First Independent Commission." *Prairie Sch R* I (no. 3, 1964), pp. 5-14.
Special issue on the Winslow house, River Forest. It includes an article by Leonard K. Eaton.

1583.   Globus, Gordon G., and Jeff Gilbert. "A Metapsychological Approach to the Architecture of Frank Lloyd Wright." *Psycho-analytic Review* LI (Su 1964), pp. 117-29. (Also issued as off-print.)

1584. Goff, Bruce. "Frank Lloyd Wright." *Arch d'Aujourd'hui* XXXIV (Ap 1964), pp. 64-71.

1585. "Grosse Baumeister-Frank Lloyd Wright." *Berliner Bauwirtschaft* XV (1 Je 1964), pp. 274-6.

1586. Hayeem, Abe. "FLloyd & Lloyd." *Architects' J* CXL (21 O 1964), pp. 897, 899.
    Observations of a visitor to some of Wright's California buildings.

1587. "A House of Leaves: The Poetry of Fallingwater." *Charette* XLIV (Ap 1964), pp. 13-16.
    Kaufmann house, Bear Run.

1588. Kalec, Donald. "The Prairie School Furniture." *Prairie Sch R* I (no. 4, 1964), pp. 5-15.

1589. Kamrath, Karl. "Frank Lloyd Wright Drawings in the AIA Archives." *AIA J* XLII (Jy 1964), pp. 50-1.
    Negative photostats of original working drawings for thirteen buildings placed in AIA archive vaults.

1590. Lewis, Charles F. "Doors Open at Fallingwater." *Carnegie Magazine* XXXVIII (Se 1964), pp. 237-40.
    Kaufmann house, Bear Run.

1591. "Perils of Frank Lloyd Wright: His Tokyo Imperial Hotel Threatened." *Progress Arch* XLV (Se 1964), pp. 89, 91.

1592. Perrin, Richard W. E. "Frank Lloyd Wright in Wisconsin: Prophet in His Own Country." *Wis Mag Hist* XLVIII (Au 1964), pp. 32-47.
    Also in *The Architecture of Wisconsin.* Madison: The State Historical Society of Wisconsin, 1967. Pp. 134-62.

1593. "Preservation/Saving What's Wright." *AIA J* XLI (My 1964), p. 12.
  Robie house, Chicago; Pope-Leighey house, Mount Vernon.

1594. "Udall Aids FLLW Landmarks." *Arch For* CXX (My 1964), p. 7.
  Robie house, Chicago; Pope house, Falls Church; Imperial Hotel, Tokyo.

1595. Van Trump, James D. "Caught in a Hawk's Eye: The House of I. N. Hagan at Kentuck Knob." *Charette* XLIV (Ap 1964), pp. 17-18.

1596. Veronesi, Giulia, and Bruno Alfieri, eds. "Civic Center, Marin County, San Rafael, California." *Lotus, Architectural Annual, 1964–1965,* pp. 18-25.

1965

Books

1597. Barney, Maginel Wright. *The Valley of the God-Almighty Joneses.* New York: Appleton-Century, [1965].
  20.2 x 13.5 cm., 156 pp., 13 ills., cloth.
  A biography of the Lloyd Jones clan, Wright's Welsh ancestors. Mrs. Barney was his sister.

REVIEW
1598. Anonymous. *Prairie Sch R* II (no. 4, 1965), p. 25.

1599. Columbia University. Libraries. Avery Architectural Library. *Catalogue of the Frank Lloyd Wright Collection of Drawings by Louis Henri Sullivan: 122 Drawings; 84 Drawings Hitherto Unpublished.* The Frank Lloyd Wright Foundation, [1965].
  An unpublished list of the drawings given to Wright by Sullivan just before his death and subsequently sold by Mrs. Wright to the Avery Library.

1600. Cresti, Carlo. *Wright: il Museo Guggenheim.* [Firenze,

Italy], Sadea/Sansoni Editori, [1965].
34.5 x 26.2 cm., 7 pp., 4 ills., 28 color pls., paper. (Forma e colore 65)
A photostudy of the Guggenheim Museum, New York. It includes a bibliography of articles on the museum.

1601. Jacobs, Herbert. *Frank Lloyd Wright: America's Greatest Architect.* New York: Harcourt, Brace & World, Inc., [1965].
20.4 x 13.6 cm., 223 pp., 23 ills., cloth.
A biography.

REVIEWS
1602. Anonymous. *Prairie Sch R* II (no. 4, 1965), p. 25.
1603. Derleth, August. *Wis Mag Hist* XLIX (W 1965–66), p. 168.

1604. Wijdeveld, H. Th., ed. *The Work of Frank Lloyd Wright: The Life-Work of the American Architect Frank Lloyd Wright,* with Contributions by Frank Lloyd Wright, an Introduction by Architect H. Th. Wijdeveld and Many Articles by Famous European Architects and American Writers. 1965 Edition Including an Introduction Written for this Edition by Mrs. Frank Lloyd Wright. [New York], Horizon Press, 1965.
See no. 165.

Periodicals

1605. Brooks, H. Allen. "La Prairie School." *Edilizia Moderna* (no. 86, 1965), pp. 65-82 and cover.

1606. Dennis, James M., and Lu B. Wenneker. "Ornamentation and the Organic Architecture of Frank Lloyd Wright." *Art J* XXV (Fa 1965), pp. 2-14.

1607. Donaldson, J. H. [Letter.] *Prairie Sch R* II (no. 4, 1965), p. 26.
Sutton house, McCook.

1608. "Gammage: From Generals to Particulars." *Progress Arch* XLVI (O 1965), pp. 210-11.

1609. "Gold in the Hills of California." *Fortune* LXXII (Ag 1965), pp. 162-4.
Marin County Civic Center, San Rafael.

1610. Griggs, Joseph. "The Prairie Spirit in Sculpture." *Prairie Sch R* II (no. 4, 1965), pp. 5-23 and cover.
Special issue devoted to Alfonso Iannelli, the sculptor who worked with Wright on Midway Gardens.

1611. "The Imperial Hotel Problem Again." *JA* (My 1965), pp. 9-10.

1612. Kaufmann, Edgar, Jr. "Frank Lloyd Wright's Years of Modernism, 1925–1935." *JSAH* XXIV (Mr 1965), pp. 31-3.

1613. Kaufmann, Edgar, Jr. "The Usonian Pope-Leighey House." *Hist Pres* XVII (My-Je 1965), pp. 96-7.

1614. "A Late Frank Lloyd Wright is Completed in Kansas." *Fortune* LXXI (Je 1965), p. 186.
Juvenile Cultural Study Center, University of Wichita.

1615. "Melody in the Glen." *AIA J* XLIV (Ag 1965), p. 82.
Pope-Leighey house opened as a museum.

1616. Messer, Thomas M. "The Growing Guggenheim. Editorial: Past and Future." *Art in Am* LIII (Je 1965), pp. 24-7 and cover.
Also includes "Evolution of a Museum," pp. 28-32.

1617. Mumford, Lewis. "The Social Background of Frank Lloyd Wright." *Kokusai Kentiku* XXXII (Mr 1965), pp. 63-72.
Japanese translation by Teizo Sugawara of an article which first appeared in 1925 (see no. 165).

1618. Pope, Loren. "Twenty-five Years Later: Still a Love Affair." *Hist Pres* XVII (My-Je 1965), pp. 98-101.
Pope house, Falls Church.

1619. "Robie House Restoration Underway." *Progress Arch* XLVI (O 1965), pp. 55-6.

1620.   "Robie House Still Imperiled." *Progress Arch* XLVI (Mr 1965), p. 53.
Note on need for restoration funds.

1621.   "Robie House Still Threatened by Lack of Contributions." *Arch Rec* CXXXVII (Ap 1965), p. 342.

1622.   Smith, Dean E. "Grady Gammage Memorial Auditorium, Arizona State University, Designed by Frank Lloyd Wright." *Arizona Highways* XLI (Fe 1965), pp. 38-47.

1623.   Stitt, F. Allen. "Frank Lloyd Wright—A Temple to Man." *Verdict Magazine* II (My 1965), pp. 15-19 and cover.

1624.   Udall, Stewart L. "Preservation and the Quality of American Life." *Hist Pres* (My-Je 1965), pp. 94-5.
The dedication of the Pope-Leighey house, Mount Vernon, 16 June 1965.

1625.   Urabe, Shizutaro. "A Personal View on Frank Lloyd Wright." *Kokusai Kentiku* XXXII (Mr 1965), pp. 55-62.

1626.   Wright, Frank Lloyd. [Quotation.] *American Registered Architect* III (Au 1965), p. 10.

1627.   "A Wright House on the Prairie." *Prairie Sch R* II (no. 3, 1965), pp. 5-19.
Special issue devoted to the Sutton house, McCook.

1628.   "Wright, Marin County." *Architettura* XI (Je 1965), pp. 108-9.

1966

Books

1629.   Committee of Architectural Heritage. *Frank Lloyd Wright: Vision and Legacy.* [Urbana], University of Illinois, [1966].
21.5 x 21.3 cm., 32 pp., 34 ills., paper.
A pamphlet which documents an exhibition of Wright's

Prairie School furniture designs presented in the context of his contemporaries. The pamphlet includes illustrations and measured drawings of furniture, illustrations of windows from the Lake Geneva Inn, Lake Geneva, and the Bradley house, Kankakee, and photographs of the construction of the Robie house. The purpose of the exhibition, held from 15 September to 1 October 1965 at the University of Illinois, was to raise funds for the restoration of the Robie house. An insert in some of the pamphlets announces the successful achievement of the committee's goal.

REVIEW
1630.   Anonymous. *Prairie Sch R* IV (no. 1, 1967), p. 23.

1631.   Hammād, Muhammad. *Frānk Lüyd Rāyt.* UAR: 1966. 21.5 x 23.1 cm., 240 pp., front., 145 ills., cloth.
    Arabic text.

1632.   Heyer, Paul. "Frank Lloyd Wright." In *Architects on Architecture: New Directions in America.* New York: Walker and Company, [1966]. Pp. 60-6.

1633.   Historic American Buildings Survey. *Chicago and Nearby Illinois Areas: List of Measured Drawings, Photographs and Written Documentation in the Survey.* J. William Rudd, Compiler. Park Forest, Illinois: The Prairie School Press, [1966].
    Includes sixteen buildings by Wright.

1634.   Oak Park, Illinois. Public Library. *A Guide to the Architecture of Frank Lloyd Wright in Oak Park and River Forest, Illinois.* Introduction by W. R. Hasbrouck, AIA. Oak Park, Illinois: The Oak Park Public Library, 1966. 21.5 x 10.6 cm., 31 pp., 37 ills., paper.
    Includes a map indicating the location of each building.

REVIEW
1635.   Hobson, Lloyd H. *Prairie Sch R* III (no. 3, 1966), p. 25.

1636.   Smith, Norris Kelly. *Frank Lloyd Wright: A Study in Architectural Content.* Englewood Cliffs, New Jersey: Prentice-Hall, [1966].

20.3 x 14.2 cm., x, 178 pp., 29 ills., cloth.

An attempt "to interpret Wright's architecture mainly in terms of what he himself had to say and in terms of the expressive forms of the buildings themselves."

□ A British paperback edition was published by Spectrum Books, Fairhaven, Lytham St. Annes, Lancs.

REVIEWS

1637. Anonymous. *Wis Mag Hist* L (W 1967), pp. 173-4.

1638. Brooks, H. A. "Frank Lloyd Wright." *Arch Rec* CXLII (Jy 1967), p. 238.

1639. Collins, Peter. "Frankleudreit?" *Progress Arch* XLVII (O 1966), pp. 262, 268.

   Reply. Mendel Glickman. "Frank Lloyd Wright and Anti-Semitism: Two Views." *Progress Arch* XLVIII (Fe 1967), pp. 10, 12, 16.

1640. Eaton, Leonard K. *Prairie Sch R* IV (no. 1, 1967), p. 21.

1641. Gowans, Alan. *JSAH* XXVIII (My 1969), pp. 140-3.

1642. Paul, Sherman. *Nation* CCIV (23 Ja 1967), pp. 121-2.

1643. Zucker, Paul. *Journal of Aesthetics and Art Criticism* XXVI (Fa 1967), p. 133.

1644. Tanigawa, Masami. *Frank Lloyd Wright.* Tokyo: Kajima Kenkyusho, 1966.

   Not seen. Cited in the bibliography published by the Oak Park Public Library. Japanese text.

1645. Wright, Frank Lloyd. *Die Zukunft der Architektur.* München-Wien: Albert Langen-Georg Müller, 1966.

   See no. 913.

1646. Wright, Frank Lloyd. *Ein Testament: Zur neuen Architektur.* Reinbek bei Hamburg: Rowohlt, 1966.

   See no. 1149.

1647. Wright, Frank Lloyd. *L'Avenir de l'architecture.* [Paris]: Gonthier, [1966].

   See no. 913.

1648. Wright, Olgivanna Lloyd. *Frank Lloyd Wright: His Life,*

His Work, His Words. New York: Horizon Press, [1966].
   25.3 x 20.2 cm., 224 pp., front., 109 ills., cloth.

   A biography by the architect's widow. It includes excerpts from Wright's writings, some published previously and others drawn from unpublished sources in the Taliesin archives. The book also contains a list of innovations by Wright, illustrations of work by the Taliesin Associated Architects, and a list of buildings and projects by Wright. This list includes biographical notes, exhibitions, speeches, and publications. Bibliography.

REVIEWS
   1649.   Brooks, H. A. "Frank Lloyd Wright." *Arch Rec* CXLII
      (Jy 1967), p. 238.
   1650.   Hardy, Hugh. "Superwright." *Progress Arch* XLVIII
      (My 1967), pp. 200, 208.
   1651.   Hines, Thomas S., Jr. *Prairie Sch R* IV (no. 2, 1967),
      pp. 27-9.
   1652.   Warren, John. *Journal of the Royal Town Planning
      Institute* LVIII (Se 1972), p. 386.

Periodicals

1653.   Banham, Reyner. "Frank Lloyd Wright as Environmentalist." *Arts & Arch* LXXXIII (Se 1966), pp. 26-30.
      Reprinted, see no. 1687. See also the author's *The Architecture of the Well-tempered Environment.* London: The Architectural Press, [1969].

1654.   Brooks, H. Allen. "Frank Lloyd Wright and the Wasmuth Drawings." *Art B* XLVIII (Je 1966), pp. 193-202.

1655.   "Drawings by Louis Sullivan from the Frank Lloyd Wright Collection, Avery Library, Columbia University." *Arch Rec* CXXXIX (Mr 1966), pp. 147-54.

1656.   Endo, R. "Forms by Frank Lloyd Wright." *Kenchiku Bunka* XXI (My 1966), pp. 74-8.
      Japanese text with English summary.

1657.   "Frank Lloyd Wright and the 17 Plaques." *Progress Arch*

XLVII (Se 1966), pp. 59-60.
17 houses designed by Wright awarded commemorative plaques by the AIA.

1658. [Frontispiece.] *Progress Arch* XLVII (My 1966), p. 114.
Doghouse, attached to Berger house, San Anselmo.

1659. "Future Projects at Civic Center." *California Architecture* II (O 1966), pp. 13, 25.
Hall of Justice, Marin County Civic Center, San Rafael.

1660. "Good Use for Robie." *Progress Arch* XLVII (Ag 1966), p. 61.
New headquarters of the Adlai E. Stevenson Institute of International Affairs.

1661. "The Guggenheim Backs Up Frank Lloyd Wright." *AIA J* XLV (Je 1966), p. 36.
Note on new 2-cent postage stamp commemorating Wright.

1662. "In Chicago." *Prairie Sch R* III (no. 1, 1966), p. 26.
Obituary of Ralph Fletcher Seymour, publisher of several books and pamphlets for Wright.

1663. Jencks, Charles. "Gropius, Wright and the International Fallacy." *Arena* LXXXII (Je 1966), pp. 14-20.

1664. Kaufmann, Edgar, Jr. "Crisis and Creativity: Frank Lloyd Wright, 1904–1914." *JSAH* XXV (D 1966), pp. 292-6.

1665. Kostka, Robert. "Frank Lloyd Wright in Japan." *Prairie Sch R* III (no. 3, 1966), pp. 5-23 and cover.

1666. Lambertucci, Alfredo. "Tendenze evolutive del concetto di spazio nell'architettura contemporanea." *Architettura* XII (O 1966), pp. 400-01.

1667. Lucie-Smith, Edward. "Pragmatists and Theoreticians." *Studio International* CLXXII (D 1966), pp. 314-15.
Includes models of the Guggenheim Museum, New York,

executed in fibreglass by Richard Hamilton.

1668.   Nyman, Thor. "Frank Lloyd Wright and His Vision."
California Architecture II (O 1966), pp. 8, 25.

1669.   "The Pope-Leighey House, Virginia USA: Historic Cypress House Re-sited Due to Threat of Destruction." *Wood* XXXI
(D 1966), p. 34.

1670.   "Recent Acquisitions by the RIBA Drawings Collection."
RIBA J LXXIII (Ja 1966), p. 7.
Yahara Boat Club, Madison (project); Francis Apartments,
Chicago; All Steel Houses, Los Angeles (project).

1671.   Robbins, Eugenia S. "Taliesin: Bard and Builder." *Art in
Am* LIV (My-Je 1966), pp. 120, 124.
Discussion of books by and about Wright.

1672.   "Robie Fund Sketches." *Prairie Sch R* III (no. 1, 1966),
p. 23.
"Frank Lloyd Wright, Vision and Legacy" exhibit.

1673.   "Robie House, Home of the Stevenson Institute." *University of Chicago Magazine* LIX (O 1966), pp. 14-15.

1674.   Ross, Irwin. "What Nature Teaches Man." *Science Digest*
LIX (Ja 1966), pp. 89-91.
Includes references to Wright's structures.

1675.   "The Stamp of Frank Lloyd Wright." *Progress Arch*
XLVII (Je 1966), p. 47.
New 2-cent postage stamp commemorating Wright.

1676.   Wright, Frank Lloyd. [Quotation.] *American Registered
Architect* IV (no. 4, 1966), p. 10.

1677.   "Wright Remembered." *Arch For* CXXIV (Je 1966), p. 30.
New 2-cent postage stamp commemorating Wright.

1678.   "Wright's Last Great Stab at Immortality." *California*

Architecture II (O 1966), pp. 10-12.
Administration Building, Marin County Civic Center, San Rafael.

1679.   Zevi, Bruno. "Los arquitectos americanos buscan el espacio perdido." *Punto* no. 28 (Ag-Se 1966), pp. 41-3.
Translated by Miguel Angel Pingarrón B.

1967

Books

1680.   [Futagawa, Yukio, photographer, and Shizutaro Urabe and Taro Amano, text.] *F. LL. Wright, 1.* [Tokyo: Bijutsu Shuppan-sha, 1967.]
25.4 x 19.4 cm., 118 pp., front., 75 ills. (part color), cloth. (Contemporary Architects Series)
A study of Wright's public buildings. A companion volume on private buildings was published in 1968 (see no. 1722). Japanese text.
□ An American edition with a new text by Martin Pawley was published as *Frank Lloyd Wright, I: Public Buildings.* New York: Simon and Schuster, [1970]. (Library of Contemporary Architects)

REVIEW of the 1970 edition
1681.   Radde, Bruce F. *Prairie Sch R* VII (no. 4, 1970), pp. 24-5.

1682.   Hasbrouck, W. R., ed. *Architectural Essays from the Chicago School: Thomas Tallmadge, Louis H. Sullivan, Jens Jensen and Frank Lloyd Wright.* [Park Forest, Illinois: Prairie School Press, 1967.]
35 x 27.5 cm., 20 pp., 90 ills., paper. (A Prairie School Press Reissue)
Includes reprints of: "The 'Village Bank' Series, V." (*Brickbuilder*, 1901); "A Home in a Prairie Town," "A Small House with 'Lots of Room in It'," and "A Fireproof House for $5000." (*Ladies' Home Journal*, 1901, 1907.)

REVIEW
1683. Anonymous. *Prairie Sch R* IV (no. 4, 1967), p. 29.

1684. Ripon, Wisconsin. Ripon College Art Gallery. *Frank Lloyd Wright: An Exhibition of Drawings.* N.d.
19.6 x 24 cm., 8 pp., 2 ills., paper.
An announcement, with a note by Bernard S. Adams, President, Ripon College.

1685. Sharp, Dennis. "Frank Lloyd Wright." In *Sources of Modern Architecture: A Bibliography.* New York: George Wittenborn, [1967]. Pp. 38-9. (Architectural Association (London) Paper Number 2)
Includes a list of 30 books and articles by and about Wright.

1686. Wright, Frank Lloyd. *The Japanese Print: An Interpretation.* New York: Horizon Press, [1967].
See no. 109.

Periodicals

1687. Banham, Reyner. "Frank Lloyd Wright as Environmentalist." *Arch Design* XXXVII (Ap 1967), pp. 174-7.
Reprinted from *Arts and Architecture* (see no. 1653).

1688. Cohen, Martin. "Peril of the Imperial." *Progress Arch* XLVIII (Se 1967), pp. 66, 68.

1689. "Committee for the Preservation of the Imperial Hotel." *Inland Arch* XI (D 1967), pp. 12-13.

1690. "Demolizioni e falsi storici." *Casabella* no. 314 (Je 1967), p. 69.
Imperial Hotel, Tokyo.

1691. DeNevi, Don. "Educational Thoughts of Frank Lloyd Wright and Their Implications for Education." *Educational Theory* XVII (Ap 1967), pp. 154-9.
Wright's influence as a teacher.

1692. DeNevi, Don. "Frank Lloyd Wright on College Teaching." *Improving College and University Teaching* XV (W 1967), pp. 48-9.

1693. Dickey, Paula. "Exploding the Box." *Arts and Activities* LXII (Se 1967), pp. 18-21.
  Houses designed by junior high school students, based on Wright's principles.

1694. "Donations May Save Wright's Imperial Hotel." *Progress Arch* XLVIII (D 1967), p. 29.

1695. Engel, Martin. "Frank Lloyd Wright and Cubism: A Study in Ambiguity." *Am Q* XIX (Sp 1967), pp. 24-38.

1696. "Frederick C. Robie House, Frank Lloyd Wright, Architect." *Prairie Sch R* IV (no. 4, 1967), pp. 10-19 and cover.

1697. Gerigk, Herbert. "An den jungen Mann in der Architektur." *Deutsche Baumeister* XXVIII (no. 12, 1967), p. 1024.

1698. Higuchi, Kiyoshi. "The Significance for Today of Wright's Architecture." *JA* no. 135 (O 1967), pp. 17-20; no. 136 (N 1967), pp. 17-20.

1699. Hines, Thomas S., Jr. "Frank Lloyd Wright—the Madison Years: Records Versus Recollections." *Wis Mag Hist* L (W 1967), pp. 109-19.
  Discussion of evidence indicating that Wright was born in 1867. Reprinted in *Journal of the Society of Architectural Historians* XXVI (D 1967), pp. 227-33. Comment, see no. 1702.

1700. Hitchcock, H.-R. "Frank Lloyd Wright 1867–1967." *Zodiac* (no. 17, 1967), pp. 6-10.
  Reprinted in slightly different form in *Prairie School Review* IV (no. 4, 1967), pp. 5-9.

1701. Kamrath, Karl. "The Stubborn Hotel Is Shaking." *AIA J* XLVIII (N 1967), pp. 70-2.
  Imperial Hotel, Tokyo.

1702.   Koehler, Robert E. "The Wright Record." *AIA J* XLVIII
(Jy 1967), pp. 3-4.
   Comment on article by Thomas S. Hines, Jr. (see no. 1699).

1703.   Meisenheimer, Wolfgang. "Der Raum in der Architektur:
Strukturen, Gestalten, Begriffe." *Kunstwerk* XXI (O-N 1967),
p. 78.

1704.   "Milestone in Madison." *Arch For* CXXVII (N 1967), pp.
30-1.
   Monona Terrace, Madison (project).

1705.   Morton, Terry Brust. "Wright's Pope-Leighey House."
Prairie Sch R IV (no. 4, 1967), pp. 20-6.

1706.   Novinger, Virginia B. "Finding His Own Way: Hero Story."
Instructor LXXVII (D 1967), p. 63.
   Biographical information on Wright's youth.

1707.   Pearson, Michael. "Pneumatic Structures." *Arch R* CXLII
(O 1967), p. 313.
   Includes a photograph of "Air House," designed by Wright
(?), exhibited at the International Home Exhibition, New York.

1708.   Pundt, Herman G. "Academia Sparked." *AIA J* XLVIII
(O 1967), pp. 53-6.
   "Vision and Legacy" exhibit; see no. 1629.

1709.   "Rilettura di tre opere di Wright." *Zodiac* (no. 17, 1967),
pp. 11-46.

1710.   Riley, Frank. "Deathwatch in Tokyo." *Sat R* L (16 D
1967), pp. 40-5.
   Imperial Hotel.

1711.   Smith, Norris K. "Frank Lloyd Wright and the Problem
of Historical Perspective." *JSAH* XXVI (D 1967), pp. 234-7.

1712.   "Squaring the Circle." *Arch For* CXXVII (D 1967), p. 46.
   Addition, designed by Taliesin Associated Architects, to the
Guggenheim Museum.

1713. "Vandalismus in Tokyo." *Baumeister* LXIV (D 1967), pp. 1494-5.
Imperial Hotel.

1714. Weisberg, Gabriel. "Frank Lloyd Wright and Pre-Columbian Art—the Background for His Architecture." *Art Q* XXX (Sp 1967), pp. 40-51.

1715. Wilson, Stuart. "The Gifts of Friedrich Froebel." *JSAH* XXVI (D 1967), pp. 238-41.
Includes references to the influence of Froebel's toys on Wright.

1716. "Wright Drawings." *Prairie Sch R* IV (no. 4, 1967), inside back cover.
Drawings of Booth house, Glencoe (project), and Stewart house (?), Montecito, given by Wright to the School of Architecture, Texas A & M University.

1717. Wright, Frank Lloyd. "Ethics of Ornament." *Prairie Sch R* IV (no. 1, 1967), pp. 16-17.
Excerpts of a lecture delivered by Wright in 1909, first published in *Oak Leaves,* 16 January 1909.

1718. "Wright's Martin House to Be Restored." *Progress Arch* XLVIII (N 1967), p. 63.

1719. "Wright's Ship of State." *Progress Arch* XLVIII (Fe 1967), p. 30.
Marin County Civic Center, San Rafael.

1720. "Wright's 'Teahouse'." *Newsweek* LXX (23 O 1967), p. 78.
Riverview Terrace Restaurant (The Spring Green), Spring Green.

1968

Books

1721. Brandon, Henry. "Beyond Modern Architecture: A Conversation with Frank Lloyd Wright." In *Conversations with Henry Brandon.* Boston: Houghton Mifflin Company, 1968. Pp. 55-62.

1722.   [Futagawa, Yukio, photographer and Tsutomu Ikuta and Hiroshi Misawa, text.] *F. LL. Wright, 2.* [Tokyo: Bijutsu Shuppan-sha, 1968.]
> 25.4 x 19.4 cm., 120 pp., 66 ills. (part color), cloth. (Contemporary Architects Series)
> A study of Wright's private buildings and companion volume to an earlier book (see no. 1680). Japanese text. An American edition was announced by Simon and Schuster, but it has not appeared as of this writing.

1723.   Historic American Buildings Survey. *The Robie House: Frank Lloyd Wright.* [Palos Park, Illinois: The Prairie School Press, 1968.]
> 27.9 x 37.9 cm., 15 pp., 14 ills., paper.
> Reproductions of measured drawings, completed by the Historic American Buildings Survey in August, 1963. Includes floor plans, elevations, sections, window details, environmental provisions, furniture, and notes which describe structural modifications to the house. See also no. 2082.

REVIEW
1724.   Cuscaden, Rob. *Prairie Sch R* V (no. 4, 1968), p. 28.

1725.   James, Cary. *The Imperial Hotel: Frank Lloyd Wright and the Architecture of Unity.* Rutland, Vermont, and Tokyo: Charles E. Tuttle Company, [1968].
> 25.7 x 18.6 cm., 79 pp., 63 ills., 6 foldout floor plans, cloth.
> A study of the hotel illustrated with photographs taken by the author in 1965. It includes a brief introduction by the author and quotations from Wright's writings.

REVIEWS
1726.   Brooks, H. Allen. "Preserved within a Book." *Progress Arch* L (Jy 1969), pp. 150, 156.
1727.   Fern, Alan. *Landscape* XVIII (Fa 1969), p. 37.
1728.   Tafel, Edgar. *Prairie Sch R* V (no. 4, 1968), p. 27.

1729. Naden, Corinne J. *Frank Lloyd Wright: The Rebel Architect.* New York: Franklin Watts, Inc., [1968].
20.9 x 13.9 cm., x, 150 pp., 31 ills., cloth. (Immortals of Engineering)
A juvenile biography.

1730. Richards, Kenneth G. *People of Destiny: Frank Lloyd Wright.* Chicago: Childrens Press, [1968].
27.8 x 21.4 cm., 96 pp., 52 ills. (A Humanities Series)
A juvenile biography.

1731. Watanabe, Yoshio, photographer, and Tachu Naito, Shindo Akashi, and Gakuji Yamamoto, text. *Imperial Hotel 1921–67.* [Tokyo]: Kajima Institute Publishing Company, [1968].
23.1 x 25.4 cm., 102 pp., 56 ills., 9 color pls.
A photostudy of the hotel, with Japanese text. Boxed.

1732. Wright, Frank Lloyd. *Frank Lloyd Wright: The Early Work.* New York: Horizon Press, 1968.
See no. 96.

Periodicals

1733. Akashi, Shindo, and Mary E. Osman. "Imperial Comes Tumbling Down." *AIA J* L (D 1968), pp. 42-9 and cover.
Includes review of James' *Imperial Hotel* (see no. 1725).

1734. DeNevi, Don. "The Education of a Genius: Analyzing Major Influences on the Life of America's Greatest Architect." *Young Children* XXIII (Mr 1968), pp. 233-40.
Includes discussion of Froebelian toys.

1735. DeNevi, Don. "The Taliesin Thesis & Frank Lloyd Wright." *Art Education* XXI (D 1968), pp. 13-15.
Education at Taliesin.

1736. "Drum along Monona." *Progress Arch* XLIX (D 1968), p. 48.
Madison Civic Auditorium (project), designed by Taliesin Associated Architects, based on Wright's earlier scheme.

1737.　Dunhill, Priscilla. "Requiem for a Masterpiece." *Arch For* CXXVIII (My 1968), pp. 70-5.
　　Imperial Hotel, Tokyo.

1738.　"Four Unitarian Churches." *Architecture Canada* XLV (Fe 1968), pp. 31-42.
　　Includes Unity Temple, Oak Park.

1739.　"Frank Lloyd Wright: His Future Influence." *Progress Arch* XLIX (Se 1968), pp. 140-3.

1740.　"Frank Lloyd Wright Items Offered for Sale by His Son." *North Carolina Architect* XV (O 1968), pp. 20-2.
　　An annotated list of sixty-six items including books, personal momentos, original manuscripts, paintings and furniture. Prices are not given.

1741.　"Imperial Hotel, Tokyo." *Arch R* CXLIII (Mr 1968), pp. 175, 178.
　　Documentation of the building during demolition.

1742.　Kirishiki, Shinjiro. "The Story of the Imperial Hotel, Tokyo." *JA* no. 138 (Ja-Fe 1968), pp. 113-38.

1743.　Kobayashi, Bunji. "Frank Lloyd Wright's Imperial Hotel in Tokyo." *Hist Pres* XX (Ap-Je 1968), pp. 62-8.

1744.　Licht, Ira. "Stained Glass Panels of Frank Lloyd Wright." *Arts Magazine* XLIII (N 1968), pp. 34-5.
　　Windows from Martin house, Buffalo, at Richard Feigen Gallery, New York.

1745.　MacCormac, Richard C. "The Anatomy of Wright's Aesthetic." *Arch R* CXLIII (Fe 1968), pp. 143-6.
　　A reply from Derek S. Bottomley, with a rejoinder, was published in volume CXLIV (Ag 1968), p. 148.

1746.　McCoy, Robert E. "Rock Crest/Rock Glen Prairie Planning in Iowa." *Prairie Sch R* V (no. 3, 1968), pp. 5-39 and cover.
　　Includes discussion of City National Bank and Hotel,

Melson house (project), and Stockman house, all in Mason City.

1747.   "On Exhibition." *Studio International* CLXXVI (D 1968), p. 274.
Windows from Martin house, Buffalo, at Richard Feigen Gallery, New York.

1748.   "Playful Precedent." *Arch For* CXXVIII (Mr 1968), pp. 84-5.
Window, Coonley playhouse, Riverside.

1749.   Ponti, Gio. "Tokyo: Imperial Hotel, 1922–1967." *Domus* no. 459 (Fe 1968), pp. 5-11.
Photographs of the hotel prior to and during demolition.

1750.   Ragon, Michel. "Wright, un genio solitario." *Punto* VII (Je 1968), pp. 10-22.

1751.   "Requiem per l'Imperial Hotel." *Architettura* XIV (Se 1968), p. 385.

1752.   "Reviews and Previews." *Art N* LXVII (N 1968), p. 79.
Windows from Martin house, Buffalo, at Feigen Galleries, New York.

1753.   Rubino, Luciano. "Flashes su Frank Lloyd Wright." *Architettura* XIII (Fe 1968), pp. 690-4; (Mr), pp. 758-64; (Ap), pp. 830-4; XIV (My), pp. 60-4; (Je), pp. 130-4; (Ag), pp. 340-4; (Se), pp. 410-14; (O), pp. 480-4; (D), pp. 620-4.

1754.   Tafel, E., and R. C. Haskett. "Tragedy of the Imperial." *Arch For* CXXVIII (Ja-Fe 1968), p. 15.

1755.   "Taliesin West's Theatre by Frank Lloyd Wright: (Scottsdale, Arizona)." *Theatre Design and Technology* no. 15 (D 1968), p. 23.

1756.   Twombly, Robert C. "Frank Lloyd Wright in Spring Green, 1911–1932." *Wis Mag Hist* LI (Sp 1968), pp. 200-17.

1757.   "Wright's Madison Plan Comes to Life." *Progress Arch*
XLIX (My 1968), pp. 66-7.
    Monona Terrace Civic Center, to be completed by Taliesin
Associated Architects.

1969

Books

1758.   Andrews, Wayne. "Frank Lloyd Wright." In *Architecture
in New York: A Photographic History.* New York: Atheneum,
1969. Pp. 147-55.
    Includes illustrations of: the Martin, Heath, and Davidson
houses, and the Larkin Company administration building,
Buffalo; Boynton house, Rochester; Friedman house, Pleasantville; and Guggenheim Museum, New York.

1759.   Braatz, Wolfgang, ed. *Frank Lloyd Wright: Humane Archi-
tecture.* [Gütersloh/Berlin]: Bertelsmann Fachverlag, [1969].
    18.2 x 13.6 cm., 273 pp., 51 ills. (Bauwelt Fundamente 25)
    German text. Includes the list of buildings compiled by
Bruce F. Radde originally published in *Frank Lloyd Wright:
Writings and Buildings* (see no. 1401).

1760.   Bullock, Helen Duprey, and Terry B. Morton, eds. *The
Pope-Leighy* [sic] *House.* Washington, D. C.: National Trust for
Historic Preservation, [1969].
    23.5 x 14.6 cm., 120 pp., 69 ills., paper.
    Includes: "Documents," by Ellen Beasley; "Frank Lloyd
Wright: His Concepts and Career," by H. Allen Brooks; "The
Challenge of Being a Taliesin Fellow," by Gordon Chadwick;
"The Usonian Pope-Leighey House," by Edgar J. Kaufmann,
Jr.; "A Testimony to Beauty," by Marjorie F. Leighey; "The
Threat, Rescue and Move," by Terry B. Morton; "Furniture
and Decoration," by John N. Pearce; "Twenty-Five Years
Later: Still a Love Affair," by Loren B. Pope; "The Challenge
of Constructing a Wright House," by Howard C. Rickert; and
"Siting and Landscaping," by Joseph Watterson.
    □ This book first appeared as the Ap-Se 1969 issue of *Historic
Preservation* (see no. 1790). It was available in a hardback

edition from the Prairie School Press.

REVIEW
1761. Kalec, Donald. *Prairie Sch R* VIII (no. 1, 1971), pp. 20-1. Correction: VIII (no. 3, 1971), p. 18.

1762. Eaton, Leonard K. *Two Chicago Architects and Their Clients: Frank Lloyd Wright and Howard Van Doren Shaw.* With an Appendix by Elizabeth M. Douvan. [Cambridge, Massachusetts, and London: MIT Press, 1969.]
25.4 x 17.6 cm., xi, 259 pp., 104 ills., cloth.
A comparative analysis of the clients of the two architects. The appendix describes the methods through which the study was made.

REVIEWS
1763. Brooks, H. Allen. *Progress Arch* LI (Ag 1970), p. 100.
1764. O'Gorman, James F. *Art Q* XXXIII (W 1970), pp. 446-7.
1765. Pawley, Martin. "To Carrying Through One Architectural Revolution—$30-40,000,000." *Arch Design* XL (Ag 1970), pp. 414-15.
1766. Smith, Norris Kelly. *JSAH* XXIX (My 1970), pp. 205-6.
1767. Townsend, Robert. *RIBA J* LXXVII (My 1970), pp. 232-3.
1768. Webster, J. Carson. *Prairie Sch R* VII (no. 1, 1970), pp. 20-1.

1769. Harris, Harwell Hamilton. *Architecture as an Art.* [Clinton, Iowa: The Fingernail Moon Press, 1969.]
12 x 12 cm., 8 pp., paper.
An essay on the Barnsdall house, "Hollyhock House," Los Angeles. It was written for the unpublished catalogue of the exhibition of Wright's work at the Museum of Modern Art in 1940. This edition was privately printed and limited to approximately 200 copies.

1770. Manson, Grant Carpenter. *Frank Lloyd Wright: la prima età d'oro.* Roma: Officina Edizioni, [1969].
See no. 1206.

1771. New York. Parke-Bernet Galleries, Inc. *Japanese Prints Including Masanobu, Harunobu, Koryusai, Shunsho, Shunko, Shunei, Kiyonaga, Utamaro, Toyokuni II, Hokusai, Hiroshige, and Works by Other Artists.* Formerly in the Frank Lloyd Wright Collection. Now the Property of the Estate of the Late Blanche B. McFetridge, San Diego, Calif. Public Auction Thursday, November 20 at 1:45 p.m., Friday, November 21 at 10 a.m. New York: Parke-Bernet Galleries, Inc., 1969.

An auction catalogue. A preface discusses Wright and the prints. Includes supplementary bid list for the 433 prints offered.

1772. Nott, C. S. "Taliesin and the Frank Lloyd Wrights." In *Journey through This World: The Second Journal of a Pupil; Including an Account of Meetings with G. I. Gurdjieff, A. R. Orage, and P. D. Ouspensky.* London: Routledge & Kegan Paul, [1969]. Pp. 138-56.

Reminiscences of a visit at Taliesin in 1940.

1773. Oak Park, Illinois. Public Library. *Frank Lloyd Wright, A Bibliography: The Local Authors Collection.* Oak Park, Illinois: Oak Park Public Library, 1969.

28 x 21.7 cm., 8 pp., paper.

Cover title. An annotated listing of the library's holdings.

1774. [Sanderson, Warren, ed.] *Frank Lloyd Wright Festival.* Oak Park-River Forest, Ill. May 30-July 4, 1969. [Oak Park, Illinois: Oak Park-River Forest Chamber of Commerce, 1969.]

20.5 x 20.1 cm., 36 pp., 44 ills., paper.

Cover title. A program including a calendar of events, a biography of Wright, and illustrations of his work in Oak Park and River Forest.

□ A new, undated edition with the cover title *Frank Lloyd Wright Architecture: Oak Park* [*and*] *River Forest, Illinois* was published in 1973.

1775. Wright, Frank Lloyd. *The Industrial Revolution Runs Away.* New York: Horizon Press, [1969].

See no. 328.

Periodicals

1776.   Banham, Reyner. "The Wilderness Years of Frank Lloyd Wright." *RIBA J* LXXVI (D 1969), pp. 512-19.
A reply from Sandra Millikin with a rejoinder was published in volume LXXVII (Ja 1970), p. 3.

1777.   "Chicago Resurrections: Frank Lloyd Wright's Robie House." *Interiors* CXXVIII (My 1969), pp. 114-17. (Also issued as offprint.)

1778.   Finch, Christopher. "Frank Lloyd Wright." *Design Quarterly* no. 74-5 (1969), pp. 13-15.
A section of a larger article on "the imagination of professional architects."

1779.   "FLW Follower." *Arch R* CXLV (My 1969), pp. 379-80.
Allan Gelbin.

1780.   DeNevi, Don. "Nature as a Teacher." *Science and Children* VII (N 1969), pp. 11-14.
Discussion of Wright's theory on the use of nature for architectural inspiration.

1781.   "Frank Lloyd Wright Was Also a Gifted Landscape Architect." *Sunset* CXLII (Fe 1969), pp. 70-3.

1782.   Greenberg, Allan. "Lutyens' Architecture Restudied." *Perspecta* no. 12 (1969), pp. 144-7.
Includes "Lutyens and Frank Lloyd Wright."

1783.   "High Bids Cloud Future of Madison Auditorium." *AIA J* LI (Je 1969), pp. 24, 28.
Madison Civic Center, designed by Taliesin Associated Architects.

1784.   Hoffmann, Donald. "Frank Lloyd Wright and Viollet-le-Duc." *JSAH* XXVIII (O 1969), pp. 173-83.

1785.   Kaufmann, Edgar, Jr. "Frank Lloyd Wright: The Eleventh

Decade." *Arch For* CXXX (Je 1969), pp. 38-41.

1786.   Marlin, William. "Taliesin 1969: Sagging and Cracking, but Alive with a Message of Man." *Inland Arch* XIII (Jy 1969), pp. 22-5.
>   Includes the Spring Green restaurant.

1787.   O'Gorman, James F. "Henry Hobson Richardson and Frank Lloyd Wright." *Art Q* XXXII (Au 1969), pp. 292-315.

1788.   Olson, Allen R., and Albert L. Hoffmeyer, eds. "Frank Lloyd Wright." *Northw Arch* XXXIII (Jy-Ag 1969), pp. 23-56, 59, 61, 63, 65, 67-8, 71, 73, 75-8 and cover.
>   A special issue, prepared with the assistance of John H. Howe. It includes articles by Howe and conversations with several of Wright's clients.

1789.   Patrulius, Radu. "Frank Lloyd Wright: 100 ani de la nastere." *Arhitectura* (Rumania) XVII (no. 5, 1969), pp. 26-9.

1790.   "The Pope-Leighy [sic] House." *Hist Pres* XXI (Ap-Se 1969), pp. 2-120 and cover.
>   See no. 1760.

1791.   Rebay, R. V. "Der aktuelle Hundertjahrige." *Baumeister* LXVI (Je 1969), pp. 804-8.

1792.   "Resurrection FLW." *Arch Design* XXXIX (Ag 1969), p. 411.
>   Robie house, Chicago.

1793.   Saltzstein, Joan W. "Taliesin through the Years." *Wisconsin Architect* XL (O 1969), pp. 14-18 and cover.
>   The author is the granddaughter of Dankmar Adler.

1794.   "Sandbags in Racine." *Inland Arch* XIII (Ag-Se 1969), pp. 18-19.
>   Note on the role of E. Willis Jones in commissioning Wright to design the S. C. Johnson and Son administration building, Racine.

1795. "Lo scempio del Guggenheim Museum." *Architettura* XIV (Ja 1969), p. 634.
Addition, designed by Taliesin Associated Architects.

1796. Segal, Walter. "Great Original: Frank Lloyd Wright." *Architects' J* CXLIX (11 Je 1969), pp. 1546-8.

1797. Short, Ramsay. "Taliesin in Tact: Frank Lloyd Wright." *Listener* LXXXII (20 N 1969), p. 699.
The author spent two weeks at Taliesin West in March, 1969 and produced a documentary film on Wright shown on BBC.

1798. Spade, Rupert. "The Other Side of Mayor Daley, or the Day Frank Lloyd Wright Changed Trains." *Arch Design* XXXIX (N 1969), p. 583.

1799. Tselos, Dimitri. "Frank Lloyd Wright and World Architecture." *JSAH* XXVIII (Mr 1969), pp. 58-72.
A follow-up on the author's earlier article (see no. 969) which discusses the influences of Japanese and pre-Columbian art on Wright's architecture. It includes a previously unpublished response to the first article from Wright.

1800. "Wright Centennial to Give Oak Park a Festive Look: Tours Set for Architects." *AIA J* LI (My 1969), pp. 12, 16.
Includes excerpts from a response from Mrs. Wright to an *AIA Journal* query about Wright's birthdate.

1801. Wright, Henry. "Unity Temple, Oak Park, Illinois." *Arch For* CXXX (Je 1969), pp. 28-37 and cover.

1802. "Wright on Sheridan Road." *Inland Arch* XIII (O 1969), pp. 14-15.
Bach house, Chicago.

1803. Zevi, Bruno. "Frank Lloyd Wright, domani." *And* Frank, Edward. "Filosofia organica, architettura organica e Frank Lloyd Wright." *Architettura* XV (N 1969), pp. 422-84.

1970

Books

1804.   Bardeschi, Marco Dezzi. *Frank Lloyd Wright.* [Firenze]:
Sansoni editore, [1970].
  30.4 x 23.9 cm., 96 pp., 65 ills., 44 color pls., cloth. (12/I
Maestri del novecento)
  A study in Italian which includes a brief text, a biographical
outline, a chronological list of works and projects, and a biblio-
graphy.
  □ An English-language edition was published by Hamlyn, Lon-
don, New York, Sydney, Toronto, [1972]. (Twentieth Century
Masters.) Some of the illustrations vary from the Italian edition.

1805.   Cavanaugh, Tom R., and Payne E. L. Thomas. *A Frank
Lloyd Wright House: Bannerstone House, Springfield, Illinois.*
Springfield, Illinois: Charles C. Thomas, [1970].
  21.3 x 14.1 cm., vi, 43 pp., 18 ills., paper.
  A discussion of the Dana house, its client and its architect,
and its use today.

1806.   Columbia University. School of Architecture. *Four Great
Makers of Modern Architecture: Gropius, Le Corbusier, Mies van
der Rohe, Wright.* The Verbatim Record of a Symposium Held at
the School of Architecture, Columbia University, March-May,
1961. New York: Da Capo Press, 1970.
  See no. 1528.

1807.   Culmsee, Carlton. "Wright and His Helix." In *Shapes for
the Deep Unrest, Three Essays: The Radiant Apex, Wright and
His Helix, Mold of Fire.* Logan, Utah: Utah State University Press,
November, 1970. Pp. 8-12. (Monograph Series Volume XVIII—
Number 1)
  Theoretical discussion of Wright's employment of geometric
forms in the Guggenheim Museum.

1808.   Futagawa, Yukio, editor and photographer, and Arata
Isozaki, text. *Frank Lloyd Wright: Johnson & Son, Administra-
tion Building and Research Tower, Racine, Wisconsin. 1936–9.*
Tokyo: A.D.A. Edita, [1970].

36.3 x 25.7 cm., 48 pp., 25 ills. (part color), paper. (The Series of Global Architecture No. 1)

A photostudy with accompanying description in Japanese. Includes plans.

1809.   Futagawa, Yukio, editor and photographer, and Paul Rudolph, text. *Frank Lloyd Wright: Kaufmann House, "Falling-water," Bear Run, Pennsylvania, 1936.* Tokyo: A.D.A. Edita, [1970].

36.3 x 25.7 cm., 48 pp., 28 ills. (part color), paper. (The Series of Global Architecture No. 2)

A photostudy with accompanying description in Japanese and English. Includes plans.

1810.   Moses, Robert. "Frank Lloyd Wright." In *Public Works: A Dangerous Trade.* New York: McGraw-Hill Book Company, [1970]. Pp. 855-72.

Includes a brief biographical sketch and the contents of correspondence dated from 1944 to 1958 of Wright, Moses, and Harry F. Guggenheim, concerning the Guggenheim Museum, New York. Another letter, from Mrs. Patrick Kinney, discusses the house Wright designed for her and her husband.

1811.   Pawley, Martin, and Yukio Futagawa. *Frank Lloyd Wright, I: Public Buildings.* New York: Simon and Schuster, [1970].

See no. 1680.

1812.   Reif, Rita. "Darwin D. Martin House, Buffalo, New York, Frank Lloyd Wright's 'Prairie House'." In *Treasure Rooms of America's Mansions, Manors and Houses.* New York: Coward-McCann, Inc., [1970]. Pp. 294-8.

Information, including five photographs, on the restoration of this house.

1813.   [Smith, Dean, ed.] *Grady Gammage Memorial Auditorium, Designed by Frank Lloyd Wright.* [Tempe, Arizona: Arizona State University, 1970.]

See no. 1569.

1814.   Tiltman, Hessell. *The Imperial Hotel Story.* [Tokyo,

Imperial Hotel, 1970.]
    20.8 x 14.8 cm., 80 pp., 8 ills., paper.
    Revised edition. Includes history of the building designed
by Wright and its use immediately after the 1923 Tokyo earthquake and during World War II.

1815. Wright, Frank Lloyd. *An Organic Architecture: The Architecture of Democracy.* The Sir George Watson Lectures of the
Sulgrave Manor Board for 1939. [London]: Lund Humphries,
[1970].
    See no. 463.

Periodicals

1816. Angrisani, Marcello. "Reyner Banham e l'environmental-
ism." *Casabella* no. 353 (O 1970), pp. 41-6.

1817. Baldridge, J. Alan. "Wright House for the Right Buyer."
AIA J LIII (Ja 1970), p. 68.
    Walser house, Chicago.

1818. Crawford, Alan. "Ten Letters from Frank Lloyd Wright
to Charles Robert Ashbee." *Architectural History* XIII (1970),
pp. 64-73.
    Written between 3 Ja 1902 and 11 My 1939. The letters are
now at King's College Library, Cambridge.

1819. "Design for Dining." *Inland Arch* XIV (Jy 1970), pp. 16-
17.
    Spring Green Restaurant, Spring Green.

1820. "Exhibitions." *Arch Rec* CXLVIII (O 1970), p. 36.
    Windows from Martin house conservatory, Buffalo, and
drawings and blueprints for Berdan house, Ludington (project),
at Richard Feigen Gallery, New York.

1821. "First Christian Church of Phoenix." *Arch Rec* CXLVII
(Je 1970), p. 42.
    Executed by Taliesin Associated Architects, based on
Wright's 1950 project for Southwest Christian Seminary.

1822. Glueck, Grace. "New York Gallery Notes." *Art in Am* LVIII (Se-O 1970), p. 39.
Windows from Martin house, Buffalo, at Richard Feigen Gallery, New York.

1823. Hartwell, Patricia. "Gala at Taliesin—Brightest Easter in the Valley…" *Phoenix* V (Mr 1970), pp. 20-3 and cover.

1824. Hasbrouck, Wilbert R. "The Earliest Work of Frank Lloyd Wright." *Prairie Sch R* VII (no. 4, 1970), pp. 14-16.

1825. "The Johnson Building, Racine, USA." *Camera* XLIX (My 1970), pp. 21, 23-5 and cover.
Photographs.

1826. *Kentiku* (Je 1970), pp. 13-24.
Japanese text. Includes: an article by Masami Tanigawa on the book *The Industrial Revolution Runs Away* (see no. 328); a translation of "Frank Lloyd Wright: The Madison Years," by Thomas S. Hines (see no. 1699); and information on the architecture of Frank Lloyd Wright in Oak Park and River Forest.

1827. *Kindaikenchiku* XXIV (Fe 1970), pp. 49-95 and cover.
Japanese text. Includes: "The Proposal of Wright for Nature," by T. Kurosawa and H. Fujii; "Liberation for Human," by Olgivanna Lloyd Wright; "Reappraisal for the Works of Wright;" six chapters about F. LL. Wright, by M. Tanigawa; and a chronological list of work of buildings and projects by Frank Lloyd Wright from 1887–1959.

1828. Koppes, Neil (photographer). "Frank Lloyd Wright's Circular Sun House." *Phoenix* V (Jy 1970), pp. 54-6.
Lykes house, Phoenix.

1829. "Landmarks: Bad News with a Few Bright Spots." *Arch Rec* CXLVIII (N 1970), p. 36.
Demolition of Lake Geneva Inn; uncertain status of hotel, Mason City, and Hickox house, Kankakee.

1830. March, Lionel. "Imperial City of the Boundless West: The

Impact of Chicago on the Work of Frank Lloyd Wright." *Listener* LXXXIII (30 Ap 1970), pp. 581-4.

1831. "Masterpieces of Two Sullivan Students: One is Destroyed, One Saved." *Arch Rec* CXLVII (Ap 1970), p. 40.
      Martin house, Buffalo.

1832. Mix, Sheldon A. "The Oak Park Years: A Walking Tour of the Frank Lloyd Wright Houses in Oak Park and River Forest." *Chicago* VII (Ap 1970), pp. 31-5, 79-80, 82.

1833. Montgomery, Roger. "Frank Lloyd Wright's Hall of Justice." *Arch For* CXXXIII (D 1970), pp. 54-9.
      Marin County Civic Center, San Rafael.

1834. "Recent Acquisitions 1968–1969." *Bulletin of Rhode Island School of Design* LVI (Su 1970), pp. 55-6.
      Windows from Martin house, Buffalo.

1835. "Restored Wright." *Arch R* CXLVII (Fe 1970), p. 157.
      Martin house, Buffalo.

1836. "Reviews and Previews." *Art N* LXIX (N 1970), p. 71.
      Windows from Martin house, Buffalo, at Feigen Gallery, New York.

1837. "Richard Neutra, Last Writings, Last Works." *Architettura* XVI (N 1970), pp. 422-72.
      Includes photographs taken at Taliesin in 1924 of Wright, Neutra, and Erich Mendelsohn.

1838. Rowe, Colin. "Chicago Frame." *Arch Design* XL (D 1970), pp. 641-7.
      A revised version of an article published in 1956, see no. 1134.

1839. Shank, Wesley I. "The Residence in Des Moines." *JSAH* XXIX (Mr 1970), pp. 56-9.
      Discussion of the Brinsmaid house, designed by Arthur Heun and completed in 1898, with references to Wright's contemporary work.

1840. Sorell, Susan Karr. "Silsbee: The Evolution of a Personal Architectural Style." *Prairie Sch R* VII (no. 4, 1970), pp. 5-13.
Includes references to Wright's early career.

1841. "Unity Temple Restoration." *Prairie Sch R* VII (no. 3, 1970), pp. 13-16. (Also issued as offprint.)

1842. Wegg, Talbot. "FLLW versus the U.S.A." *AIA J* LIII (Fe 1970), pp. 48-52.
Cloverleaf housing, Pittsfield (project).

1843. "Weiner and Wright." *Inland Arch* XIV (My 1970), p. 19.
Egon Weiner sculpted a bust of Wright; note on their meeting at Taliesin.

1844. "Wright House in Danger of Dissection." *Progress Arch* LI (Ja 1970), p. 25.
Walser house, Chicago.

1845. Wright, Frank Lloyd. "The New Larkin Administration Building." *Prairie Sch R* VII (no. 1, 1970), pp. 14-19.
Reprinted from *Larkin Idea,* see no. 67.

1846. Zevi, Bruno. "L'idea di Oskar Stonorov." *Architettura* XVI (Jy 1970), pp. 142-3.

1971

Books

1847. Gebhard, David, and Harriette Von Breton. *Lloyd Wright, Architect: 20th Century Architecture in an Organic Exhibition.* Santa Barbara: University of California, 1971.
An exhibition catalogue. It includes information on the contributions of Lloyd Wright to many of his father's buildings before 1930.

1848. Salsini, Paul. *Frank Lloyd Wright: The Architectural Genius of the Twentieth Century.* D. Steve Rahmas, ed. Charlotteville, New York: SamHar Press, 1971.

21.3 x 14.2 cm., 32 pp., paper. (Outstanding Personalities No. 2)
A juvenile biography.

1849. Wright, Frank Lloyd. *Genius and the Mobocracy.* New York: Horizon Press, [1971].
See no. 750.

Periodicals

1850. Bowman, Ned A. "Stalking Theatre Scenography through the American Southwest with Gun and Camera." *Theatre Design and Technology* no. 26 (O 1971), pp. 4-13.
Includes: Grady Gammage Memorial Auditorium, Tempe; and Cabaret Theatre, Taliesin West, Scottsdale.

1851. Brooks, H. Allen. "Chicago Architecture: Its Debt to the Arts and Crafts." *JSAH* XXX (D 1971), pp. 312-17.
Includes references to Wright and two previously unpublished interior photographs of his house in Oak Park.

1852. Cordier, Gilbert. "Architectonic Reflexions on the Written Work of F. L. Wright c. e. Le Corbusier." *Review of the International Union of Architects* no. 12 (1971), pp. 34-50.
Translated by William Burke.

1853. "Dallas Theater Center." *Arch Rec* CXLIX (Fe 1971), p. 42.
Award from Dallas A.I.A. chapter; photograph of addition by William Wesley Peters.

1854. "Early Wright Work Destroyed." *Arch Rec* CXLIX (Ap 1971), p. 41.
Harlan house, Chicago.

1855. Eisenstaedt, Alfred (photographer), and Loudon Wainwright. "Guardian of a Great Legacy." *Life* LXX (11 Je 1971), pp. 44-55.
Frank Lloyd Wright Foundation.

1856. Hallmark, Donald P. "Richard W. Bock, Sculptor, Part II: The Mature Collaborations." *Prairie Sch R* VIII (no. 2, 1971), pp. 5-29 and cover.

Includes discussion of the sculpture executed by Bock for several of Wright's early buildings.

1857. Michels, Eileen. "The Early Drawings of Frank Lloyd Wright Reconsidered." *JSAH* XXX (D 1971), pp. 294-303.

Comment, see no. 1886.

1858. "New Frank Lloyd Wright and Louis H. Sullivan Papers in the Burnham Library of Architecture." *Calendar of the Art Institute of Chicago* LXV (Ja 1971), pp. 6-15.

Letters from Wright concerning the Frank L. Smith Bank, Dwight.

1859. "Parasol for the Arts." *Arch For* CXXXV (Jy-Ag 1971), p. 5.

Veteran's Memorial Auditorium, Marin County Civic Center, designed by William Wesley Peters.

1860. Smith, Nancy K. Morris, ed. "Letters, 1903–1906, by Charles E. White, Jr. from the Studio of Frank Lloyd Wright." *Journal of Architectural Education* XXV (Fa 1971), pp. 104-12.

1861. Tarfel [i.e., Tafel], Edgar. "Windows by Frank Lloyd Wright." *Stained Glass* LXVI (Su 1971), pp. 20-1.

1862. "3 Projects." *Arch R* CXLIX (My 1971), pp. 317-18.

Masieri Memorial Building, Venice (project).

1863. Tulecke, Rose, and Jerome B. Tulecke. "Summer Sojourn in Spring Green." *Phoenix* VI (O 1971), pp. 23-4, 60.

1864. "Will the Real Communist Please Stand up." *Arch Design* XLI (Ag 1971), p. 516.

Note concerning the attitude of the Frank Lloyd Wright Foundation toward researchers.

1865. Wright, Frank Lloyd. "The Language of an Organic

Architecture." *Structurist* (no. 11, 1971), pp. 80-2.
  Reprinted from *The Future of Architecture* (no. 913).

1866.   Zevi, Bruno. "Bomba Mendelsohniana: perché la quarta,
se sprecate la terza?" *Architettura* XVII (My 1971), pp. 2-3.

1867.   Zevi, Bruno. "Urbanistica/architettura e la commedia
Gropius +/-/:/x Wright." *Architettura* XVI (Mr 1971), pp. 702-3.

1972

Books

1868.   Bardeschi, Marco Dezzi. *Frank Lloyd Wright.* London,
New York, Sydney, Toronto: Hamlyn, [1972].
  See no. 1804.

1869.   Brooks, H. Allen. *The Prairie School: Frank Lloyd Wright
and His Midwest Contemporaries.* [Toronto and Buffalo]: University of Toronto Press, [1972].
  21.5 x 21.5 cm., 373 pp., 247 ills., cloth.
  A study of a group of architects working in the American
midwest in the early twentieth century. Wright is treated as
the member who gave the movement prominence and who
supplied guidance to some twenty other architects.

REVIEWS
1870.   Eaton, Leonard K. "Frank Lloyd Wright and Friends."
  Progress Arch LIII (Je 1972), pp. 120, 128.
1871.   Hasbrouck, Wilbert R. *Arch For* CXXXVII (D 1972),
  pp. 12-13.
1872.   Hines, Thomas S. *JSAH* XXXI (D 1972), pp. 332-5.
  Correction: XXXII (My 1973), p. 192.
1873.   O'Gorman, James F. *Art B* LIV (D 1972), pp. 564-5.
1874.   Sprague, Paul E. *Prairie Sch R* VIII (no. 4, 1971), pp.
  14-18.

1875.   Clark, Robert Judson, ed. "Frank Lloyd Wright." In *The
Arts and Crafts Movement in America, 1876-1916.* An Exhibition
Organized by the Art Museum, Princeton University, and the Art

Institute of Chicago. With texts by the editor and Martin Eidel-
berg, David A. Hanks, Susan Otis Thompson, and others. [Prince-
ton]: Princeton University Press, [1972]. Pp. 68-75, 101.

An exhibition catalogue with a brief essay on Wright and
ten illustrations of his decorative arts. Another section, "The
Arts and Crafts Book," by Susan Otis Thompson, contains a
reproduction and description of the title page from *The House
Beautiful* (see no. 18).

1876. Futagawa, Yukio, editor and photographer, and Masami
Tanigawa, text. *Frank Lloyd Wright: Taliesin East, Spring Green,
Wisconsin, 1925– ; Taliesin West, Paradise Valley, Arizona,
1938– .* Tokyo: A.D.A. Edita, [1972].
36.3 x 25.7 cm., 48 pp., 25 ills. (part color), paper. (The Series
of Global Architecture No. 15)
A photostudy with Japanese text.

1877. Jordy, William H. "The Encompassing Environment of
Free-Form Architecture: Frank Lloyd Wright's Guggenheim
Museum." In *American Buildings and Their Architects, Volume 4:
The Impact of European Modernism in the Mid-Twentieth Cen-
tury.* Garden City, New York: Doubleday & Company, Inc.,
1972. Chapter V, pp. 279-359.

1878. Jordy, William H. "The Organic Ideal: Frank Lloyd
Wright's Robie House." In *American Buildings and Their Architects, Volume 3: Progressive and Academic Ideals at the Turn of
the Twentieth Century.* Garden City, New York: Doubleday &
Company, Inc., 1972. Chapter III, pp. 180-216.

1879. Muggenberg, James. "Frank Lloyd Wright in Print, 1959–
1970." *In* O'Neal, William B., ed. *The American Association of
Architectural Bibliographers, Papers, Volume IX, 1972.* Char-
lottesville, Virginia: The University of Virginia, [1972]. Pp. 85-
132.

An annotated bibliography in which books and periodical
articles are listed alphabetically by author. It also includes
motion pictures, recordings, and manuscript collections.

1880. Streich, Eugene R. "An Original Owner Interview Survey of Frank Lloyd Wright's Residential Architecture." *In* Mitchell, William J., ed. *Environmental Design: Research and Practice.* Proceedings of the EDRA 3/ AR 8 Conference, University of California at Los Angeles, January, 1972. Pp. 13-10-1 to 13-10-8.

The text of a paper presented at the environmental Design Research Conference held at UCLA. It consists of data compiled after interviews with thirty-three original owners of Wright's houses.

1881.   Willard, Charlotte. *Frank Lloyd Wright: American Architect.* New York: The Macmillan Company, [1972].
20.9 x 14 cm., 183 pp., front., 21 ills., cloth.

A biography. It includes a chronology of major events in the architect's life.

1882.   [Wright, Frank Lloyd.] *Kyu Teikoku Hoteru no Jisshoteki Kenkyu.* [*Frank Lloyd Wright in Imperial Hotel.*] [By] Nobumichi (i.e., Shindo) Akashi. [Tokyo: Tōkōdo Shoten, 1972.]
33.2 x 25.6 cm., xi, 420 pp., 917 ills. (part color), cloth.

A photographic survey of the hotel prior to and during demolition. It includes an appendix containing elevation and plan drawings, detail and furniture drawings, and sections. Japanese text with English subtitles for illustrations. An English translation was announced, but has not yet appeared. English title from book jacket. Boxed.

Periodicals

1883.   "Arizona Church Builds Wright Design 22 Years Later." *Progress Arch* LIII (Se 1972), pp. 59-62.

Chapel, Southwest Christian Seminary, Phoenix (project), 1950.

1884.   Bach, Ruth. "It Happened Only Once." *AIA J* LVIII (O 1972), p. 65.

A letter concerning a visit by Wright to the Balch house, Oak Park.

1885.   Barnett, Jonathan. "Rethinking Wright." *Arch For* CXXXVI (Je 1972), pp. 42-7.

An analysis of Wright's views of our society and cities.

1886. Besinger, Curtis. "Comment on 'The Early Drawings of Frank Lloyd Wright Reconsidered'." *JSAH* XXXI (O 1972), pp. 216-20.
See no. 1857.

1887. Besinger, Curtis. [Letter.] *JSAH* XXXI (My 1972), p. 159.
Concerning Wright's birthdate.

1888. Bowly, Devereux, Jr. "Unity Temple, a Masterpiece on the Way to Restoration." *Inland Arch* XVI (D 1972), pp. 18-19.

1889. Bradshaw, Jon. "The Stern Shining Brow." *Los Angeles Times West Magazine* (16 Ap 1972), pp. 9-12.

1890. Cohen, Stuart E. "Trailing Frank Lloyd Wright." *Arch Design* XLII (N 1972), pp. 663-4.
National Mobile Homes.

1891. Cox, James A. D. "Frank Lloyd Wright and His Houses in Virginia." *Arts in Virginia* XIII (Fa 1972), pp. 10-17.

1892. Cutler, Anthony. "The Tyranny of Hagia Sophia: Notes on Greek Orthodox Church Design in the United States." *JSAH* XXXI (Mr 1972), pp. 41-4.
Includes Annunciation Greek Orthodox Church, Wauwatosa.

1893. "First Prairie House." *Arch For* CXXXVII (D 1972), p. 62.
Wright house, Oak Park.

1894. Higuchi, Kiyoshi. "F. L. Wright and Le Corbusier." *Architecture and Urbanism* II (Fe 1972), pp. 7-8; (Mr), pp. 45-6; (Ap), pp. 6-7; (My), pp. 80-1; (Je), pp. 116-17; (Jy), pp. 88-9; (Ag), pp. 105-6; (Se), pp. 127-8; (O), pp. 100-1; (N), pp. 144-5; (D), pp. 124-7.
Japanese text.

1895. Jernow, Stanley Kenneth. "Richardsonian Tradition and

Frank Lloyd Wright, with an Excursus on the Flower Pot That Grew into a Church." *JSAH* XXXI (O 1972), pp. 234-5.

Abstract of a paper presented at the twenty-fifth annual meeting of the Society of Architectural Historians, 26-30 January 1972. It includes a comment on Annunciation Greek Orthodox Church, Wauwatosa.

1896.   Joedicke, Jürgen. "Frank Lloyd Wright, 1893–1909: die Entstehung einer neuen Raumkonzeption." *Bauen und Wohnen* XXVII (N 1972), 510-14.

1897.   Marlin, William. "The Quality of 'More-to-it-Than': Wright's Johnson Wax Building Today." *Inland Arch* XVI (Ag-Se 1972), pp. 13-17 and cover.

1898.   McCoy, Esther. "Architecture West." *Progress Arch* LIII (Se 1972), p. 76.

Concrete block houses, Los Angeles and Pasadena.

1899.   McDaniel, Joyce Pelham. "The Evolution of a House." *Alabama Architect* VIII (Je-Jy-Ag 1972), pp. 10-15 and cover.

Rosenbaum house, Florence.

1900.   "19th-Century Architecture for the American Wing: Sullivan and Wright." *Metropolitan Museum of Art Bulletin* XXX (Je-Jy 1972), pp. 300-05.

Little house, Deephaven, living room.

1901.   Pica, Agnoldomenico. "Quattro progetti per Venezia alla XXXVI Biennale." *Domus* no. 515 (O 1972), pp. 1-3.

Includes Masieri Memorial Building, Venice (project).

1902.   "Possible Destruction of the Yamamura House by Frank Lloyd Wright." *JA* XLVII (Fe 1972), p. 15.

1903.   Powell, Eileen. "The Frank Lloyd Wright Designed Munkwitz Apartments: Will What We Say Affect What Is Done?" *Wisconsin Architect* XLIII (Jy-Ag 1972), pp. 7-10.

Concerning possible demolition of duplex apartments, Milwaukee. Includes measured drawings by Brian Spencer. Reply: Richard W. Perrin, (O-N), p. 5.

1904. "Preservation: The Met to the Rescue." *Arch For* CXXXVI (Je 1972), p. 22.
Little house, Deephaven.

1905. Schaefer, Inge. "Marin County Civic Center von F. L. Wright." *Werk* LIX (Ja 1972), p. 5.

1906. Severens, Kenneth W. "Frank Lloyd Wright House in Oberlin." *Oberlin College Bulletin* XXIX (W 1972), pp. 90-105.
Weltzheimer house.

1907. Twombly, Robert C. "Undoing the City: Frank Lloyd Wright's Planned Communities." *Am Q* XXIV (O 1972), pp. 538-49.

1908. "Wrightmobile." *Arch For* CXXXVI (Mr 1972), p. 61.
Mobile homes, designed by Taliesin Associated Architects, based on Wright's designs.

1909. Zevi, Bruno. "Attualità dell'urbanistica wrightiana." *Architettura* XVIII (O 1972), pp. 352-3.

1973

Books

1910. Billings, Montana. Yellowstone Art Center. *Frank Lloyd Wright.* 1973.
27.9 x 21.5 cm., 16 pls. in folder.
A catalogue of a traveling exhibition of photomurals and color lithographs of Wright's drawings, and seven pieces of furniture designed by him for Heritage Henredon in 1955, and built for the first time for this show. It includes statements by Bruce Brooks Pfeiffer, Director of Archives, Frank Lloyd Wright Foundation, and John A. Armstrong, Director, Yellowstone Art Center.

1911. Crocker, Mary Wallace. "Louis Sullivan Cottages." In *Historic Architecture in Mississippi.* Jackson: University Press of Mississippi, [1973]. Pp. 96-9.
Sullivan and Charnley houses, Ocean Springs.

1912.   Futagawa, Yukio, editor and photographer, and William
Marlin, text. *Frank Lloyd Wright: Houses in Oak Park and River
Forest, Illinois, 1889–1913.* Tokyo: A.D.A. Edita, [1973].
    36.4 x 25.7 cm., 48 pp., 34 ills. (part color), paper. (The Series
of Global Architecture No. 25)

1913.   Gol'dshtein, Arkadii Fedorovich. *Frank Lloid Rait.*
Moskva: Stroiizdat, 1973.
    21.5 x 16.8 cm., 136 pp., front., 93 ills., cloth.
    Russian text.

1914.   Heckscher, Morrison, and Elizabeth G. Miller. *An Architect and His Client: Frank Lloyd Wright and Francis W. Little.*
[New York]: The Metropolitan Museum of Art, May 2, 1973.
    22.2 x 17.1 cm., 24 pp., 19 ills., paper.
    A catalogue of an exhibition of furniture, glass, original
drawings, photographs, and correspondence from the Little
house, Deephaven.

1915.   Hitchcock, Henry-Russell. *In the Nature of Materials:
1887–1941, the Buildings of Frank Lloyd Wright.* New York:
Da Capo Press, 1973.
    See no. 573.

1916.   Raymond, Antonin. "Frank Lloyd Wright at Taliesin"
and "Rendezvous with Japan: The Imperial Hotel." In *An Autobiography.* Rutland, Vermont, Tokyo: Charles E. Tuttle Company, [1973]. Pp. 46-53, 65-77.
    Raymond first worked for Wright at Taliesin in 1916. He
assisted with a scheme for prefabricated housing for the
Richards Company and also made the drawings for promotional literature for this project (see no. 130). Later he accompanied the architect to Japan to help with the Imperial Hotel.
These chapters offer Raymond's reminiscences of their association and include references to Wright's private life with
Miriam Noel. The texts of letters from Wright appear on pages
56-7 and 77.

REVIEW
1917.   Richards, J. M. *JSAH* XXXIII (D 1974), pp. 360-1.

1918.   [Sanderson, Warren.] *Frank Lloyd Wright Architecture, Oak Park [and] River Forest, Illinois.* Oak Park, Illinois: Oak Park-River Forest Chamber of Commerce, [1973].
   See no. 1774.

1919.   Starosciak, Kenneth, and Jane Starosciak. *Frank Lloyd Wright: A Bibliography.* Issued on the Occasion of the Destruction of the Francis W. Little House, Deep Haven, Minnesota. 1913-1972. [New Brighton, Minnesota: Kenneth Starosciak, 1973.]
   18.7 x 18.7 cm., 44 pp., 3 ills., paper.
   A "checklist of Frank Lloyd Wright's separately published first editions." It includes an introduction describing the destruction of the Little house, Deephaven. This edition is limited to seven hundred fifty hand numbered copies.

1920.   Twombly, Robert C. *Frank Lloyd Wright: An Interpretive Biography.* New York, Evanston, San Francisco, London: Harper & Row, Publishers, [1973].
   20.9 x 13.9 cm., x, 373 pp., 50 ills., cloth.
   A biography developed from the author's University of Wisconsin doctoral dissertation. It includes extensive source notes, notable for a large number of newspaper citations, and a bibliography. A copy of the original dissertation can be obtained from University Microfilms, Ann Arbor. Portions of this work appeared previously in *Wisconsin Magazine of History* (see no. 1756) and in *American Quarterly* (no. 1907). A paperback edition also was published by Harper Colophon Books, [1974].

REVIEWS
1921.   Anonymous. *New Yorker* (2 Je 1973), p. 124.
1922.   Brooks, H. Allen. *JSAH* XXXIII (D 1974), pp. 359-60.
1923.   Gillespie, Bernard. "Frank Lloyd Wright: An Interpretive Biography." *Canadian Architect* XIX (Se 1974), p. 64.
1924.   Hoffmann, Donald. *Arch For* CXXXVIII (Ap 1973), p. 14.
1925.   Kalec, Donald G. *Prairie Sch R* XI (no. 2, 1974), pp. 19-21.
1926.   Severens, Kenneth W. *Prairie Sch R* XI (no. 2, 1974), pp. 22-5.

1927. Wright, Olgivanna Lloyd. *[Frank Lloyd Wright.]* [New York]: Winthrop Laboratories, 1973.
    31.1 x 23.2 cm., 8 pp., 10 ills., paper. (What Makes it Great?)
    A brief biographical summary of Wright's philosophies of architecture and education. One of a series of publications distributed nationally to the medical profession by Winthrop Laboratories.

Periodicals

1928. "Architect and His Client: Frank Lloyd Wright and Francis W. Little." *Interiors* CXXXII (Je 1973), p. 10.

1929. Chaitkin, William. "Frank Lloyd Wright in Russia." *Architectural Association Quarterly* V (Su 1973), pp. 45-55.

1930. Hanks, David. "A Desk by Frank Lloyd Wright." *Bulletin of the Art Institute of Chicago* LXVII (Se-O 1973), pp. 6-8.
    From the Coonley house, Riverside.

1931. Hanks, David A. "The Arts and Crafts Movement in America, 1876–1916." *Apollo* n. s. XCVII (Fe 1973), pp. 183-8.
    Review of exhibit (see no. 1875).

1932. Martinson, Tom. "A Loss of Consequence." *Northw Arch* XXXVII (Mr-Ap 1973), pp. 82-5.
    Little house, Deephaven.

1933. Miller, Nory. "Four Architects with Their Own Design for Living." *Inland Arch* XVII (Je 1973), pp. 8-13.
    Includes Mrs. Thomas Gale house, Oak Park.

1934. Pfeiffer, Bruce Brooks. "Out of the Desert's Mystery." *AIA J* LIX (My 1973), pp. 54-5.
    Wright house, "Taliesin West," Scottsdale.

1935. "Plaque Marks Offices of Adler, Sullivan, Wright." *Progress Arch* XIV (Ja 1973), p. 43.
    In Auditorium Building, Chicago.

1936. Sherrill, Sarah B. "Frank Lloyd Wright." *Antiques* CIII (Je 1973), pp. 1054, 1058.
Little house living room at Metropolitan Museum.

1937. "Taliesin West 1973: Frank Lloyd Wright Foundation." *Arch d'Aujourd'hui* XLV (Jy-Ag 1973), pp. 104-13.

1938. Item number not used.

1939. "World." *Canadian Architect* XVIII (Fe 1973), pp. 6, 9.
Note on commemorative plaque in the Auditorium Building, Chicago.

1940. Wright, Frank Lloyd. "The Annual Distribution of Prizes —1950." *Architectural Association Quarterly* V (Ja-Mr 1973), pp. 46-7.

1974

Books

1941. Davis, Patricia Talbot. *Together They Built a Mountain.* [Lititz, Pennsylvania]: Sutter House, [1974].
26.8 x 15 cm., xvi, 179 pp., front., 45 ills., cloth.
Beth Sholom Synagogue, Elkins Park.

1942. Frank Lloyd Wright Foundation and Hubbard Associates. *Nakoma, Nakomis, Winnebago Indian Memorials: Two Sculptures by Frank Lloyd Wright, 1924; Bronze Edition, 1974.* 1974.
23 x 20.3 cm., 14 pp., 20 ills., paper.
A pamphlet which describes the recent casting of Wright's sculpture. It includes reproductions of original drawings and photographs as well as "The Sculpture of Frank Lloyd Wright," by Bruce Brooks Pfeiffer.

1943. Frank Lloyd Wright Foundation. *The Arizona Biltmore Hotel: History and Guide.* 1974.
22.7 x 20.3 cm., 20 pp., 9 ills., paper.
A pamphlet which includes: "Frank Lloyd Wright and the Arizona Biltmore Hotel," by Olgivanna Lloyd Wright; "The

Arizona Biltmore Hotel 1929–1973," by Bruce Brooks Pfeiffer; reproductions of six original drawings of the hotel by Wright; and photographs. Wright's abstract drawing, "Phoenix-1927," is reproduced on the cover.

1944. Los Angeles. Cultural Heritage Foundation, Inc. and Southern California Chapter, Architectural Secretaries Association, Inc. *Frank Lloyd Wright Week.* 1974.

21.6 x 14.1 cm., 11 pp., paper.

A pamphlet with notes on the Barnsdall ("Hollyhock House"), Ennis, Freeman, Sturges, and Storer houses, Los Angeles, and Anderton Court Shops, Beverly Hills.

1945. Moisescu, Anton. *Wright;* [monografie]. Bucuresti: Editura tehnică, 1974.

Not seen. Summary in English, French, Italian, and Russian (Library of Congress).

1946. Oak Park, Illinois. Public Library. *Frank Lloyd Wright, Prairie School Architecture: A Selection of Materials in the Oak Park Public Library.* Oak Park, Illinois: 1974.

23 x 15.3 cm., 7 pp., paper.

1947. Radford, Evelyn Morris. *The Bridge and the Building: The Art of Government and the Government of Art.* New York: A Hearthstone Book; Carlton Press, Inc., [1974].

A discussion of Wright's Marin County Government Center, San Rafael, and the Golden Gate Bridge.

1948. Storer, William Allin. *The Architecture of Frank Lloyd Wright: A Complete Catalogue.* Cambridge, Massachusetts and London, England: The MIT Press, [1974].

20.2 x 12.8 cm., 450 pp., 400 ills., cloth.

A catalogue of Wright's executed buildings illustrated with photographs taken by the author. The structures are arranged chronologically and include many that had not been published previously. The book also contains eleven residential floor plans representing the transition of Wright's designs, and maps illustrating the geographical distribution of completed buildings by time periods. And, a geographical index arranged by zip codes lists all buildings in the text, with street addresses usually given. The foreword is by Henry-Russell Hitchcock.

1949. Teske, Edmund. *Edmund Teske.* [Los Angeles: Municipal Art Gallery, 1974.]
A catalogue of an exhibition of photographs at the Los Angeles Municipal Art Gallery, Barnsdall Park, 18 September-20 October 1974. It includes photographs of the Barnsdall house "Hollyhock House," and residence B, Los Angeles, and Wright house, "Taliesin," Spring Green. Teske was a member of the Taliesin Fellowship in 1936–37, and from April, 1944, through 1949 he lived in Miss Barnsdall's studio residence B.

Periodicals

1950. Bell, Robert A. "Shotcrete Restoration of a Historic Landmark." *Concrete Construction* XIX (Ap 1974), pp. 161-3.
Unity Temple, Oak Park.

1951. Dymond, Lura. "New Life for a Landmark." *Westways* LXVI (N 1974), p. 22.
Barnsdall house, Los Angeles.

1952. Fowles, Aggie. "Oak Park's Unique Heritage." *Nation's Cities* XII (My 1974), pp. 22-3.

1953. Johnson, Kathryn C. "Frank Lloyd Wright's Mature Prairie Style." *Minneapolis Institute of Arts Bulletin* LXI (1974), pp. 54-65.
Little house, Deephaven.

1954. Panerai, Ph. "Frank Lloyd Wright: de la Prairie house à la maison Usonienne." *Architecture Française* XXXV (My-Je 1974), pp. 21-3.

1955. Pedio, Renato. "Casa Pfeiffer a Taliesin West, Scottsdale, Arizona." *Architettura* XX (Ag 1974), pp. 240-6.
Based on the Jester house, Palos Verdes (project).

1956. Pica, Agnoldomenico. "Wright oggi." *Domus* no. 531 (Fe

1974), pp. 6-8.
    S. C. Johnson and Son administration building, Racine.

1957.   Reiach, Alan. "Meetings with Frank Lloyd Wright." *Concrete Quarterly* no. 100 (Ja-Mr 1974), pp. 38-40.
    Reminiscences of visits with Wright between 1935 and 1957.

1958.   Ronnie, Art. "Hollyhock—The Wright House." *Westways* LXVI (N 1974), pp. 18-22, 86.
    Barnsdall house, Los Angeles.

1959.   "Strong Room." *Architects' J* CLX (18 Se 1974), p. 655.
    Kaufmann office, Pittsburgh, now at Victoria and Albert Museum, London.

1960.   Treiber, Daniel. "Frank Lloyd Wright." *Cree* no. 30 (Ag-Se 1974), pp. 104-14.
    Includes superimposed plans of Wright house, "Taliesin," Spring Green, in 1911, 1914, and 1925. French text. English summary, p. 38.

1961.   Twombly, Robert C. "Organic Living: Frank Lloyd Wright's Taliesin Fellowship and Georgi Gurdjieff's Institute for the Harmonious Development of Man." *Wis Mag Hist* LVIII (W 1974-75), pp. 126-39.

1962.   Walker, Virginia E. "Prejudgment of History." *Canadian Architect* XIX (N 1974), pp. 39-41.
    Analysis of Wright's comments concerning historical architectural styles.

1963.   "Wright in Japan." *Architecture Plus* II (Se-O 1974), p. 115.
    Exhibit at Takumi Gallery, Koriyama City.

1975

Books

1964.   Asselbergs, Fons, and others. *Nederlandse architectuur,*

1880–1930: Americana. [Otterlo: Rijksmuseum Kröller-Müller, 1975.]

Cover title. A catalogue to accompany an exhibition held between 24 August and 26 October 1975. It includes "20 jaar belangstelling voor Frank Lloyd Wright," "Frank Lloyd Wright en De Stijl," "Frank Lloyd Wright en de Amsterdamse school," and "Frank Lloyd Wrights invloed in de jaren twintig," all by Auke van der Woud. Another section contains excerpts of correspondence between Wright and Berlage, Oud, and Wijdeveld. The letters were written between 30 November 1922 and 6 March 1934 and are now in the Architectural Museum in Amsterdam.

1965. Futagawa, Yukio, ed., and photographer. *Frank Lloyd Wright: Solomon R. Guggenheim Museum, New York City, N.Y., 1943–59; Marin County Civic Center, California, 1957–1970.* Text by Bruce Brooks Pfeiffer. Tokyo: A.D.A. Edita, [1975].

36.4 x 25.6 cm., 48 pp., 31 ills. (part color), paper. (Global Architecture No. 36)

A photostudy. Includes a reproduction of an original perspective drawing of Marin County Civic Center and plans and sections of the Civic Center and the Guggenheim Museum. Introduction by Bruce Brooks Pfeiffer. Japanese and English text.

1966. Futagawa, Yukio, editor and photographer. *Houses by Frank Lloyd Wright 1.* Tokyo: A.D.A. Edita, [1975].

28 x 22.3 cm., 184 pp., 204 ills. (part color), paper. (Global Interior no. 9)

Interior and exterior photographs of: Wright house and studio, W. E. Martin, Fricke, Heurtley, Mrs. Thomas Gale, and Cheney houses, all in Oak Park; Winslow, Davenport, Roberts, and Ingalls houses, River Forest; Bradley house, Kankakee; Willits house, Highland Park; Dana house, Springfield; Gilmore house, Madison; Hardy house, Racine; Gridley house, Batavia; Robie house, Chicago; Coonley house, Riverside; Irving house, Decatur; Little house, Deephaven; Bogk house, Milwaukee; Wright house, "Taliesin," Spring Green; Storer, Freeman, and Ennis houses, Los Angeles; and Jones house, Tulsa. Also includes a list of structures, 1889–1934. Japanese text. A companion volume of later houses was published in 1976 (see no. 1999).

1967.   Kalec, Donald G., and Thomas A. Heinz. *Frank Lloyd Wright Home and Studio, Oak Park, Illinois.* Oak Park: Frank Lloyd Wright Home and Studio Foundation, 1975.
   18.7 x 19.1 cm., 24 pp., 25 ills., paper.
   A pamphlet describing the research done to date on these buildings, which are now a property of the National Trust for Historic Preservation. It includes early and recent comparative photographs, floor plans illustrating the alterations made by Wright, and a chronology. Printed in red and black.

REVIEW
1968.   Vinci, John. "More on the Work of Frank Lloyd Wright." *Chicago History* V (Fa 1976), p. 172.

1969.   New York. Solomon R. Guggenheim Museum. *The Solomon R. Guggenheim Museum, New York: Frank Lloyd Wright Architect.* [New York: The Solomon R. Guggenheim Foundation, 1975.]
   27.3 x 21 cm., 47 pp., 29 ills. (part color), paper.
   A photostudy with an introduction by Peter Lawson-Johnston and Thomas M. Messer; a history of the museum by Louise Averill Svendsen; the text of a letter from Wright to Guggenheim; and a history of the building by Henry Berg.

1970.   Wright, Frank Lloyd. *Studies and Executed Buildings by Frank Lloyd Wright. Ausgeführte Bauten und Entwürfe von Frank Lloyd Wright.* Palos Park, Illinois: The Prairie School Press, 1975.
   See no. 87.

1971.   Wright, Frank Lloyd. *In the Cause of Architecture.* Edited by Frederick Gutheim. Essays by Frank Lloyd Wright for Architectural Record 1908–1952. With a Symposium on Architecture with and without Wright by Eight Who Knew Him. [New York]: An Architectural Record Book, [1975].
   27.6 x 21.5 cm., viii, 246 pp., front., 154 ills., cloth.
   A reprint of Wright's "In the Cause of Architecture" articles

which appeared in the *Architectural Record* between March, 1908 and May, 1952. His drawings from "The Wright Legacy Evaluated," (*Architectural Record*, O 1960), and a group of photographs taken at Taliesin West in 1958 by Mildred F. Schmertz are included. Wright's essays are preceded by a preface by Frederick Gutheim and eight articles by Wright's associates: "The Whole Man," by Elizabeth Kassler; "Wright, the Man," by Henry Klumb; "Wright: Then and Now," by Andrew Devane; "Now More than Ever," by Elizabeth Wright Ingraham; "Toward an American Architecture," by Karl Kamrath; "A Humane and Environmental Architecture," by Victor Hornbein; "Wright: the Eleventh Decade," by Edgar Kaufmann, Jr.; and "A Language after Wright," by Bruno Zevi. The dust jacket design is a modification of the abstraction by Eugene Masselink which appeared on the cover of the January, 1948 *Architectural Forum.*

Periodicals

1972.   "Benefit Tour of FLLW Homes Nets $24,000." *Arch Rec* CLVIII (Se 1975), p. 37.
> Includes a description of the tour by Jack L. Gordon.

1973.   "Bock Collection at Greenville College." *National Sculpture Review* XXIV (Su-Fa 1975), p. 5.
> Exhibition including a number of objects related to Wright.

1974.   Cohen, Stuart. "Wright's Studio Home Open to the Public." *Progress Arch* LVI (My 1975), p. 32.

1975.   del Renzio, Toni. "Frank Lloyd Wright & the Pop Traditions." *Art & Artists* IX (Ja 1975), pp. 28-31.
> Kaufmann office, Pittsburgh, now at Victoria and Albert Museum, London.

1976.   "Designers' Showhouse, Frank Lloyd Wright's Charnley House, Chicago." *Interior Design* XLVI (N 1975), pp. 118-19.

1977.   "FLLW Sculpture Offered in Limited Edition." *Arch Rec* CLVII (Fe 1975), p. 35.

1978. Fox, Terry Curtis. "Living Wright." *Chicago* XXIV (O 1975), pp. 152-60.
Information on several houses in the Chicago area designed by Wright.

1979. "From the Editors." *Prairie Sch R* XII (no. 3, 1975), p. 4.
Charnley house, Chicago.

1980. Geran, Monica, ed. "Frank Lloyd Wright Revisited." *Interior Design* XLVI (N 1975), pp. 96-101.
S. C. Johnson and Son administration building, Racine.

1981. Geselbracht, Raymond H. "Transcendental Renaissance in the Arts: 1890–1920." *New England Quarterly* XLVIII (D 1975), pp. 463-86.
A discussion of Wright, Charles Ives, and Isadora Duncan.

1982. Guerrero, Pedro E. "Frank Lloyd Wright: An Unpublished Portfolio." *Sat R* III (4 O 1975), pp. 18-23 and cover.
Photographs of Wright taken between 1940 and 1959 by a former member of the Taliesin Fellowship. Reprinted, see no. 2012.

1983. Heckscher, Morrison. "Frank Lloyd Wright's Furniture for Francis W. Little." *Burlington Magazine* CXVII (D 1975), pp. 866, 869, 871-2.

1984. Hildebrand, Grant. "Privacy and Participation: Frank Lloyd Wright and the City Street." University of Washington, College of Architecture and Urban Planning, *Development Series* I (Sp 1975), pp. 23-39.

1985. "In Progress: Teliesen [sic] Design for Hotel Wing." *Progress Arch* LVI (O 1975), pp. 52-3.
Arizona Biltmore Hotel, Phoenix.

1986. Kugler, Silvia. "Der grosse Arbeitsraum." *Du* XXXV (My 1975), pp. 64-73.
S. C. Johnson and Son administration building and research tower, Racine.

1987. Lynes, Russell. "On Knowing Wright from Wrong." *Architectural Digest* XXXII (N-D 1975), pp. 24, 32, 36.

Barton house, Buffalo; Kaufmann house, "Fallingwater," Bear Run.

1988. Marlin, William. "Frank Lloyd Wright, The Enduring Presence." *Sat R* III (4 O 1975), pp. 14-17.

Biographical sketch with an evaluation of the pertinence of Wright's theories today. Includes observations by Anne Baxter, Alistair Cooke, Buckminster Fuller, Frederick Gutheim, John C. Harkness, and Lewis Mumford. Reprinted, see no. 2017.

1989. "Max Fry: Inspirations, Friendships, and Achievements of a Lifetime in the Modern Movement." *Building* CCXXIX (31 O 1975), pp. 52-8.

Includes Wright.

1990. Sembach, Klaus-Jürgen. "Fünf Villen des frühen 20. Jahrhunderts." *Du* XXXV (Se 1975), pp. 10-49 and cover.

Includes Robie house, Chicago and Coonley house, Riverside.

1991. Severens, Kenneth W. "The Reunion of Louis Sullivan and Frank Lloyd Wright." *Prairie Sch R* XII (no. 3, 1975), pp. 5-21 and cover.

1992. Stamm, Gunther. "Modern Architecture and the Plantation Nostalgia of the 1930s: Stone's 'Mepkin' and Wright's 'Auldbrass Plantation'." *JSAH* XXXIV (D 1975), p. 318.

Abstract of a talk delivered to the Society of Architectural Historians, April, 1975.

1993. Twombly, Robert C. "Saving the Family: Middle Class Attraction to Wright's Prairie House, 1901–1909." *Am Q* XXVII (Mr 1975), pp. 57-72.

1994. Wright, Frank Lloyd. "The Master's Work." *American Art Review* II (My-Je 1975), pp. 133-6.

From *Genius and the Mobocracy* (see no. 750).

1995. "Wrightian Revival." *Interiors* CXXXV (O 1975), pp. 76-81.
  Arizona Biltmore Hotel, Phoenix.

1996. "Wright Windows Stolen from Rochester House." *AIA J* LXIV (Jy 1975), p. 14.
  Boynton house.

1976

Books

1997. Blake, Peter. *The Master Builders: Le Corbusier, Mies van der Rohe, Frank Lloyd Wright.* New York: W. W. Norton & Company, [1976].
  See no. 1379.

1998. Futagawa, Yukio, editor and photographer, and Bruce Brooks Pfeiffer, text. *Frank Lloyd Wright: Pfeiffer Chapel, Florida Southern College, Lakeland, Florida, 1938; Beth Sholom Synagogue, Elkins Park, Pennsylvania, 1954.* Tokyo: A.D.A. Edita, [1976].
  36.4 x 25.6 cm., 48 pp., 23 ills. (part color), paper. (Global Architecture no. 40)
  A photostudy. It includes reproductions of original drawings and plans for the buildings.

1999. Futagawa, Yukio, editor and photographer. *Houses by Frank Lloyd Wright 2.* Tokyo: A.D.A. Edita, [1976].
  28 x 22.3 cm., 184 pp., 226 ills. (part color), paper. (Global Interior no. 10)
  Interior and exterior photographs: the Willey house, Minneapolis; Kaufmann house, "Fallingwater," Bear Run; Hanna house, Palo Alto; Johnson house, "Wingspread," Racine; Lewis house, Libertyville; Pope-Leighey house, Mount Vernon; Schwartz house, Two Rivers; Sturges house, Los Angeles; Pew house, Madison; Affleck and Smith houses, Bloomfield Hills; Baird house, Amherst; Wall house, Plymouth; Jacobs house II, Middleton; Walter house, Quasqueton; Mossberg house, South Bend; Walker house, Carmel; Laurent house, Rockford;

Zimmerman and Kalil houses, Manchester; Robert Wright house, Bethesda; Boomer and Lykes houses, Phoenix; Price house, Bartlesville; Price house, Paradise Valley; and Hoffman house, Rye. The book also includes "The Usonian House," by Bruce B. Pfeiffer in Japanese and English and a list of structures, 1933–1959. A similar volume of photographs of earlier houses was published in 1975 (see no. 1966).

2000.   Izzo, Alberto and Camillo Gubitosi. *Frank Lloyd Wright: Disegni, 1887–1959.* [Firenze: Centro Di, 1976.]
   23.1 x 21.6 cm., 189 pp., 232 ills. (part color), paper.
   A catalogue of a traveling exhibition of photographic reproductions of Wright's drawings. The introductory articles by the authors are in Italian. A chronology, a list of work, and a bibliography are included.

2001.   Sergeant, John. *Frank Lloyd Wright's Usonian Houses: The Case for Organic Architecture.* New York: Whitney Library of Design, an imprint of Watson-Guptill Publications, [1976].
   25.2 x 22.6 cm., 207 pp., 200 ills., cloth.
   A scholarly reassessment of Wright's late career. It includes a Chronological List of Frank Lloyd Wright's Chief Designs, 1929–1943 with notes about discrepancies in dates, a foreword by Lionel March, six chapters analyzing Usonian architecture and Broadacre City, extensive footnotes, a bibliography, and six appendixes. Appendix A: "A Spatial Analysis of Usonian Houses." Appendix B: "The Personal Architectural Services of Frank Lloyd Wright." Appendix C: "Agreement between Contractor and Owner for Construction of Usonian Buildings." Appendix D: "Organic Architecture Meets the International Style." Appendix E: "Taliesin Memorabilia." Appendix F: "Broadacre City Petition, 1943."

REVIEWS
2002.   Hoffmann, Donald. *JSAH* XXXVI (My 1977), pp. 128-9.
2003.   Loeffler, Jane Canter. *AIA J* LXVI (My 1977), pp. 68, 72.
2004.   Tafel, Edgar. *Arch Rec* CLX (N 1976), p. 43.
   Replies from Robert C. Twombly and John Sergeant were published in volume CLXI (Mr 1977), p. 4.

2005. Sprague, Paul E. *Guide to Frank Lloyd Wright and Prairie School Architecture in Oak Park.* Oak Park, Illinois: Oak Park Bicentennial Commission of the American Revolution; Oak Park Landmarks Commission; Village of Oak Park, [1976].

22.8 x 14.5 cm., 96 pp., 113 ills., paper.

An annotated guide with maps indicating the locations of the buildings. It includes a foreword by H. Allen Brooks, an introduction, and a short biography of the architects.

REVIEW

2006. Anonymous. *AIA J* LXV (Jy 1976), p. 200.

2007. Wodehouse, Lawrence. "Frank Lloyd Wright." In *American Architects from the Civil War to the First World War: A Guide to Information Sources.* Detroit: Gale Research Company, [1976]. Pp. 226-58.

An annotated bibliography which lists one hundred sixty-one books and periodical articles by and about Wright. The entries are all in English and are cited alphabetically in one list. A brief introduction identifies some of Wright's drawings in public collections, and lists some of his books. There is one additional citation in the Addendum, p. 276.

Periodicals

2008. Bowly, Devereux, Jr. "Saving the Idea of Wright's 1895 'Model Tenement'." *Inland Arch* XX (Fe 1976), pp. 18-20.

Francisco Terrace, Chicago.

2009. Brown, Dan. "Wright Prairie House Burns in Oak Park." *Arch Rec* CLIX (Ap 1976), p. 34.

Hills house.

2010. Downs, Arthur Channing, Jr. "Victorian Premonitions of Wright's Prairie House in Downing and Scott." *Nineteenth Century* II (Su 1976), pp. 35-9.

2011. "Frank Lloyd Wright Revisited." *Architectural Digest* XXXII (Ja-Fe 1976), pp. 92-9.

Hoffman house, Rye, redecorated by John F. Saladino.

2012.   Guerrero, Pedro E. "Frank Lloyd Wright: An Unpublished Portfolio." *Design* (Bombay) XX (Ja 1976), pp. 19-21.
Reprinted from *Saturday Review* (see no. 1982).

2013.   Gutheim, Frederick. "Frank Lloyd Wright and the American Home." *Architect and Builder* XXVI (Fe 1976), pp. 2-4.

2014.   Jacobs, Herbert. "Our Wright Houses." *Hist Pres* XXVIII (Jy-Se 1976), pp. 9-13.

2015.   " 'Japan's Williamsburg' Gets Part of Wright's Imperial." *AIA J* LXV (Ag 1976), pp. 8-9.

2016.   Jensen, Robert. "Where F. L. Wright Meets Le Corbusier." *Parametro* VII (Mr 1976), pp. 48-51, 63-4.
Paolo Soleri's Arcosanti.

2017.   Marlin, William. "Frank Lloyd Wright: The Enduring Presence." *Design* (Bombay) XX (Ja 1976), pp. 22-4.
Reprinted from *Saturday Review* (see no. 1988).

2018.   "Mile High Skyscraper—'The Illinois.' Frank Lloyd Wright, 1956." *AIA J* LXV (N 1976), p. 59.
Abridged from *Architectural Record* (N 1956).

2019.   Skurka, Norma. "Revisiting Frank Lloyd Wright." *NYTM* (4 Ja 1976), pp. 36-7.
Hoffman house, Rye, redecorated by John F. Saladino.

2020.   Sprague, Paul. "Frank Lloyd Wright Home and Studio: Homeward Bound." *Hist Pres* XXVIII (Jy-Se 1976), pp. 4-8.
Reply, see no. 2028.

1977

Note: research on this bibliography ended in October, 1977, and items that came to the compiler's attention after that date have not been included.

Books

2021. Hoag, Edwin and Joy Hoag. *Masters of Modern Architecture: Frank Lloyd Wright, Le Corbusier, Mies van der Rohe, and Walter Gropius.* Indianapolis and New York: The Bobbs-Merrill Company, Inc., [1977].
   22.8 x 15 cm., xiii, 209 pp., 36 ills., cloth.
   A juvenile biography; each architect is treated in a separate section. A paperback edition also was published.

2022. Wright, Frank Lloyd. *An Autobiography.* New York: Horizon Press, [1977].
   See no. 303.

2023. Wright, Frank Lloyd. *Frank Lloyd Wright: Selected Drawings Portfolio.* New York: Horizon Press, [1977].
   52.2 x 38 cm., 50 color plates in portfolio.
   A portfolio of fifty drawings reproduced in color. They were selected and arranged by A.D.A. EDITA, Tokyo Co., Ltd. and were printed in Japan. The plates are mounted on heavy cardboard and are housed in a black cloth portfolio with ivory fasteners. An introduction by the architect's widow, Olgivanna Lloyd Wright, is included. This edition is limited to five hundred numbered copies of which ten are not for sale. Although the works represented are not listed individually in this description, an entry for each one appears in the building index.

Periodicals

2024. "Doing it Wright." *Progress Arch* LVIII (Ja 1977), p. 28.
   Tour in Oak Park.

2025. Dring, William B. [Letter.] *Hist Pres* XXIX (Ja-Mr 1977), p. 47.

Concerns the restoration of the Wright studio, Oak Park.

2026. "Frank Lloyd Wright." *Architecture* no. 403 (Je 1977), pp. 42-60 and cover.
Exhibition of drawings.

2027. Grabow, Stephen. "Frank Lloyd Wright and the American City: The Broadacres Debate." *Am Inst Plan J* XLIII (Ap 1977), pp. 115-24.

2028. Johannesen, Eric. [Letter.] *Hist Pres* XXIX (Ja-Mr 1977), p. 47.
A reply to an article by Paul Sprague (see no. 2020).

2029. Peatross, C. Ford. "Architectural Collection of the Library of Congress." *Quarterly Journal of the Library of Congress* XXXIV (Jy 1977), pp. 276-7.
Includes information on Wright and a reproduction of his 1914 copyright deposit design for an Embassy for the USA, Tokyo (project).

2030. Pica, Agnoldomenico. "F. Ll. Wright, ineditie e non." *Domus* no. 569 (Ap 1977), pp. 1-5.
Drawings exhibition.

2031. Rudd, J. William. "Sullivan and Wright: A Duality of Difference." *Journal of Architectural Education* XXX (Ap 1977), pp. 28-32.

2032. "Story Behind the Book: 'An Autobiography'." *Publishers Weekly* CCXII (25 Jy 1977), p. 55.
Interview with Ben Raeburn, publisher of Wright's works since 1953.

2033. Zevi, Bruno. "Frank Lloyd Wright, Designs 1887–1959: Exhibition of Some 300 of His Drawings." *Architecture* no. 401 (1) (Fe 1977), p. 35.
Not seen.

APPENDIX A

Taliesin Publications

Unless otherwise noted, Wright was the author or editor of the following publications. Dates for several undated items were established from internal evidence or from a list of Taliesin Press publications provided by the Frank Lloyd Wright Foundation.

1931

2034. *The Hillside Home School of the Allied Arts: Why We Want This School.*
18.6 x 21.6 cm., 16 pp.
A prospectus dated October, 1931. The sheets are printed on both sides and folded once but are not bound.

1933

2035. *The Taliesin Fellowship.*
21.3 x 21.5 cm., 16 pp., 7 ills.
A prospectus dated January 1, 1933. It includes drawings and plans for the remodeled Hillside Home School building, an application for the fellowship, and a list of charter applicants. The pages are double folded and printed in black.

2036. *The Taliesin Fellowship.*
21.6 x 21.6 cm., 10 pp., 3 ills.
A prospectus dated December, 1933. It includes a perspective drawing and plan of the proposed Taliesin Fellowship building and photographs of Taliesin and some fellowship members. Lists of Friends of the Fellowship and Fellows and an application for fellowship are provided. The sheets are

printed in red and black on one side only, with one exception, and folded variously to form loose, unbound gatherings of two or four pages each. The cover is illustrated on Plate 10 of this volume.

1934

2037. *Taliesin* I, no. 1, [1934].
22.1 x 26.5 cm., 27 pp., 20 ills.

This is the first number of the "characteristic monograph" of the Taliesin Fellowship. Each yearly volume was to consist of nine numbers. The next issue, also volume I, no. 1, did not appear until 1940. This issue includes: "Matter: In the Cause of Architecture," by Frank Lloyd Wright; "Architectural Education in Germany," by Heinrich de Fries; "Architecture of the Present and the Taliesin Standpoint," by Stamo Papadaki; "A Mother Looks at Taliesin," by Pauline Schubart; "Colossus," by Yen Liang; a letter from Dorothy Johnson Field; and "The Modern Museum Show: Institutionalized Poverty," by Edgar A. Tafel. Wright's two-zone house project is illustrated. Photographs of members of the Taliesin Fellowship are included. An editorial by Wright is printed in the minor column of each page. The typographic design is by Wright. His Four Organic Commandments (see no. 2057) are printed on the back cover. The sheets are printed on one side only in black and red and folded into unbound gatherings of four pages each.

1938

2038. *Taliesin Eyes* I (1 O 1938).

A one-page newspaper published in broadside formats of various sizes by the apprentices of the Fellowship. It has various contributors, and includes news, editorials, and other miscellaneous items. Additional issues, all volume I, were published October 8, October 15, October 22, November 5, November 12, November 19, and November 24, 1938. The final three numbers have linoleum-cut illustrations.

1939

2039. *Taliesin.*
18.4 x 13.3 cm., 4 pp., 2 ills.
A pamphlet describing the Taliesin Fellowship and inviting visitors to tour the buildings and attend programs on Sunday afternoons in the playhouse. It includes a map of Taliesin and the Fellowship buildings. It is printed in red and black on only one side of a single sheet of newsprint and folded twice into quarters. It is undated, but internal evidence supports the date of approximately 1939.

1940

2040. *Taliesin* I, no. 1 [sic] (O 1940).
21.8 x 21.7 cm., 38 pp., 14 ills.
On cover: Taliesin. Taliesin Fellowship Publication. Frank Lloyd Wright Editor. The New Frontier. Broadacre City. The second issue of the magazine of the Taliesin Fellowship, this number is devoted to the Broadacre City project. It includes: "A New Success Ideal," by Frank Lloyd Wright; "Mr. Wright Talks on Broadacre City to Ludwig Mies van der Rohe; and other articles describing the project. An editorial by Wright, and a statement, "A Way to Beat Hitler," by the English publisher Stanley Nott, are printed in red on the top one-third of each page. The illustrations are photographs of the model of Broadacre City constructed by the Taliesin Fellowship. The typography for the magazine was designed by Wright. It was printed in red and black by the Democrat-Tribune Press, Mineral Point, Wisconsin. The cover is reproduced on Plate 12 of this volume.

1941

2041. *Taliesin* I, no. 2 (Fe 1941).
21.8 x 21.7 cm., 34 pp., 51 ills.
On cover: Taliesin. The Taliesin Fellowship Publication. Frank Lloyd Wright, Editor. This is the third and final issue of

Taliesin that was published. It is devoted to the Taliesin Fellowship, and includes: "Our Work," by Frank Lloyd Wright; "Social Life," by Olgivanna Lloyd Wright; "Fellowship at Work: Significance and Direction," by William Wesley Peters; "The Playhouse and its Visitors," and "Concerning Superintendence," by Eugene Masselink; "Music," by Robert Carroll May; "How to Stay Out of the War (The American Way)," by Burton J. Goodrich; "An Englishman Looks at Taliesin," by Stanley C. Nott; and "In the Arizona Desert: Taliesin West," by Robert Mosher. An editorial by Wright printed mostly in red ink occupies the top third of each page; the other texts and illustrations run along the lower two-thirds of each page. The illustrations are photographs of the apprentices and buildings of the Fellowship. Views and a plan of Taliesin West are included. The typography for the magazine was designed by Wright and printed in red and black.

2042. *A Taliesin Square-Paper: A Nonpolitical Voice from Our Democratic Minority.* [No. 1, 25 Ja 1941.] "To London."

An article on rebuilding postwar London. It was written in response to a request from the *News Chronicle of London* and printed in numerous English newspapers. The *Taliesin Square-Paper* was published sporadically between 1941 and 1953. The text is printed as a broadside in red and black on one side of a sheet of newsprint, and the cover appears on the other side. The sheet is folded twice to form a cover and four pages measuring approximately 21.5 x 21.5 cm. All issues follow this basic format, but number 13 consists of two sheets folded one within the other, and number 16 consists of a cover and six printed pages.

2043. *A Taliesin Square-Paper: A Nonpolitical Voice from Our Democratic Minority.* [No. 2] (15 My 1941). "Of What Use Is a Great Navy with No Place to Hide?"

2044. *A Taliesin Square-Paper: A Nonpolitical Voice from Our Democratic Minority.* [No. 3, Je 1941.] "Good Afternoon, Editor Evjue," *and* "Again 'Good Afternoon,' Mr. Editor."

Two articles by Wright which defend his views on our participation in World War II. They were written during an exchange with William J. Evjue, editor of the *Madison Capital Times*, in which they first appeared on 29 May and 6 June, 1941.

2045. *A Taliesin Square-Paper: A Nonpolitical Voice from Our Democratic Minority.* No. 4 (4 Jy 1941). "Defense."
A statement on World War II. It also includes Wright's response to a telegram requesting a statement for publication in the Soviet Union concerning support for the Soviet Union against German attack.

2046. *A Taliesin Square-Paper: A Nonpolitical Voice from Our Democratic Minority.* No. 5 (Jy 1941). "To Beat the Enemy."

2047. *A Taliesin Square-Paper: A Nonpolitical Voice from Our Democratic Minority.* No. 6 (24 Ag 1941). "Usonia, Usonia South and New England. A Declaration of Independence."
A proposal for regrouping the United States into a tri-state Federal Union.

1943

2048. *An Autobiography, Book Six: Broadacre City.*
21.1 x 21.3 cm., ii, 30 pp.
A chapter intended for, but not used in, the revised and expanded edition of Wright's *An Autobiography,* published in 1943. The text is dated summer, 1943, and is printed in red and black on newsprint. (See no. 2049.)

1944

2049. *An Autobiography, Book Six: Broadacre City.*
21.5 x 21.4 cm., 32 pp.
A revised printer's proof of no. 2048. The text is dated spring, 1944.

2050. *A Taliesin Square-Paper: A Nonpolitical Voice from Our Democratic Minority.* No. 7 (14 Ag 1944). "To the Mole."

1945

2051. *A Taliesin Square-Paper: A Nonpolitical Voice from Our Democratic Minority.* No. 8 (My 1945). "The Price of Peace."

2052. *A Taliesin Square-Paper: A Nonpolitical Voice from Our Democratic Minority.* No. 9 (Ag 1945). "Nature."

1946

2053. *A Taliesin Square-Paper: A Nonpolitical Voice from Our Democratic Minority.* No. 10 (29 O 1946). "Building a Democracy."
Text of a speech delivered on the occasion of the *Herald Tribune* Forum, 29 October 1946.

2054. "To Svetlana."
4 pp. (single sheet folded once).
A poem written by Iovanna Lloyd Wright after the death in 1946 of her half-sister Svetlana.

1947

2055. *A Taliesin Square-Paper: A Nonpolitical Voice from Our Democratic Minority.* No. 11 (6 Mr 1947). "Mimic No More."
Text of a speech concerning education and democracy, delivered on the occasion of the Princeton Bicentennial Conference on Planning Man's Physical Environment, 6 March 1947.

1948

2056. *A Taliesin Square-Paper: A Nonpolitical Voice from Our Democratic Minority.* No. 12 [5 My 1948]. "Harum-Scarum."
A discussion of Communism and Democracy.

2057. "Taliesin to Friends."
Single folded sheet.

It includes Wright's "Four Organic Commandments." It has been reprinted several times, most recently as a Christmas greeting by the Frank Lloyd Wright Foundation in 1974.

1949

2058. *A Taliesin Square-Paper: A Nonpolitical Voice from Our Democratic Minority.* No. 13 (17 Mr 1949). "The American Institute of Architects Citation. The Speech of Acceptance." (Cover and 8 pp., i.e., 2 sheets)

2059. *A Taliesin Square-Paper: A Nonpolitical Voice from Our Democratic Minority.* No. 14 (2 N 1949). "We Want the Truth."
    Text of a speech concerning the commercialized state of this country, written for, but not delivered on, the occasion of the award of the Peter Cooper Medal for the Advancement of Art at the 90th Anniversary Convocation of the Cooper Union, 2 November 1949.

1950

2060. *A Demonstration of the Gurdjieff Movements by the Taliesin Fellowship at Taliesin in Wisconsin on October 29th, 1950.*
    20.5 x 21.1 cm., 8 pp.
    A program which includes the text of an address delivered by Wright prior to the demonstration.

1951

2061. *The Art and Knowledge in the Ritual Exercises of Gurdjieff, Presented by the Taliesin Fellowship at the Unitarian Church of Madison on Tuesday, November 6, 1951.*
    21.5 x 21.4 cm., 8 pp.
    A program.

2062. *Fourth Demonstration of the Gurdjieff Movements by*

the Taliesin Fellowship at Taliesin West, Easter, 1951.
21.7 x 21.6 cm., 8 pp.
A program.

2063. *The Sovereignty of the Individual: In the Cause of Architecture.* Frank Lloyd Wright. Preface to Ausgeführte Bauten und Entwürfe Published by Wasmuth Berlin 1910. Reprinted as Introduction to Exhibition Palazzo Strozzi Florence Italy 1951.
30 x 23.8 cm., 19 pp.
The text in English from *Ausgeführte Bauten und Entwürfe* (see no. 87).

2064. *A Taliesin Square-Paper: A Nonpolitical Voice from Our Democratic Minority.* [No. 15] (25 Ja 1951). "On an Architecture for Democracy."
The foreword from *When Democracy Builds* (see no. 609), reprinted on the occasion of the preview of the exhibition of Wright's work at Gimbel Brothers, Philadelphia.

1953

2065. *In the Cause of Architecture.*
21.4 x 21.4 cm., 7 pp.
An undated editorial which attacks the International Style. It was also published in *House Beautiful* (Jy 1953) and in an edited form in *Architectural Record* (Je 1953).

2066. *In the Cause of Architecture: The "International Style."*
21.5 x 21.4 cm., 8 pp.
Another editorial which attacks the International Style. This version is dated February, 1953. According to the Wright Foundation, this is issue no. 17, the last of the *Taliesin Square-Paper* series, but it carries no such identification, and its format as a conventional pamphlet matches that of item no. 2039.

2067. *Music, Ritual Exercises, and Temple Dances by Georges Gurdjieff.* Introduced by Frank Lloyd Wright. Presented by Members of the Taliesin Fellowship Under the Auspices of the Art Institute of Chicago at the Goodman Theatre, November 3, 1953.

23.5 x 15.8 cm., 8 pp.

A program.

2068. *Organic Architecture: Language of an Organic Architecture.*

21.4 x 18.8 cm., 6 pp.

A slightly revised version of Wright's explanation of organic architecture. It is dated 20 May 1953. (See no. 2069.) Also in *The Future of Architecture* (1953).

2069. *A Taliesin Square-Paper: A Nonpolitical Voice from Our Democratic Minority.* No. 16 [Fe 1953]. "The Language of Organic Architecture." Also published in *Architectural Forum* (My 1953).

An explanation of Wright's buildings and writings on organic architecture. (See no. 2068.)

2070. *Taliesin Tract, Number One.* (Christmas morning, 1953.) "Man."

14.6 x 19 cm., 5 folded pp. (single sheet).

This is the first number of a series planned for annual distribution at Christmas. It is printed in red and black. No additional issues were published.

1956

2071. *Man: Frank Lloyd Wright Birthday.* (8 Je 1956).

20.3 x 13.8 cm., 6 folded pp. (single sheet).

A slightly revised version of the above item.

1959

2072. "To My Father."

A poem by Iovanna Lloyd Wright read to her father in December, 1958 and published after his death.

1965

2073. *Taliesin.*

20.4 x 28 cm., 12 pp., 28 ills. (part color).

A pamphlet which describes the Taliesin Fellowship and the Taliesin Associated Architects. It includes an article by Olgivanna Lloyd Wright and quotations by Frank Lloyd Wright. The cover was designed by Eugene Masselink.

APPENDIX B

Frank Lloyd Wright Buildings Recorded by the Historic American Buildings Survey

*Items marked with an asterisk are in the HABS office files as of June, 1977. When completed, they will be transferred to the Library of Congress. The others are in the Prints and Photographs Division, Library of Congress, Washington, D. C. 20540, and may be ordered there.

California

2074. Barnsdall, Aline, house ("Hollyhock House") (HABS No. CAL-356), 4800 Hollywood Boulevard, Los Angeles
   9 ext. photos., 4 int. photos.

2075. Barnsdall, Aline, residence A (HABS No. CAL-357), 1645 North Vermont Avenue, Los Angeles
   6 ext. photos., 8 data pp.

*2076. Freeman, Samuel, house (HABS No. CAL-1935), 1962 Glencoe Way, Los Angeles
   7 Micromasters of Wright's plans, 4 data pp.

Illinois

2077. Bach, Emil, house (HABS No. ILL-1088), 7415 North Sheridan Road, Chicago
   6 sheets measured dwgs. (site plan; first floor plan; second floor plan; south and west elevations; north and east elevations; cross sections), 2 ext. photos., 1 int. photo., 11 photocopies of orig. dwgs., 7 data pp.

2078. Charnley, James, house (HABS No. ILL-1009), 1365

Astor Street, Chicago
  7 sheets measured dwgs. (site plan; first floor plan, second
  floor plan; third floor plan, molding details; section; west elevation; stair hall details; living room bookcase door detail,
  soffit plan, cornice detail), 4 ext. photos., 3 int. photos., 6
  data pp.

2079. Francis Apartments (HABS No. ILL-1076), 4304 South
Forestville Avenue, Chicago
  5 ext. photos., 4 data pp.

2080. Glasner, W. A., house (HABS No. ILL-1098), 850 Sheridan Road, Chicago
  4 sheets measured dwgs. (site plan; first floor plan; ground
  floor plan; elevations)

2081. Heller, Isadore, house (HABS No. ILL-1046), 5132 Woodlawn Avenue, Chicago
  4 sheets measured dwgs. (site plan; first and second floor plans;
  east and south elevations and section; four details of staircase
  windows), 4 ext. photos., 3 int. photos., 1 photocopy of old
  view, 6 data pp.

2082. Robie, Frederick C., house (HABS No. ILL-1005), 5757
South Woodlawn Avenue, Chicago
  14 sheets measured dwgs. (site plan; ground floor plan; main
  floor plan; third floor plan; longitudinal section and south
  elevation; west, east, and north elevations; fireplace elevations;
  window patterns and details; window patterns; environmental
  provisions; four pages of furniture), 3 ext. photos., 2 int.
  photos., 3 photocopies (1911), 17 data pp.
    The measured drawings were published separately; see no.
  1723.

2083. Steffens, Oscar, house (HABS No. ILL-1063), 7631
North Sheridan Road, Chicago
  6 sheets measured dwgs. (site plan, elevations, sections; ground
  floor plan, living room fireplace detail, schedule of heights;
  second floor plan, master bedroom fireplace detail and elevations, second floor sill and continuous trim detail, overhang

detail; west, north, south, and east elevations; sections; window details), 2 photocopies, 4 data pp.

2084. Unity Temple (HABS No. ILL-1093), Lake Street at Kenilworth Avenue, Oak Park
7 sheets measured dwgs. (site plan, north elevation, west elevation, auditorium level plan, ground floor plan, balcony level plan, longitudinal section), 3 ext. photos., 2 int. photos., 12 data pp.

2085. Winslow, William H., house (HABS No. ILL-1061), 515 Auvergne Place, River Forest
5 sheets measured dwgs. (site plan; first floor plan; second floor plan; west elevation; reception hall plan and section), 6 ext. photos., 5 int. photos., 2 photocopies, 17 data pp.

2086. Wright, F. L., house and studio (HABS No. ILL-1099), Forest and Chicago Avenues, Oak Park
4 ext. photos., 3 int. photos., 16 data pp.

Kentucky

2087. Ziegler, Rev. J. R., house (HABS No. KY-103), 509 Shelby Street, Frankfort
14 sheets measured dwgs. (vicinity plan; sections, basement plan; first floor plan; second floor plan; roof plan; west elevations, fireplace elevations, details; south elevation; east elevation, sections, details; north elevation; 2 sheets sections; cabinet details and sections; 2 sheets window glazing details)

Michigan

*2088. Amberg, D. M., house (HABS No. MICH-242), 505 College Avenue, Grand Rapids
5 ext. photos., 11 data pp.

*2089. May, Meyer, house (HABS No. MICH-241), 450 Madison Avenue, S. E., Grand Rapids
4 ext. photos., 1 photocopy, 11 data pp.

New York

*2090.   Boynton, E. E., house (file in preparation), 16 East Boulevard, Rochester
   2 ext. photos., 5 int. photos., 4 data pp.

2091.   Martin, Darwin D., house (HABS No. NY-5611), 125 Jewett Parkway, Buffalo
   5 ext. photos., 8 photocopies, 13 data pp.

Virginia

2092.   Pope-Leighey house (HABS No. VA-638), Woodlawn Plantation, U.S. Rte. 1 and State Rte. 235, Mount Vernon
   9 sheets measured dwgs. (site plan; plan; east elevation; south elevation; west elevation; north elevation; 2 sheets sections; details), 4 ext. photos., 2 int. photos., 5 data pp.
   *Also 18 ext. photos., 18 int. photos., 7 photocopies of plans, clippings, correspondence

Wisconsin

2093.   Bogk, F. C., house (HABS No. WIS-252), 2420 North Terrace Avenue, Milwaukee
   5 ext. photos., 7 int. photos., 7 data pp.

*2094.   Lake Geneva Inn (file in preparation), Lake Geneva
   2 ext. photos., 4 int. photos.

*2095.   Johnson, S. C., and Son administration building and research tower (file in preparation), 1525 Howe Street, Racine
   14 ext. photos., 17 int. photos.

BUILDING & PLACE INDEX

This index attempts to list references to as many individual buildings and projects by Frank Lloyd Wright as possible. It includes all references to buildings mentioned in this bibliography. In addition, bibliography items 41, 58, 85, 87, 96, 101, 165, 172, 201, 573, 745, 864, 1206, 1265, 1298, 1489, 1948, and 2023 are indexed in full, although the individual buildings and projects discussed in each are too numerous to list individually in the bibliography citations. In several cases alternative schemes for a project have been grouped together with the note (schemes not distinguished).

1569, 1574, 1608, 1622, 1813, 1850, 1948

Grand Beach, Mich. *see* Bagley (J.), Carr (W. S.), Vosburgh

Grand Rapids, Mich. *see* Amberg, May

Grant, Douglas, house, Cedar Rapids, Iowa 745, 864, 1265, 1948

Great Neck, N.Y. *see* Rebhuhn

Greenberg, Dr. Maurice, house, Dousman, Wisc. 1948

Greene, William, house, Aurora, Ill. 1948

Greenville, South Carolina *see* Austin

Gridley, A. W., house, Batavia, Ill. 85, 573, 1206, 1948, 1966

Griggs, Chauncey, house, Tacoma, Wash. 1948

Grouped apartment towers, Chicago, Ill. (project) 1489

Guggenheim Museum (schemes not distinguished), New York, N.Y. 596, 600, 626-30, 634-5, 637-40, 643, 645, 659, 669, 671, 673-4, 678, 681, 695, 703, 713-14, 744-5, 821, 887, 889, 953, 966, 1004, 1062, 1076, 1110, 1123, 1136, 1176, 1187, 1226, 1233, 1236, 1238, 1243, 1276, 1279, 1282, 1293, 1298, 1313, 1317, 1328-9, 1331, 1333, 1340, 1351, 1368, 1392, 1405, 1410, 1417-18, 1420-1, 1423, 1426-7, 1432, 1434-6, 1442-5, 1447, 1458, 1489, 1517, 1600, 1616, 1661, 1667, 1712, 1758, 1795, 1807, 1810, 1877, 1948, 1965, 1969, 2023

Guthrie, William Norman, house, Sewanee, Tenn. (project) 87, 1206, 1489

Guthrie, William Norman, steel cathedral 573, 1489

Hagan, I. N., house, Uniontown, Penn. 1439, 1595, 1948

Hagerstown, Maryland *see* Motel for Weiland

Hakone, Japan *see* Fukuhara

Haldorn, Stuart, house, Carmel, Calif. (project) 745

Hanna, Paul, house (including later alterations), Palo Alto, Calif. 413, 442, 445, 457, 573, 858, 1489, 1548, 1948, 1999

Hanover, Ind. *see* Sigma Chi

Hardy, Thomas, house, Racine, Wisc. 62, 68, 85, 87, 573, 1206, 1265, 1489, 1948, 1966

Harlan, Dr. Allison, house, Chicago, Ill. 23, 41, 573, 1206, 1854, 1948

Harper, Dr. Ina Morris, house, St. Joseph, Mich. 1250, 1948

Hartford, Huntington, house, Hollywood, Calif. (project) 1489

Hartford, Huntington, resort (schemes not distinguished), Hollywood, Calif. 721, 745, 1265, 1489, 2023

Hartford, Conn. *see* New Theatre

Hastings, Minn. *see* Fasbender

Hawaii *see* Hilo, Kona Coast

Hayashi, Aizaku, house, Tokyo, Japan 573, 1948

Heath, W. R., house, Buffalo, N.Y. 66, 85, 87, 96, 101, 201, 573, 700, 1206, 1265, 1758, 1948

Hein, M. N., house, Chippewa Falls, Wisc. (project) 745

Helena Valley, Wisc. (*see also* Spring Green, Wisc.) *see* Country residence, Hillside Home School, Unity Chapel

Helicopter (project) 1489

Heller, Isadore, house, Chicago, Ill. 41, 54, 87, 96, 101, 573, 1206, 1265 (frieze, identified as Husser), 1948, 2081

Henderson, F. B., house, Elmhurst, Ill. 49, 85, 87, 573, 1206, 1948

Heritage-Henredon furniture 1085, 1101, 1115, 1910

Heurtley, Arthur, house, Oak Park, Ill. 76, 85, 87, 96, 101, 201, 573, 1206, 1948, 1966

Heurtley, Arthur, house remodeling, Marquette Island, Mich. 1948

NAME & TITLE INDEX